D1606296

Environmental Security

Environmental Security

A Guide to the Issues

Elizabeth L. Chalecki
Foreword by Stacy VanDeveer

Contemporary Military, Strategic, and Security Issues

 PRAEGER

AN IMPRINT OF ABC-CLIO, LLC
Santa Barbara, California • Denver, Colorado • Oxford, England

Library of Congress Cataloging-in-Publication Data

Chalecki, Elizabeth L.
    Environmental security : a guide to the issues / Elizabeth L. Chalecki; foreword by
Stacy VanDeveer.
        p. cm. — (Contemporary military, strategic, and security issues)
    Includes index.
    ISBN 978-0-313-39151-4 (hardcopy : alk. paper) — ISBN 978-0-313-39152-1
(ebook)   1. National security.   2. Environmental policy.
3. Environmental protection.   I. Title.
    UA10.5.C39   2013
    363.7—dc23   2012037985

ISBN: 978-0-313-39151-4
EISBN: 978-0-313-39152-1

17 16 15 14 13   1 2 3 4 5

This book is also available on the World Wide Web as an eBook.
Visit www.abc-clio.com for details.

Praeger
An Imprint of ABC-CLIO, LLC

ABC-CLIO, LLC
130 Cremona Drive, P.O. Box 1911
Santa Barbara, California 93116-1911

This book is printed on acid-free paper ∞

Manufactured in the United States of America

Contents

Foreword

Security and the environment are deeply interconnected. Humans are dependent on our environments for basic human needs and for the resources we have used to grow wealthier than ever and improve our quality of life as a species. Yet, as human impacts on our local, national and global environments accelerate, we are seeing more—not fewer—challenges to our safety and well-being as a result. Environmental security issues are here to stay.

Environmental security was once a new and untested concept—but no longer. For decades, debate raged as evidence and high-quality research mounted. Elizabeth Chalecki's analysis here demonstrates that national security and human security are deeply and complexly connected to aspects of our environment around natural resource extraction and use, food and climate change issues, and war-making and military-security operations around the world. Today, academics, activists, and policy makers in many countries grapple with these issues every day. Environmental security analysis and planning are now the subjects of offices in the U.S. Central Intelligence Agency, the Department of State, and the Department of Defense. National security institutes around the world, long the bastions of traditional national security ideas, have taken environment and security connections into their portfolios, as have military academies in the United States and abroad.

As this book demonstrates, the growing threats to human security posed by increasing environmental change are already altering our thinking and theories about international relations and civil war, as well as the everyday policy decisions made in national capitals and defense and security planning offices around the world. Students, like other citizens and many public officials, are beginning to grapple with environmental security questions: How will climate change impact our food and water supplies? How will it change migration patterns for people, animals, insects, viruses, and bacteria? If demand for oil, gas, and mineral resources grows indefinitely, will we need more

international law and cooperation or more military assets—or both—to protect our access to the things we need and want? How much will it cost to
adapt to climate and other environmental changes, if we have to rebuild
large portions of our infrastructure even as we seek to help people in other
countries to adapt to changes in their areas? Are our governments up to these
tasks?

From classrooms to boardrooms and the corridors of government power,
environmental security is of growing concern—and there is much to be done.
Chalecki's *Environmental Security: A Guide to the Issues* not only identifies
governance challenges and security threats posed on ongoing environmental
change, it seeks to identify what we can do about these growing problems.
A modern, high-tech military consumes enormous amounts of oil, gas, and
electricity just as it consumes massive mineral and industrial resources to continue its operations in peacetime and in war. Security planners the world
over seek to secure their access to the materials they need. Small and large
businesses face the same challenge. If they are to profit and grow, they need
secure and reliable access to the resources required to make the products and
services they sell. But access to the resources any of us might want is not the
only concern. If a powerful nation secures its access to scarce water or oil
either by paying a higher price or by using force to get what it wants, it may
well end up denying such resources to others. These scarcities can result in
greater trading and innovation to meet growing demand, or they may result
in increased violence or poverty or oppression. This growing competition for
resources takes place in a warming world, which can change national borders,
food production patterns, and the frequency and strength of extreme weather
events.

Pursuing national security is a complicated task. Should Americans build
massive pipelines to bring oil and gas from Canada and open their parks and
offshore areas for more oil and gas exploration to avoid being dependent on
other, less friendly or less stable countries? Many Americans would say yes,
but if climate change is also a threat to security, and oil and gas and coal
consumption increases climate change, which choice makes Americans more
secure? Likewise, many Europeans do not want to be dependent on Russia
for oil and gas, but the choices between becoming more energy efficient and
investing in renewable energy production, nuclear power, or coal-fired power
plants have very different implications for European and global security.

Defending a nation's interests, people, and borders from foreign enemies
is complicated and unpredictable, as the long history of defense strategizing
and war making by governments makes clear. Yet traditional defense looks
straightforward compared to aspects of environmental security. Consider, for
example, that a world with a changing global climate makes it harder to predict where humanitarian crises are likely to occur and where and how food

production is likely to increase or decline. Consider that, as one nation tries to address climate change by substituting more biofuels for fossil fuels like gasoline and diesel, it might drive up the costs of food around the world, resulting in food riots or worse. What if a nation makes a big push for electric cars or wind turbines to produce renewable energy, but the minerals in batteries and other components of these "cleaner" technologies have to be mined in the Democratic Republic of the Congo or other conflict zones? What if one country invests foreign aid to improve food production in another country, only to see those funds go up in smoke when drought or civil war ensues? Which policy choices leave us more secure?

Despite the fact that food-related issues have been central to domestic and international security for generations—high prices and bread riots, for example, have long histories as important components of conflict—food security is too often underappreciated in contemporary security discussions. Pressing scarcities in available clean water, arable land, fisheries, and soil quality combine with uncertainties about the local impacts and variability associated with a changing climate to put millions of people at risk around the world. If policy makers are not careful and well informed, the policies and private sector investments designed to address one set of problems, such as the lack of electricity in poorer regions, can make other problems much worse through their actions. Electricity generation—from nuclear power, fossil fuel resources, or hydrological sources—requires huge amounts of water, as do manufacturing and many improvements in agricultural productivity. Poorly analyzed and regulated water management can easily result in gains for some, and dangerous scarcities for others. As examples around the world demonstrate, huge demonstrations, violence and repression can all result when people are denied access to water or land, or fear that they are about to be excluded. Consequently, water management or electricity investments are not only developmental or environmental questions. They are also issues of central concern for social order, peace, and security.

Elizabeth Chalecki's *Environmental Security* identifies the critical issues facing citizens and policy makers, offering well-supported arguments for actions designed to reduce environmental degradation and enhance national and human security. Meeting these challenges, as she makes clear, requires policy and behavior changes at home and abroad. Americans, Europeans, and other citizens of the world's wealthier countries have much to do to put their own houses in order, just as they face a host of foreign and security challenges abroad. This book makes it clear we need to get busy.

Stacy VanDeveer
University of New Hampshire

Preface and Acknowledgments

When Praeger first approached me about writing the *Environmental Security* volume for their Contemporary Security Issues series, I thought that this would be a great opportunity to put the basic ideas of environmental security in front of a whole new audience. This volume, like the others in the series, is a primer aimed at students, policy makers, and the curious public. The topic is very large and connected to very many other issues in security and international relations such as economic development; demographic trends; social, cultural, and religious issues; and domestic politics. I could not possibly address every facet of every related issue, or this book would have become too heavy to lift. However, there should be enough here to make clear the links between environmental issues and security concerns, and spark further study.

I would like to thank several people: my colleague and friend Stacy VanDeveer for his excellent introduction, and his encouragement when I told him I wanted to write "not another academic tome" about a topic that interests both of us; my editor Steve Catalano at Praeger, who was patient with my occasional disappearance off the grid; Robin Tutt at ABC-CLIO, who did a heroic job dealing with the graphics and pictures contained herein; and my colleagues and students at Boston College and Goucher College who inspire me with their questions and insights. Special appreciation and gratitude go to my invaluable research assistants Katya Rucker and Peter Morizio, who cheerfully tracked down obscure references and proofread endless pages. I expect world-changing things from you guys, so get busy.

Beth Chalecki
Goucher College
October 2012

CHAPTER 1

Historical and Current Overview of the Issue

The United States is providing the leadership to promote global peace and prosperity. We must also lead in safeguarding the global environment on which that prosperity and peace ultimately depend.
—Former U.S. Secretary of State Warren Christopher

National security has traditionally been seen as a matter relating to the military defense of state borders. Now, however, global environmental phenomena such as climate change, deforestation, and extreme weather events all have an impact on national security. This means that any nation wishing to preserve or strengthen its national interest must not only be ready to deal with environmental issues within its own territory, but must cooperate with other nations on the world stage to ameliorate environmental problems.

Traditional Views of National Security

When most people think of national security, they think of war. War and the preparation for war have been the constant focus of security practitioners since the birth of the modern nation-state. Although different countries give greater or lesser priority to different national values, a nation's ability to defend itself has always been its paramount value. Political realists follow Hans Morgenthau's lead in equating the national interest with national security and hence with the preservation and expansion of state power (see Morgenthau 1948). Since the military has been the traditional means of securing this power, national security has come to mean military might.

When viewed as a military outcome, national security was calculated with a simple metric. One nation's armed forces met another nation's armed forces on the battlefield, and whichever side had superior strength, cunning, and tenacity won the battle and was awarded the prize of national security. War could be started by decree, as when Lincoln requested troops in response to the Confederacy's firing on Fort Sumter before the U.S. Civil War. War could be started by sudden attack, as in the Japanese attack on Pearl Harbor, or by stealth and creeping encroachment, as in Hitler's Anschluss before World War II. War could even be started by the act of a single individual, as in the assassination of an Austrian official before World War I. However, the deciding factor in victory was the military might of one state or a combination of states. War would be over when the government of one nation surrendered to the government of the other. Security was defined as a wholly state-based affair: the government proposed and the military disposed.

Zero-Sum Realism

For political realists, this makes perfect sense. The international system is anarchic and always has been, and each nation that values its existence (that is to say, every nation) has the right and duty to act to protect itself against its enemies. Although countries give greater or lesser priority to different national values, the ability of a country to defend itself has always been its paramount value. Since the only force that was seen to threaten the existence of a nation was another nation's armed forces, security as defined in the context of power was logical and just. National security in an anarchic system is a zero-sum game: if one nation gains a certain measure of security, it means that another nation has lost security in that same measure.

Morality is irrelevant to realists of the Morgenthauian persuasion, as are alliances between nations. A state's only moral goal is its survival, and any action which supports that survival is allowable, if not strictly moral, in a realist world. Because one state can never know with certainty what another state will do to ensure its survival, alliances are temporary at best and never to be chosen over national interest. Consequently, decisions are best made on a unitary basis. Morgenthau wrote these rules down in 1948, after decades of world wars and economic turmoil. Modern students of environmental security will have to ask themselves whether these assumptions about national interest and power are still true.

Although the ability of a state to defend and preserve itself has always been its supreme value, states give different national values greater or lesser priority depending upon their own internal security calculus (see Wolfers 1952, Baldwin 1997). Other national values might include political systems, cultural homogeneity, religious purity, economic openness, or ecological health, though this last value occurs only rarely as a specific national interest. Realists argue that without security, none of these other interests can be protected, though what constitutes security itself changes from time to time and from nation to nation. Arnold Wolfers wrote at mid-century:

> Security is a value, then, of which a nation can have more or less and which it can aspire to have in greater or lesser measure. . . . (Wolfers 1952, 484)

Security, then, is not an absolute value, but a derivative one. A nation will identify its core values and take steps to secure them from threat. How secure the nation wishes to make those values will then lead it to ask more or less of its citizens in sacrifice, so if a country greatly fears attack from a foreign army, it might require military conscription. If a nation wishes to insulate itself from economic shock, it may disallow imports. If it wishes to be secure in energy supplies, it may build nuclear reactors. But in recognizing the range of values that a nation wishes to secure, it is important to realize that there are values that will not be secured by power.

Realism's contrasting theory, the theory of liberalism, posits that security is achieved collectively. Because states are embedded in an international system that constrains their actions, improved security for one state does not automatically result in decreased security for others. Liberals argue that while the international system is anarchic because there is no overarching authority to compel the behavior of sovereign states, the gains and losses incurred by a state after a particular action or policy are encouragement or deterrent enough. Because security under liberalism is not zero-sum, collective gains can be made by strengthening the international institutions that guide state behavior. The role of collective gains in the pursuit of environmental security will be reexamined in Chapter 6.

What is axiomatic in any discussion of national security in the traditional sense is that the threat to security is always exogenous; it comes from another nation or group of people (e.g., tribe, ethnic group, terrorist cell). Nowhere in traditional security studies, except for those forward thinkers discussed later in this chapter, appears the idea that a security threat may be *endogenous*, that is to say, coming from within, from our own peacetime behaviors. Further, nowhere in the discussion of national interest is any mention made that a country's legitimate national interest would include a stable ecosystem. Only recently have we recognized that human activities could alter the global ecosystem to the point where our economic capabilities, territorial integrity, and public health could be jeopardized.

High Politics vs. Low Politics

Now the question arises: how are nations defending themselves and from what sorts of threats? Modern national security is no longer merely a function of state-based military capabilities, and does not wholly resemble national security in Morgenthau's time. State capabilities are asymmetric in power and their strategies are asymmetric in aim.

Modern military forces in most countries are very powerful and equipped with new and increasingly destructive technology. This confidence in technological capability may lead powerful nations into wars of choice by fooling them into thinking that their weapons are so superior that war will be easy, as in the American invasion of Iraq. However, most wars now are not likely to occur between one state and another—though this is always a possibility—but between a state and a nonstate actor like Al Qaeda, or between two tribes or ethnic groups within a state as in Sudan or Yemen.

It is interesting to note—though such analysis lends itself to bias—to what degree the definitions and assumptions about national security have been colored by the perception that security is guaranteed by mostly male military forces and is not something in which women play a significant role. **High politics,** in its Hobbesian form, refers to those things that are critical to the survival of the state, such as armies, weapons, nuclear missiles—anything related to national and international security. **Low politics,** by contrast, encompasses policies that are thought not to be critical to state survival, such as the environment, demographics, education, culture, and public health—all the things in which women have had greater representation. A thorough discussion of the role of women in national security is beyond the scope of this volume, but for further consideration of the gender dimensions of security and international relations see Elshtain 1985, Cohn 1987, Tickner 1992, and Wibben 2004.

Low politics, ecological health included, are not to be discounted as factors in the high politics calculations of national and international security. When we look at the current security crises around the world, we can see that many of them have their roots in low politics. For example, war has raged in Afghanistan for over 30 years, as the Afghans have faced attack first from the Soviet Union and then from NATO and the United States. The outward rationale for this interference in Afghanistan was Cold War politics, but when examined more fundamentally, population growth, agricultural resources including opium, and religious extremism have been the drivers of war. The most horrific examples of ethnic cleansing in Bosnia, Kosovo, and most recently, Darfur, have also been fueled by religious and cultural differences and growing population. More recently, the stability and economic recovery of Haiti, already a mammoth task, has been shaken by the news that UN peacekeeping troops recently arrived from Nepal brought with them a new and deadly strain of cholera that killed over 5,500 people and sickened hundreds of thousands more. Even now, the political unrest spreading across the Middle East and North Africa stems in part from food shortages, and it is instructive to realize that something as quotidian as food can bring down a state regime.

History of Environmental Security Thinking

Breaking the Mold

Beginning in the late 1960s, a few thinkers began to view threats to national security through a larger lens and consider environmental issues as drivers of national security threats. In 1968, Paul Ehrlich wrote *The Population Bomb* in which he posited three scenarios for future development in a world of overpopulation and scarce resources; all three ended in starvation and war, with the most "optimistic" scenario predicting the death of only one-fifth of the world's population (Ehrlich 1968, 72–80). The connections between overpopulation, resources, and war were elucidated further two years later, when he and coauthors Anne Ehrlich and John Holdren concluded that,

> Finite resources in a world of expanding populations and increasing per-capita demands create a situation ripe for international violence. The perceived need to control resources has been a major factor is U.S. military and paramilitary involvements around the globe since World War II. (Ehrlich et al. 1970, 909)

In 1977, Lester Brown, founder of the Worldwatch Institute, argued that systemic environmental issues such as climate change, deforestation, and loss of arable land could be nonmilitary drivers of insecurity, and that military forces would be ineffective against these new threats. To counter them would require a new vision of security. Brown recommended reallocation of budgetary assets to meet the spectrum of threats to security, military as well as nonmilitary, though he warned that "few individuals are trained or able to weigh and evaluate such a diversity of threats and then to translate such an assessment into the allocation of public resources that provides the greatest national security" (Brown 1977, 38).

In 1983, Richard Ullman argued for the "redefinition" of what constitutes a national security threat to include endogenous threats like environmental conditions in addition to traditional state and military concerns. He defined a national security threat as,

> an action or sequence of events that (1) threatens drastically and over a relatively brief span of time to degrade the quality of life for the inhabitants of a state, or (2) threatens significantly to narrow the range of policy choices available to the government of a state or to private,

non-governmental entities (persons, groups, corporations) within the
state. (Ullman 1983, 134)

This definition of national security significantly expands the realms of
what can be viewed as a threat. No longer is military protection of a state's
borders sufficient to guarantee security, and in fact Ullman warned that
defining national security primarily in terms of military threats conveyed
a false image of reality because it allowed states to ignore other harmful
dangers, such as civil conflicts, overpopulation, and public health crises
that reduced their overall security. However, the Cold War was a time of
zero-sum security metrics measured in ICBM throw weights, Trident submarine MIRVs, and megatons of nuclear destruction. National security meant
that one side had more, or at least better-targeted, nuclear missiles than the
other side, and concerns such as fresh water, arable cropland, and greenhouse gases were either ignored or shoved into the portfolio of low politics.
At the time, Brown's and Ullman's admonitions to focus on nonnuclear,
nonstate, environmentally based strategic threats were not well received or
widely heeded.

As Much Security through Trees as through Tanks

However, as the Cold War began winding down, environmental issues
began to emerge from their nuclear eclipse, and what came to be known
as environmental security theory was reexamined beginning in 1989. Jessica
Mathews called for redefining security to include environmental threats, stating that the institutions and assumptions that governed international relations and national security since the end of World War II were "a poor fit"
with the new realities of environmental stresses, demographic changes, and
the decline of U.S. economic hegemony (Mathews 1989, 162), in particular
the obsolete assumption that national interests end with territorial borders.
In the same year, David Wirth, writing in *Foreign Policy*, pointed out that the
United States would suffer significantly from warming-induced sea level rise
and warned that "policymakers should give the most serious consideration
to the security implications of the ongoing failure to anticipate and arrest
greenhouse warming" (Wirth 1989, 10). Norman Myers was more specific,
pointing out that environmentally driven problems such as water security
in the Middle East, soil erosion in El Salvador, and outmigration in Mexico
have the potential to become conflicts; he also noted that the time could
"be coming when as much lasting security can be purchased through trees as
through tanks" (Myers 1989, 41).

In 1991, three critical articles came out spotlighting the link (or
nonlink) between environmental conditions and security threats. Thomas

Homer-Dixon (1991), in "On the Threshold," argued that environmental degradation can cause conflict, especially in poor countries with less robust adaptive capacity, in one of four ways: reduced agricultural production, economic decline, population displacement, and/or disruption of legitimate social relations. In turn, this would cause scarcity disputes between countries or ethnic groups. Examples will be discussed in later chapters.

Homer-Dixon pointed out that the modern realist perspective in international relations was insufficient to deal with issues of environmental security because it viewed states as rational power maximizers in an otherwise anarchic system (Homer-Dixon 1991, 84). In Morgenthauian terms, states are territorially distinct and mutually exclusive. With each nation in a zero-sum system looking to advance its own interests over those of its neighbors, there is no incentive to solve transboundary ecological problems cooperatively. Rather, there is incentive to free-ride on the good behavior of your neighbor.

At the same time, Peter Gleick and Daniel Deudney published pro and con articles surrounding the topic in the same journal. Gleick argued that a redefinition of national security was not required, but rather an expanded understanding of the nature of threats to security, especially links between natural resources and international behavior. He saw the growing economic and technical inequity between the developed countries in the global North and the developing countries in the global South as a possible security problem. In order to forestall environmentally driven conflict, he recommended a transfer of resources from North to South, both to counter arguments of environmental inequity and to curb the environmentally destructive development practices demanded by Northern institutions such as the World Bank and the IMF that would be fueling much of the coming degradation (Gleick 1991, 21). In this way, the development gap between the North and the South would not spiral into conflict.

Deudney, on the other hand, argued that national security has traditionally concerned itself with protection from organized violence, and if redefined (i.e., conflated with environmental degradation), the term "national security" would lose all analytical usefulness. Since the two concepts are fundamentally different in nature and in scope (security has "them and their behavior" as the enemy, whereas environmentalism has "us and our behavior" as the enemy), the traditional national security apparatus is insufficient to deal with the new environmental problems, and in Deudney's eyes, this meant that they were not security problems (Deudney 1991, 25). The Cold War definition of national security that restricted the field of security studies to military affairs largely prevailed in the security community during the following decade (see Levy 1995).

In the early scholars' attempts to clarify the relationship between environmental issues and national security, the definition of security was rewritten once again:

> A national security issue is any trend or event that (1) threatens the very survival of the nation; and/or (2) threatens to drastically reduce the welfare of the nation in a fashion that requires a centrally coordinated national mobilization of resources to mitigate or reverse. (Goldstone 1996, 66)

While Goldstone should have added the word "external" to his description of trend or event, this definition and the ones preceding it are important to consider because they were instrumental in prying open the domain of security studies for input from other disciplines. Since Westphalia, the function of national security has revolved around protecting a state's borders, and up until the age of global environmental phenomena, the only thing that could penetrate a state's borders was another state's military force (or, on occasion, refugees in large numbers). Now, however, forces that can pose a security threat to a state's citizens are not always military in nature.

Environmental security in this instance is not to be confused with *human security*; the two concepts are related, but they are not identical. The redefinition of the idea of national security in the 1980s and 1990s broadened it significantly to include many nonmilitary threats. However, human security, as it is understood in a modern academic sense, deals with forces such as development, famine, and disease that are threats to the well-being of individuals regardless of their status as citizens, thereby making the human the referent of security (see generally Gasper 2005, Uvin 2004). While many of the forces acting to threaten human security are created or exacerbated by environmental degradation, the referent of security for this volume is the state and the international system as a whole.

Countervailing Arguments

Some scholars have argued that the term "environmental security" is misleading or incomplete, and have leveled three types of countervailing arguments against the linkage of environmental and national security. Much of the disagreement has to do with the definitions of "environment" and "security," respectively.

The first and most commonly made argument is that environmental issues cannot be security problems because they do not involve a traditional security apparatus like the military. Consequently, any attempt to link national security and environmental drivers is merely an attempt to attract some of the high politics glamour of security to the low politics topic of the environment; far from environmental issues threatening national security, the security establishment itself appears to be threatened by an undue emphasis on the environment (Deudney 1991). Because the military is the customary frame in which to place issues of national security, it appears to be used with exclusion.

> A common thought experiment used to separate security threats from other threats . . . is to ask whether the values affected and the degree of degradation threatened are sufficient to provoke a military defense. For any alleged security threat, one can ask, "Would we fight over it?" (Levy 1995, 41)

In asking this question, Levy is relying on traditional security thinking to assess this connection, and it is not surprising that those who make this argument cannot fit endogenous drivers into the nation-state–based security framework. Dalby (2002) agrees, arguing that classifying particular environmental threats as security threats causes the solution to be misframed as a military one and not one of economic development. However, we now know that military capability is not necessarily the barometer for determining a critical national security interest. Even when assessing a traditional security situation, the military may still be the wrong instrument to use. Some international issues are of such critical concern that they can legitimately be considered security threats (e.g., oil, Islamic fundamentalism), and yet a military response has not only *not* secured the threat in question, but it has arguably made the condition worse.

The second countervailing view against environmental security argues that linking national security and the environment smacks of **eco-colonialism**, or environmental rule-setting by the global North for its own benefit at the expense of the developing South. To this end, Jon Barnett thinks that the economic exploitation of the South by the North has driven much of the environmental degradation that the North is now trying to address. By labeling it a security problem, the North's considerable resources will now be directed toward ensuring that this inequality is permanent and militarized (Barnett 2001). His view contains a necessary cautionary element—that military means to attain security can be environmentally destructive (see Chapter 5 for further discussion of collateral environmental damage) and that a defensive war mentality on the part of states can obscure cooperative solutions to global or transboundary environmental problems.

However, the eco-colonialism frame is misplaced for two reasons. First, and consistent with the argument above, security is not always something best guaranteed by the military. If an environmental problem presents a security risk, military involvement may make the situation worse, not better. Second, Barnett thinks that environmental degradation is something the North has perpetrated on the South. Although colonialism has historically involved the transfer of natural resources from South to North, environmental security should not be viewed through a simple North vs. South framework. Developing countries have allowed plenty of environmental degradation within their own states in pursuit of economic development. Population, an environmental stressor second to none, has been rising in the global South much faster than in the North, and is predicted to account for 86 percent of the total global population by 2050 (Population Reference Bureau 2008). Finally, developing states themselves are concerned about South-South environmental security issues. Not all developing states are developing at the same rate, and what once appeared to be a clear have–have not divide is more nuanced in reality.

The third argument is not so much a countervailing view of the concept as a search for proof by making the idea of environmental security fit within a predefined academic framework. Scholars at the Peace Research Institute Oslo have attempted to uncover a rigorous statistical correlation between indicators of environmental change of various kinds and the severity of conflict in the area affected by the change. Their research has yielded mixed results, which leads them to conclude that the connection between environmental drivers and security outcomes is yet unproven. Their use of conflict models and databases is predicated upon the assumption that the future is becoming more peaceful (Nordås & Gleditsch 2007, 635).

While academic frameworks and peer review are necessary to demonstrate the durability of a thesis, statistically based assumptions about real world events suffer from key weaknesses. Statistical models are not and cannot be as complex as the real world. Consequently, any representation of a relationship between two variables (e.g., lack of rainfall and violence) will not account for all the intervening variables that govern the outcome. A statistical mean that averages data over a country or a set time period will often hide substantial regional or temporal variations, so what looks to be a nonsignificant trend can in fact be very significant for a particular subset of the data. Conversely, the exclusion of information about one country or region can make an otherwise significant result statistically insignificant. Data gathered at a national level may not reflect local conditions (see Raleigh & Urdal 2007), so if the results of a statistical model show a lack of apparent correlation between two variables, this does not mean that they are not in fact correlated in any situation. Just because a large-N study does not find a statistically significant relationship between two variables across the entire sample does not mean that the relationship should not be examined on a case-by-case basis.

The first argument assumes that security is a unitary problem viewed through a military lens and possessing a unitary solution. In order to maintain this exclusionary frame, Deudney drops the environment as an acceptable driver. The second argument assumes that since a sovereign nation in an anarchic international system is permitted to do anything it can to ensure its national security, "environmental security" is the perfect label to use to justify status quo–preserving behavior. Therefore Northern interest in environmental security is a thinly disguised attempt at colonialism, and Barnett drops national security as an acceptable outcome. The third argument is only justified within a particularly narrow methodological straitjacket. All three of these countervailing arguments attempt to predefine the terms "environment" and "security" and then fit them into existing frameworks rather than examine the connection on a messy, inconsistent, and wholly necessary case-by-case basis.

Modern Environmental Security

From 1991 to 2006, the study of environmental security in the United States lagged, not on the academic side, but on the policy side. Much of the reason for this gap had to do with the dearth of environmental legislation during the Bill Clinton administration, including the passage of the Byrd-Hagel Resolution in the U.S. Senate in 1997 which preemptively rejected the Kyoto Protocol for ratification. After the *Bush v. Gore* Supreme Court decision awarding the 2000 election to George W. Bush, his administration and the Republican-controlled Congress subsequently refused to address environmental issues in any form. It wasn't until 2006, when the Democrats retook both the Senate and the House of Representatives, that the logjam broke and discussion of the environment could again take place in the political sphere.*

That same year, two studies were released which examined the role of climate change as a security driver: one from the Center for Naval Analyses (CNA) and one from the Center for Strategic and International Studies and the Brookings Institution. These could have been just another academic exercise, but the CNA study in particular was noteworthy because it was

---

* The only exception occurred in 2003, when a research office in the U.S. Department of Defense commissioned a study from an independent research firm looking at the international security implications of a large climate shift. Their conclusion that climate was intimately connected to security and that the United States would suffer hugely under a changed climate was not popularly received by the president's political advisors, and the report was subsequently disavowed by the administration (see Schwartz & Randall 2003).

authored by a number of retired three- and four-star military officers who wrote about the effects of environmental degradation and resource scarcity from their own careers (CNA 2006; see also Campbell ed. 2008).

Ecosystem Services

A key component in any discussion of security is the different national values that states are seeking to protect. These could be liberty, religious expression, capitalism, and political dominance of one social group, among many values. What makes the environment so valuable? The answer is **ecosystem services**. These are the goods and services that a healthy ecosystem provides for us, including but not limited to those outlined in Table 1.1.

In 1997, Robert Costanza, an ecological economist at the University of Maryland, attempted with his colleagues to calculate the dollar value of the world's ecosystem services. Using conservative estimates of value wherever possible, they reached the range of $15–58 trillion 1997 dollars, with an average value of $33 trillion (Costanza et al. 1997). To compare that to a more traditional economic measure, the global GDP at that time was $18 trillion. This means that nature gives us almost twice the value of what we can provide for ourselves, and it does so for free. Human technology can replace some of these services *temporarily*, such as purification of water (e.g., we can build a water treatment plant to do artificially what a wetland does naturally, but at much greater expense). However, it is all but impossible for humans to duplicate all these services on a global scale over the long term. Nature is simply too complex a system for human knowledge to reproduce.

Table 1.1 Examples of Ecosystem Services

Climate stabilization	Air and water purification
Moderation of weather extremes, such as hurricanes and storms	Disease regulation
Pollination of plants, including grains, crops, and vegetables	Dispersal of seeds
Protection against ultraviolet radiation	Mitigation of floods and droughts
Detoxification and decomposition of wastes	Pest control
Generation and preservation of fertile soils	Cycling and moving nutrients
Erosion protection	Generation and maintenance of biodiversity

Methods of Attaining Security Are Changing

As we expand the definition of national security to include consideration of threats from nontraditional drivers, we must also reconsider how security is to be attained in the face of these drivers. The realist view of international power assumes that states are the guarantors of security, that all states have the same strategic goals, and that security comes at the expense of other states. This means that nations compete to become more secure than their neighbors, a problem known as the **security dilemma**. Actions that nations may take to increase their security, such as building up military forces, leaves neighboring states less secure. These states then build up their own forces, reducing the global security balance to its original condition (see Jervis 1978). Is the security dilemma relevant to environmental security? In a limited way, yes. Nations that wish to secure particular resources like fresh water or food may view the acquisition of these resources as a type of security dilemma: if I don't dam this river, my upstream neighbor might. But when considering the stability of the global environment as a whole, the security dilemma does not apply.

Due to the very nature of climate change and other global environmental phenomena, environmental security *cannot* be addressed in an anarchic fashion. For example, if the United States works to retool its economy and bring down its greenhouse gas emissions, it will not accrue that climate benefit solely for itself. It must involuntarily share that benefit with all other nations on earth. Similarly, if the United States continues to emit GHGs and destabilize the climate, not only will it suffer the ecological consequences, but so will everyone else. No amount of power or policy will make the atmosphere directly above the United States "American atmosphere," a space in which the United States can unilaterally do what it wishes. Consequently, its security now involuntarily rests, at least in part, on the actions and decisions of other nations.

If the physical environment cannot be governed by means of political boundaries, then it should not be surprising that traditional military strength is no longer sufficient to guarantee state security, as the recent American experiences with Al Qaeda have demonstrated. Asymmetrical aims and capabilities in modern international relations can nullify the advantage of superior military technology and superior numbers of powerful nations, and bring strong vs. weak conflicts to a stalemate. If combat has traditionally been the main competency of military forces, their capabilities now need to stress **stability operations**, or operations other than war (OOTW). Stability ops include the power to "maintain or reestablish a safe and secure environment, provide essential government services, emergency infrastructure reconstruction, and humanitarian relief" (FM3–07, vi). Specific instances of OOTW will be addressed in later chapters. The U.S. Army is already emphasizing stability operations in its planning and training, and has declared that stability operations are not secondary to combat operations, but are parallel in importance. The need for any nation's armed forces to provide stability ops can arise from a number of situations, irrespective of whether they are environmentally related or not. However, as environmental issues contribute to insecurity and possibly conflict, the OOTW capabilities of the world's military forces will be called upon to a greater degree.

Confounding Problems

A new consideration of national and international security means that we must now include new methods of thinking in our study. This is, of course, easier said than done, for both academics and policy makers. First, because the intersection of global ecology and international relations is so rich and complex, there is rarely one causal chain to follow when tracing the connection between environmental drivers and security outcomes. This means that two variables can relate in different ways, directly and via a feedback loop. For example, increasing temperatures in the Arctic will cause reflective ice and snow to melt, uncovering darker ground and ocean beneath. The darker surfaces generate more heat, raising temperatures. Such self-reinforcing loops are known as positive, while a loop that cancels itself is negative. Since feedback loops occur both in environmental sciences and in social sciences, we may expect that they occur at the intersection of these two fields. Unfortunately, they can make solutions harder to achieve because our understanding of global ecological science and our ability to predict the consequences of human activity are still incomplete.

Second, complex environmental security issues occur across varying scales of time and space. Transboundary resources like forests or watersheds and global environmental commons like the oceans or the atmosphere exist independently of national political boundaries, which makes solutions dependent upon international cooperation. Issues like climate change or ozone depletion, in which the effect may be separated in time from the cause by years or decades, require nations to shoulder the cost of the solution now without enjoying the benefit at the same time. This means that effective solutions require a policy-making time horizon well ahead of the two- and four-year election cycles politicians favor, much less the year-to-year reassessment of national security needs. This is a confounding effect because politicians and security planners do not generally operate under long time horizons, and prefer to push the search for solutions into the future.

Upcoming Environmental Security Threats

In the subsequent chapters of this volume, we will examine the various types of resources and environmental conditions that can become drivers of insecurity, and in some cases, where the quest for security can in turn affect the environment.

Natural Resources

Most discussions of natural resource security are driven by the competing notions of scarcity and plenty: does a lack of natural resources cause insecurity and conflict, or does their abundance? Depending upon the type of resource, its uses, and the places where it is found, both of these conditions are true.

Resource scarcity is the most obvious environmental security concern, because basic natural resources like food and water are critical for survival. British demographer Thomas Malthus argued in 1798 that humanity was perfectly capable of overreproducing and if human populations were left unchecked, we would outgrow and outstrip our food supply, resulting in death from famine and disease. Malthus, a clergyman in the Church of England, thought this constant threat of famine was God's way of keeping humanity from the sin of laziness. Sin aside, Malthusians regard resource shortages as the limiting factor for civilization, and warn that humanity must lower its population growth or suffer possibly catastrophic famine.

Global population has surpassed 7 billion, however, and we have not yet seen a worldwide famine (localized famines usually have a political or distributional component, discussed further in Chapter 3 of this volume). This is due largely to two factors. First, nations generally do not operate in conditions of autarky (no trade). If one nation is facing a food or energy shortfall, it can generally buy what it needs on the world market. Nations that have open trading policies generally do not face resource shortages. Second, technological advances can obviate shortages of critical goods by providing substitutes where possible. For example, copper was predicted to be in short supply as construction of telephone lines increased. Once fiber optics was invented, substituting glass cable for copper, the demand for copper dropped and the upcoming "shortage" disappeared. As humanity invents new technology, the demand for resources can increase or decrease depending upon the technology involved.

Water Resources

For some basic goods like water, however, there is no substitute. Water resources are critical not only for human life and health, but also for ecological diversity, economic development, energy, and national security.

Although 70 percent of the earth's surface is covered with water, only 2.5 percent of that water is fresh, and only 0.7 percent is available to humans. Shortage of fresh water, not its abundance, is the security issue. Although there is plenty of water on earth if measured on a global per capita basis, it is not distributed equally around the world and is certainly not plentiful in all populated areas.

Increasing population globally means greater need for fresh water, and competition between users of this limited resource means that existing supplies can be oversubscribed. Surface water such as rivers and lakes are withdrawn for municipal water supplies, irrigation of farmland, and power plant cooling. Groundwater is pumped up from aquifers for agriculture at an increasingly unsustainable rate. Climate change will affect water availability by changing the form and timing of precipitation: rain may fall earlier or later than expected, it may fall in the form of rain rather than snow, or it may fall in greater or lesser quantity. These changes will affect food production, transportation, energy, economic production, and general public health, as discussed further in Chapter 2.

How does fresh water affect national security? Watershed boundaries do not line up neatly with political and state boundaries, so nations that are able will construct water infrastructure to alter the hydrological cycle and increase their domestic water supply. Water use is linked to energy production (e.g., nuclear power, hydroelectricity, hydraulic fracturing), and hence to energy security, so nations that are developing will find it necessary to obtain and secure water supplies to build industry. However, countries facing water stress (less than 1,667 m^3/year) may find themselves at a development impasse.

Since water is becoming an increasingly scarce resource, environmental security theory states that nations may fight over it (see Homer-Dixon 1991, 1995). However, while the potential for conflict over water exists and will be exacerbated by growing populations and climate change, this does not mean that water conflicts are guaranteed. Recent environmental security research, discussed further in Chapter 2, finds that nations with shared water resources will negotiate and cooperate over the allocation of these resources rather than enter into conflict.

Diamonds/Timber/Minerals

Unlike the case of fresh water, where scarcity is the environmental security driver, abundance of commodity resources like diamonds, timber, gold, and other minerals can exacerbate conflict by providing a source of funds. Several examples of this type of environmental security issue have occurred since the end of the Cold War. During the 1990s and 2000s, Charles Taylor used the revenue from sales of diamonds to continue his violent 15-year regime across Liberia and Sierra Leone. Tropical hardwoods have provided the means for continuation of civil war in Cambodia, Indonesia, and Myanmar (Burma), and the Democratic Republic of the Congo has paid for the death of over 5.5 million people since the mid-1990s with diamonds, copper, zinc, and coltan.

Nations that have significant wealth in commodity resources often suffer from lower levels of development and higher levels of corruption and violent conflict than would be expected for so-called rich nations. This is known as the **resource curse**. Why do some resource-rich states fall prey to corruption and conflict and others don't? By itself, the existence of natural resources does not mean a nation will become corrupt. Rather, conflict is dependent upon other political, economic, and military factors such as the lack of democratic tradition, tribal loyalties, and the lack of diversity in the economy. If a nation is already developed and subject to the rule of law when valuable resources are discovered, then it will likely not suffer the resource curse because it already has transparent institutions in place to govern new wealth and a sufficiently developed economy that new resource money is not a significant portion of its GDP. Examples of nations that have avoided the resource curse include Canada, the United Kingdom, Norway, and Australia. However, if a nation is poor and less developed, or has little tradition of democracy or public accountability, then a sudden influx of new wealth is more likely to engender corruption, fuel traditional social and political divides, and prolong violence.

Conflicts triggered by resource abundance are generally not international in nature, since natural resource commodities such as diamonds and minerals are freely traded on the global market. Rather, resource abundance furthers internal conflicts, and even though they are not technically international wars, they are connected to international security in several ways. First, ongoing conflicts provide new markets for small arms trade, and several large developed countries enjoy robust arms exports to nations fighting civil wars. Second, civil conflicts can require international peacekeeping or peace enforcement troops, and will certainly require food and medical aid from the international community. Third, civil conflicts that last long enough can proliferate for-hire private security forces, also called mercenaries. In addition, because natural resources are extractive industries, collateral damage to the environment is often severe in resource abundance conflicts (addressed further in Chapter 5).

Petroleum

Petroleum resources are a unique natural commodity because both shortage and abundance of the resource are security issues. Oil is critical to the functioning of the modern global economy, used around the world for transportation fuel and for manufacturing of various goods including plastics. It is the number one traded commodity around the world, whether measured by value, by volume, or by the carrying capacity needed to move it (EIA n.d.). The environmental security aspect of petroleum is not generally a function of shortage or abundance. Since both oil and natural gas are traded transparently on the global market, price fluctuations are a clear signal of supply and demand. Rather, it is the nonmarket aspects of oil production and consumption that give rise to security concerns.

Oil-exporting nations face a unique set of security issues. Because global demand for oil increases every year, oil-exporting states have felt economically justified in basing significant portions of their entire national income on revenue from oil and very little else. Eighty percent of the Saudi Arabian treasury is funded by income from oil exports, as are 95 percent of the Nigerian treasury and 55 percent of the Venezuelan treasury (CIA World Factbook 2011). If the global price of oil drops, this leaves them with very little economic cushion. Terry Lynn Karl argues that oil-exporting states suffer from a special version of the resource curse. Called "petro-states," their oil wealth means that they have not had to develop politically transparent governance structures, so money and political power within the state is skewed toward a small minority. Moreover, their economic foundation has not diversified much beyond oil, which means that development is precarious (Karl 1997). Many petro-states like Saudi Arabia and Venezuela subsidize the price of gasoline and other basic goods to keep their populations pacified. Should these subsidies be curtailed due to the falling price of oil, the population can get restive and start demanding economic and political reforms, as we are currently seeing in countries across the Middle East and North Africa. Because oil wealth generally flows to an elite segment of the population, disenfranchised populations can also resort to violence and terrorism against the government and against any foreign oil companies working with the government. Militants can sabotage petroleum infrastructure, take hostages, usually from among foreign oil workers, and terrorize local populations (e.g., Colombia, Nigeria).

Oil-importing nations face their own security issues. Developed nations that rely heavily on imported oil, such as the United States, will state energy security as one of their national strategic interests. But what is energy security, and is it realistically achievable? Energy security, in the common political use of the term, means having access at all times to sufficient quantities and types of affordable energy to pursue a nation's development goals. However, most developed nations consume more oil than they produce, and in order to secure supply, may assist petro-states with economic or military aid. The quest for energy security can lead democracies to deal on a favorable basis with regimes that have questionable to poor human rights records, like Sudan and Saudi Arabia. Even the United States declared in 1980 that it would use all available tools of national power, including military force, to keep oil flowing from the Persian Gulf. As global oil prices increase, the people of oil-importing nations often agitate politically for energy independence, but is self-sufficiency in energy realistic? Not without a significant reduction in oil demand.

Food Security

Provision or lack of food is not traditionally considered to be key to national security, and yet a nation that cannot produce or import its food is not secure at the most fundamental level. Food security, defined by the UN as people having access to sufficient stock and supplies of food to provide a nutritionally adequate diet, derives from the availability of food, access to food for the entire population, optimal utilization of food, and the stability of the national food system over time. The majority of people facing food insecurity live in the developing world. Humans have dealt with food insecurity by increasing food production where possible, and our estimates of worldwide agricultural output, and hence global food security, are predicated upon our assumptions of a stable climate. However, environmental, political, and distributional factors will all affect food production and availability.

Climate change–induced fluctuations in temperature and precipitation will have a net negative effect on crop production by shifting the growing seasons and the expected rainfall. Extreme weather events such as flooding or droughts of the magnitude we are now seeing across North America can also affect crops at critical points in their growth. In addition, arable land has been redirected away from food crop production toward biofuel crop production, taking food off the global market and increasing food insecurity. Although biofuels are considered to be both better for the climate and an important alternative to oil from unstable regions of the world, the Intergovernmental Panel on Climate Change (IPCC) predicts that the world's nations will need to increase food production by 55 percent by 2030 just to keep up with growing population (IPCC AR4 WGII, 280–281). It is unclear as to where that increase in arable land is going to come from. Finally, as the world's population gets wealthier, they demand more animal protein, and this compounds food insecurity: 70 percent of the world's grain supply currently goes to feed livestock.

Global food prices are rising every year, and this relentless upward pressure means uncertainty and instability in the world's food markets. Climate-induced supply shocks such as the recent ban on wheat exports from Russia in the wake of a punishing drought exacerbate this instability, and can lead food-insecure nations to hoard stocks, further driving up prices. Political factors such as trade sanctions and social and cultural factors such as the status of women or the access of low-caste people to food can contribute to food insecurity.

Changes in the ability to produce food can lead to a shift in relative economic and political power between agricultural exporting states and importing countries. State governments can draw down national food stockpiles to offset shortages, but this is a stopgap measure at best. Food shortages and rising prices have already caused riots in over 60 countries and underlie much of the current unrest across North Africa and the Middle East. Food itself can be used as a weapon of war by governments which selectively withhold food to certain portions of the population to achieve political aims, even escalating to what one legal scholar calls "faminogenic" behavior (Marcus 2003). Food insecurity writ small is a tragedy, but food insecurity writ global can destabilize the entire international system and affect the national security interests of even food-plentiful nations (Brown 2009).

Climate Change

Article I of the 1992 UN Framework Convention on Climate Change defines climate change as "a change in climate which is attributed directly or indirectly to human activity that alters the composition of the global atmosphere and which is in addition to natural climate variability observed over comparable time periods." In its most recent assessment report, the IPCC concluded with a greater than 90 percent certainty that the earth's climate is warming and that humans are contributing to this warming. Climate change will have significant short- and long-term effects on the natural environment that we take for granted and the national security strategies and tactics that nations pursue.

The Arctic

The Arctic is the bellwether for the effects of climate change, both geographically and politically. The 2007 IPCC Assessment has forecast considerable loss of sea ice in the Arctic Ocean during the 21st century, and newer estimates have moved this date up as close as 2030. The last time the Arctic was substantially ice-free was 125,000 years ago, well before modern human civilizations, so climate change is physically making the Arctic into a world that humans have not inhabited before. What does this mean for modern international security?

First, less ice means more open water, which in turn means more cross-Arctic transit. Merchant ships, naval and coast guard vessels, submarines, cruise ships and other recreational boats, and smugglers will all find a regularly ice-free Arctic easier to navigate. Commercial ships transporting goods across continents can save time and money along one of two passages: the

Northern Sea Route, above the coast of Russia, and the Northwest Passage, above the coast of Canada and the United States. Greater commercial transit will result in greater national presence by the circumpolar nations in order to maintain their security interests in the region.

Significant mineral resources lie under the Arctic sea floor, including oil and natural gas. The U.S. Geological Survey estimated that approximately 22 percent of the world's known recoverable petroleum reserves lie north of the Arctic Circle (USGS 2008). Climate change will make these resources easier to extract. The area also holds the potential for cold-water aquaculture, a significant food security issue. Even nonpolar nations such as Japan and Korea have sent exploratory vessels up to Arctic waters to estimate resources.

There is no overarching legal regime governing the Arctic. The UN Convention on the Law of the Sea currently represents the operant body of law, although the United States, a significant world power with an Arctic coastline, has not ratified it. In addition, the Government of Canada argues that because the Northwest Passage lies in the midst of the Canadian archipelago, it is considered internal waters and any ship wishing to transit the passage needs Canadian permission. However, an international strait is defined as any strait of water connecting two portions of the high seas; this definition allows for innocent passage of any warship or merchant vessel, and could put the Canadians on the wrong side of UNCLOS. The Arctic is the most profound example of the effects of a changing environment on national and international security, and it is yet unknown if a new legal, economic, and security regime is needed to govern a globally warmed Far North.

Migration

Populations faced with resource shortages, changing environmental conditions, extreme weather events, and possible public health impacts may make the decision to migrate, if they are able. Migration is a complex phenomenon and is governed by economic and political factors as well as environmental conditions, but if the same environmental conditions populations rely on for agriculture and livelihood are sufficiently changed, this might provide enough of an impetus, a push factor, to increase marginal levels of migration. Climate change is predicted to increase the intensity and possibly the frequency of extreme temperature events, precipitation events, floods and droughts, and hurricanes and storms. The recent experience in Japan shows us that even the wealthiest and most robust nations cannot adapt readily to a large disaster; how much harder will it be for populations without wealth and strong government support to adapt.

The migration of large numbers of people fleeing extreme events or environmental change can affect national security in several ways. The sheer numbers of refugees, or internally displaced persons (IDPs) if they have not crossed an international border, might overwhelm any resources the host government has set aside to assist them. Crossing an international border itself can become administratively problematic if refugees do not have proper visas or identification papers. Governments may be unwilling to accept refugees if they can't keep track of them. If the refugees are of a different ethnicity, race, or religion, neighboring governments may not accept them at all, fearing political or social unrest within their own population.

Disease and Public Health

Finally, climate change will affect disease vector ecology, increase the global spread of infectious diseases, and affect public health worldwide. Gradual changes in temperature and precipitation can alter the behavior of the vector, the host, or the target species, including human behavior. Mosquito-vectored diseases like malaria and dengue, rodent-vectored diseases like hantavirus, or human-vectored diseases like influenza are likely to increase under climate change. Sudden events such as storms, hurricanes, and floods can cause a localized spike in disease exposure, whereas incremental environmental changes can affect the baseline epidemiology of a country or region.

Infectious diseases then affect security by opening up new areas of instability due to geographical and social attrition. If the outbreak is acute, such as after a natural disaster, it can precipitate outmigration of a large number of people from the stricken area, some of whom are likely to be infected. This then presents a national security problem, or if the individuals cross a border, an international problem. If changing environmental conditions allow the disease to migrate into new areas, then it can affect national development by depressing economic productivity, as AIDS has done across much of sub-Saharan Africa. Governments that are unable to provide basic levels of public health care may face domestic instability.

Disease can also deplete the operational capability of a nation's armed forces. Deployment into areas that face newly endemic diseases means that soldiers must increase inoculations and take precautionary measures in order to maintain readiness. If they face a new and unknown disease, no inoculation may exist. In addition, societies that face high levels of chronic disease will see the effects in the military recruitment pool, as increasing numbers of young people will be unfit for military service due to poor health.

Collateral Damage

It is not only resources and degradation of the environment that drive insecurity, but war itself and the preparation for war can in turn drive environmental degradation. In decisions of national strategic interest, the ability to wage war has always been considered more important to state survival than the maintenance of a healthy ecosystem. Consequently, any restrictions on collateral environmental damage during war have generally been ignored in favor of military advantage.

More troublesome from an environmental standpoint is the occasional use of the environment itself as a weapon of war, or the deliberate targeting of environmental resources in an effort to defeat the enemy by denying them cover or sustenance. Actions such as these have been an accepted part of warfare for millennia, and it is only within the last century that the destruction inherent in these types of actions has been judged to be destructive beyond the military advantage gained. Several international legal instruments now exist to prohibit or limit environmental damage during war, including the Geneva Protocols and the Environmental Modification Convention, but these have yet to be tested in any international court.

As our awareness of the global ramifications of environmental problems increases, we can begin to recognize the implications for national security. Militarily strong nations may be prepared for combat operations, but are unprepared for environmental security threats, particularly those presented by global climate change. The world's population surpassed 7 billion people in October 2011, and emissions of heat-trapping gases into the atmosphere are increasing every year. Consequently, the examination of environmental phenomena as a threat to security has never been more timely.

References

Barnett, Jon. 2001. *The Meaning of Environmental Security.* London: Zed Books.

Brown, Lester. 1977. *Redefining National Security.* Worldwatch Papers. Washington: Worldwatch Institute.

Campbell, Kurt M., ed. 2008. *Climatic Cataclysm: The Foreign Policy and National Security Implications of Climate Change.* Washington: Brookings Institution Press, 235 pp.

Cohn, Carol. 1987. "Sex and Death in the Rational World of Defense Intellectuals." *Signs.* Vol. 12, No. 4, Summer 1987, pp. 687–718.

Costanza, Robert, Ralph d'Arge, Rudolf de Groot, Stephen Farber, Monica Grasso, Bruce Hannon, Karin Limburg, Shahid Naeem, Robert V. O'Neill, Jose Paruelo, Robert G. Raskin, Paul Sutton, and Marjan van den Belt. 1997. "The Value of the World's Ecosystem Services and Natural Capital." *Nature.* Vol. 387, May 15, 1997, pp. 253–260.

Dalby, Simon. 2002. *Environmental Security.* Minneapolis: University of Minnesota Press.

Deudney, Daniel. 1991. "Environment and Security: Muddled Thinking." *Bulletin of the Atomic Scientists.* Vol. 47, No. 3, April 1991, pp. 22–28.

Ehrlich, Paul R. 1968. *The Population Bomb*. New York: Ballantine Books.

Ehrlich, Paul R., Anne H. Ehrlich, and John P. Holdren. 1970. *Ecoscience: Population, Resources, Environment*. San Francisco: W. H. Freeman & Co.

Elshtain, Jean Bethke. 1985. "Reflections on War and Political Discourse: Realism, Just War, and Feminism for a Nuclear Age." *Political Theory*. Vol. 13, No. 1, February 1985, pp. 39–57.

FM3–07. 2008. *Stability Operations*. Department of the Army. October 2008, 208 pp.

Gasper, Des. 2005. "Securing Humanity: Situating Human Security as Concept and Discourse." *Journal of Human Development*. Vol. 7, No. 2, pp. 221–245.

Gleick, Peter H. 1991. "Environment and Security: The Clear Connections." *Bulletin of the Atomic Scientists*. Vol. 47, No. 3, April 1991, pp. 17–21.

Goldstone, Jack A. 1996. "Environmental Security and Violent Conflict: A Debate." *Environmental Change and Security Project Report*. Issue 2, pp. 66–71.

Homer-Dixon, Thomas F. 1991. "On the Threshold: Environmental Changes as a Cause of Acute Conflict." *International Security*. Vol. 16, No. 2, pp. 76–116.

Homer-Dixon, Thomas F. 1994. "Environmental Scarcities and Violent Conflict: Evidence from Cases." *International Security*. Vol. 19, No. 1, Summer 1994, pp. 5–40.

Jervis, Robert. 1978. "Cooperation under the Security Dilemma." *World Politics*. Vol. 30, No. 2, January 1978, pp. 35–65.

Karl, Terry Lynn. 1997. *The Paradox of Plenty: Oil Booms and Petro-States*. Berkeley, CA: University of California Press.

Kay, Sean. 2006. *Global Security in the Twenty-First Century: The Quest for Power and the Search for Peace*. Lanham, MD: Rowman & Littlefield.

Keohane Robert O., and Joseph S. Nye. 1977. *Power and Interdependence: World Politics in Transition*. New York: Little Brown, & Co.

Levy, Marc. 1995. "Is the Environment a National Security Issue?" *International Security*. Vol. 20, No. 2, Fall 1995, pp. 35–62.

Mathews, Jessica T. 1989. "Redefining Security." *Foreign Affairs*. Vol. 68, No. 2, pp. 162–77.

Morgenthau, Hans. 1948. *Politics Among Nations: The Struggle for Power and Peace*. New York: Alfred A. Knopf.

Myers, Norman. 1989. "Environment and Security." *Foreign Policy*. No. 74, pp. 23–41.

Nordås, Ragnhild, and Nils Petter Gleditsch. 2007. "Climate Change and Conflict." *Political Geography*. Vol. 26, No. 6, August 2007, pp. 627–638.

Population Reference Bureau. 2008. "2008 World Population Data Sheet." http://www.prb.org/Publications/Datasheets/2008/2008wpds.aspx

Raleigh, Clionadh, and Henrik Urdal. 2007. "Climate Change, Environmental Degradation, and Armed Conflict." *Political Geography*. Vol. 26, No. 6, August 2007, pp. 674–694.

Schwartz, Peter, and Doug Randall. 2003. "An Abrupt Climate Change Scenario and its Implications for United States National Security." A report prepared for the Office of Net Assessment, U.S. Department of Defense, October 2003, 22 pp.

Wolf, Aaron T., Annika Kramer, Alexander Carius, and Geoffrey D. Dabelko. 2005. "Managing Water Conflict and Cooperation." In *State of the World 2005: Redefining Global Security*. Linda Starke, ed. New York: W.W. Norton, pp. 80–99.

Ullmann, Richard. 1983. "Redefining Security." *International Security*. Vol. 8, No. 1, pp. 129–153.

USGS. 2008. "Circum-Arctic Resource Appraisal: Estimates of Undiscovered Oil and Gas North of the Arctic Circle." U.S. Geological Survey, Department of the Interior, 4 pp.

Uvin, Peter. 2004. "A Field of Overlaps and Interactions." *Security Dialogue*. Vol. 35, No. 3, September 2004, pp. 352–353.

Wibben, Annick T.R. 2004. "Feminist International Relations: Old Debates and New Directions." *Brown Journal of World Affairs*. Vol. X, No. 2, Winter/Spring 2004, pp. 97–114.

Wirth, David A. 1989. "Climate Chaos." *Foreign Policy*. No. 74, pp. 3–22.

Wolfers, Arnold. 1952. "'National Security' as an Ambiguous Symbol." *Political Science Quarterly*. Vol. 67, No. 4, December 1952, pp. 481–502.

CHAPTER 2

Natural Resources

We are drowning in the devil's excrement.
    —Juan Pablo Pérez Alfonzo, founder of OPEC (1976)

There is no peace. We are getting tired of being attacked daily. We used to flee to the forest before but now there is nowhere to escape. The conflict is everywhere.
    —Bandu Kaberuka, Congolese farmer (Al Jazeera 2010)

Security of natural resources is a seemingly obvious form of environmental security. However, not all natural resources are secured in the same way. Depending on the type and quantity of the resource, where it is found, and how it is used, too little of one resource can be a security threat while too much of another can also be a security threat.

Environmental resource shortage can cause conflict directly in at least three different ways. A reduction in the quantity or quality of the resource shrinks the amount of the resource pie available to everyone. Population growth divides the pie into smaller and smaller pieces for each person. Unequal resource distribution within a society means that some groups get disproportionately large pieces (Homer-Dixon 1994, 8–9). These are not mutually exclusive occurrences, but can happen together. In countries with few economic resources, control of this natural capital equates to control of both political and military power.

The primary cause of resource scarcity is population growth, and global population has already surpassed 7 billion, most of which lives in the developing world.[†] Sustained population growth will intensify the effects of human activity on the environment, and can exacerbate scarcity of fresh water, arable land, fish stocks, and forest resources. So, logic would say that competition for these resources would be a great reason to fight. However, resources usually act as a contributing factor in conflicts, not a primary factor. In this chapter, we will examine water resources, extractable commodity resources like diamonds and metals, and petroleum for their relationship with environmental security.

Water Resources

There is no life without water, no civilization without water, and no development without water. It flows freely past political boundaries, it fluctuates in both space and time, and there are multiple and conflicting demands on its use. The major uses of fresh water include not only basic drinking, cooking, and sanitation, but also irrigation, transportation and navigation, electricity production, fisheries, and aesthetic uses. Any environmental security agenda in the future will have to address water security and scarcity. There are approximately 1.4 billion km^3 of water on earth, of which 97.5 percent is salt water, contained in the oceans and seas. Only 2.5 percent of earth's water is fresh. Of that, 1.7 percent is found in the form of glaciers and permanent snow cover, inaccessible to humans. The remaining 0.7 percent is found in rivers, lakes, ponds, and groundwater (Shiklomanov 1999). This less than 1 percent of the earth's water is all the water that humanity has on which to survive and develop, and although there is plenty of water on earth if measured on a global per capita basis, it is not distributed equally around the world and is certainly not plentiful in all populated areas.

How does fresh water affect national security? Watershed boundaries do not line up neatly with political and state boundaries, so nations that are able will construct water infrastructure to alter the hydrological cycle and increase their domestic water supply. Water use is linked to energy production (e.g., nuclear power, hydroelectricity, hydraulic fracturing for natural gas extraction), and hence to energy security, so nations that are developing will find it necessary to obtain and secure water supplies to build industry. However, countries facing water stress (less than 1,667 m^3/year) may find themselves at a development impasse, since it has been posited that a certain amount of water is necessary for economic advancement.

[†] Unless stated otherwise, country-specific statistics for this chapter have been taken from the CIA World Factbook 2011. https://www.cia.gov/library/publications/the-world-factbook/index.html.

Uses of Fresh Water

Because there is no substitute for fresh water in any of its ecolog-ical, agricultural, industrial, or personal uses, this resource is currently di-vided between many competing users. Human society uses approximately 70 percent of the freshwater that it appropriates for agriculture, 20 percent for industry, and 10 percent for domestic and personal use, though of course this varies by region (e.g., in the United States approximately 34% of fresh water is used for agriculture and 49% for thermoelectric power [USGS 2009]). In the industrial sector, the biggest share of fresh water is stored in reservoirs for electrical power generation. Regionally, people in developing countries use roughly one-tenth of the water that people in developed countries use, but as overall global population grows, water withdrawals will increase to meet this demand, as indicated in Figure 2.1.

While the minimum amount of fresh water that a human being needs to live on is 13 gallons per person per day, including drinking, sanitation, and hygiene, many developed nations like the United States use considerably more (80–100 gallons per person per day) and many developing nations like Bangladesh use considerably less than the recommended minimum amount. Currently, approximately 1.1 billion people lack access to safe drinking water, and 2.6 billion people lack access to proper sanitation (World Water Council).

Water quantity is naturally variable. Precipitation, streamflow, riverflow, and snowfall can change over the course of a year by up to 70 percent due to normal variation, and climate change may have the effect of magnify-ing natural variation further in time and in location. Precipitation may fall earlier or later than expected, or it may fall in a different form. Fluctua-tion of the water supply may not significantly affect nations that are water plentiful, like Canada or Russia. However, drier nations like India or South Africa suffer from **water stress**, defined by the UN as 1,667 m^3 per capita per year or less. The driest nations such as Saudi Arabia and Egypt suffer from **water scarcity**: 1,000 m^3 per capita per year or less, as shown in Figure 2.2. Nations that do not have enough fresh water to meet their development or basic human health needs face what Swedish hydrologist Malin Falkenmark called a **water barrier**. This is not a physical barrier; rather, it is a hypoth-esis that economic development requires a certain amount of fresh water, and nations that do not have at least 500 m^3 per capita per year, naturally or with the use of technology, will not develop (Falkenmark & Widstrand 1992). Figure 2.2 shows the levels of absolute water scarcity in major river basins around the world, by calculating a withdrawal-to-availability ratio for each basin.

Figure 2.1 Water Withdrawals as a Percentage of Total Available Water

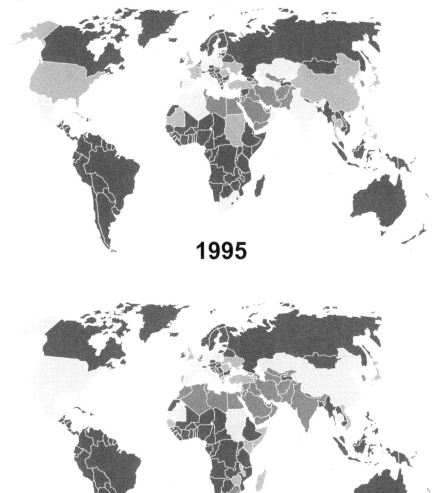

1995

2025

Water withdrawal as a percentage of total available water
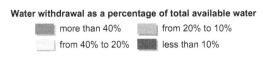

(UNEP/Grid-Arendal. Philippe Rekacewicz (Le Monde diplomatique), February 2006. Available at http://www.grida.no/graphicslib/detail/increased-global-water-stress_5694. Used by permission.)

Figure 2.2 Water Scarcity Index, 2004

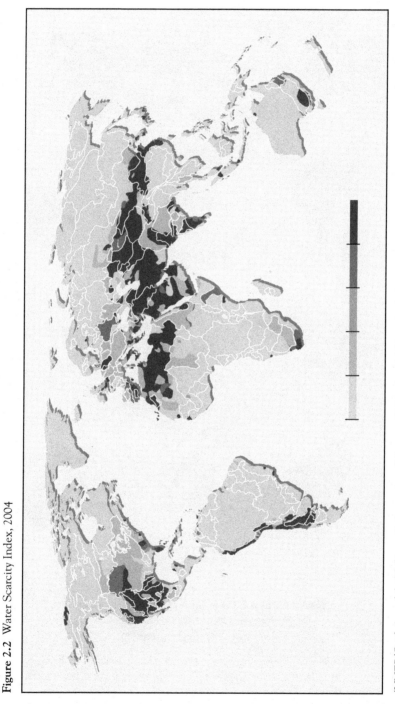

(UNEP/Grid-Arendal. Philippe Rekacewicz, February 2006. Available at http://www. grida.no/graphicslib/detail/water-scarcity-index_14f3. Used by permission.)

Climate Change and Water Stress

As mentioned previously, natural water supplies will fluctuate seasonally in amount and in quality. Climate change can exacerbate these fluctuations, increasing natural variability, and the IPCC concludes with high confidence that the net negative effect of climate change on fresh water systems will be greater than the net positive effect (IPCC AR4 WGII 2007, 175).

For every 1°C rise in ambient air temperature, the atmosphere can hold approximately 7 percent more moisture. As a result, the global hydrological cycle will become more intense, as water circulates through faster. However, since the climate/hydrological cycle interaction is very complex, the effect of climate change on precipitation is one of the most difficult relationships to model. None of the climate model runs included in the data gathered by the IPCC showed a significant global trend, but the IPCC did identify some significant regional trends. Precipitation has increased over the eastern parts of North and South America, over Northern Europe, and over Northern and Central Asia. Precipitation has decreased over the Sahel and the Mediterranean areas, over southern Africa, and over parts of southern Asia (IPCC AR4 WGI 2007, 41). Overall, a greater increase in extreme precipitation is expected, as compared to events of average intensity (Bates et al. 2008, 16).

As for water on or under the ground, average annual runoff is projected to increase by 10–40 percent at high latitudes and in wet tropical areas, and to decrease by 10–30 percent over dry regions at midlatitudes and in the dry tropics (IPCC AR4 WGII SPM 2007, 11). This means that wet areas are likely to get wetter and dry areas dryer. Snow and ice cover will decrease as air temperatures increase, meaning less water will be stored in frozen form (NRC 2010, 261). Since more than one-sixth of the world's population relies on melting glaciers and snowpacks for its water supply (IPCC AR4 WGII 2007, 35), this can presage significant water shortages for human and ecosystem use.

The effects of climate change on water quality have not been studied extensively, but water quality can be negatively affected by climate change in several ways. As sea levels rise, coastal aquifers can become contaminated with salt water, an event called saline intrusion. Increasing water temperatures can increase algal blooms and reduce dissolved oxygen, affecting water-based biota. Higher precipitation levels leading to greater runoff can wash sediment and pollutants into the water from land-based sources (IPCC AR4 WGII 2007, 186–188; for a more thorough discussion of the effects of climate change on water resources and on confidence levels expressed in these findings, see NRC 2010, Bates et al. 2008 and IPCC AR4 2007 WGI Chapter 3, and WGII, Chapter 3).

Put all of these factors together and we can expect that climate change will lead to declining water availability and increased water stress. Some areas are predicted to have more water available, such as Alaska, South Asia and parts of China, the Sahara and the lower part of the Arabian peninsula, though this is a relative measure in these last two areas as they are extremely dry to begin with. Areas that are predicted to lose water include much of the United States and southern Canada, the Amazon River basin, much of southern Africa, Europe and western Russia, and most of the Middle East. The areas with declining water availability are currently some of the most fertile and populous areas in the world. This will have ramifications for international security by increasing food insecurity and social instability, contributing to militarization of natural resources, and breeding international mistrust of wealthy nations by developing nations (Brown & Crawford 2009).

Given the expected changes in water supply, there are various physical ways by which humans can alter the hydrological cycle to allocate more water for their needs. Damming rivers provides flood control and power generation in the form of hydroelectricity. Constructing reservoirs provides drinking water storage and recreational areas. Pumping groundwater from aquifers brings up fresh water to dry lands for drinking and irrigation. However, each of these changes can have ecological downsides. Blocking river flows with dams can interrupt fish migration and lead to sedimentation. Flooding large areas for reservoirs can destroy ecosystems both upstream and downstream, and drawing down groundwater stocks can lead to land subsidence and saltwater intrusion into freshwater aquifers. Trade-offs such as these indicate that the water security needs of both humans and ecosystems should be achieved together, a principle that has generally not been implemented in either rich or poor countries (Vörösmarty et al. 2010). As the effects of climate change become stronger, the number of nations facing water stress will only increase if measures aren't taken to ensure water security for both humans and ecosystems.

Water Wars?

The term **"water wars"** has become popular when discussing issues of environmental security; it refers to the idea that states could and would go to war with each other over access to fresh water. The degree of water scarcity, the extent to which water is shared among various users, the relative power of the states within the catchment basin, and the existence of alternative sources of water will all factor into a nation's decision to engage in conflict over water. In 1995, Ismail Serageldin, who was World Bank Vice President for Sustainable Development at the time, said, "wars of the next century will be over water." This idea has captured the imagination of politicians and the public, but we must examine if this is strictly true.

There are 263 international river basins in the world. This makes water an international resource in one of two ways. First, many nations share a river with other nations within the same basin. The Nile River, for example, flows through 10 nations, the Amazon River through 6 nations, and the Danube River through 17 nations. The imperative to share this resource among potentially competitive states, in the absence of an overarching water allocation authority, gives upstream nations little incentive to conserve water within their borders. For example, the United States and Mexico signed a treaty in 1944 that requires the United States to deliver 1.5 million acre feet of water from the Colorado River to Mexico every year. However, due to upstream overuse, agricultural runoff, and periodic drought, the United States often delivers less than the agreed amount, and the water that is delivered is often of poor quality.

Second, a river can delineate a border between nations, as the Rio Grande separates Mexico and the United States, the Jordan River separates Jordan and Israel, and the Yalu River separates China and North Korea. For co-riparians that do not have good relations with each other, this can lead to militarization of the river and loss of access to the river and its resources for civilians. For example, both the Chinese and North Korean governments have fortified their borders along the Yalu River to prevent refugees from North Korea crossing into China.

Nations often go to war to protect their vital national interests, and since water is critical for agriculture, industry, and economic development, water scarcity could logically engender conflict in at least one of several ways. International conflicts can arise between riparian states that share a river as a border, or upstream and downstream neighbor states that share one river moving through their respective territories. National-level conflicts arise from disputes between sub-national entities such as states or tribes over water resources. Conflicts within nations are likely to be more violent than international conflicts, and other nations are less likely to get involved due to sovereignty concerns. Finally, local conflicts can stem from loss of irrigation water or other water services leading to politically destabilizing migrations (Wolf et al. 2005, 83).

If fresh water is such a critical national interest, how likely are actual "water wars"? Not likely. Water is not a "lootable" resource like diamonds or precious metals. Because water is too heavy and hence too expensive to transport secretly, it must be used *in situ* or infrastructure such as pipelines must be built to carry the water from the source to the desired location. This means that any nation or group wishing to possess water resources has to occupy the land where the water is found. Short of invading another country, nations with shared water resources will generally negotiate and cooperate over the allocation of these resources rather than enter into conflict. Consequently, conflicts over water that do occur are more likely to occur within states, not between them (Carius et al. 2004, 63).

It is worth noting that the potential for conflict over water continues to exist, and will be exacerbated by water stresses arising from growing populations and climate change. As discussed in Chapter 1, environmental issues such as a lack of fresh water can have an indirect effect on conflict, not through simple scarcity of resources, but through changes in the underlying environmental conditions that nations rely on to develop. Water scarcity could be only one of several underlying factors contributing to conflict, but that one factor might be the tipping point. Decreased agricultural production (discussed further in Chapter 3), economic decline, the disruption of legitimate institutions and social relations, and population migration (discussed further in Chapter 4) can all be exacerbated by the lack of fresh water.

Although countries rarely go to war over water, they do argue over water quite frequently. Countries have often faced geopolitical disputes over shared waters, though most of them have not escalated into violent conflict. Researchers at Oregon State University have compiled the Transboundary Freshwater Dispute Database of the nearly 450 freshwater treaties that have been signed between two or more nations since 1820. Likewise, the Pacific Institute has developed a Water Conflict Chronology which highlights some of the water resource–related incidents, both real and threatened, that have occurred since 3000 BC, most of which are local or small-scale. Geographical points of contention include access to rivers, lakes and other sources of fresh water; fishing rights; and riverine access to coastlines or ports. Physical points of contention include water infrastructure, such as dams, pipelines, and pumping stations; water quantity; and water quality, as affected by temperature and pollution. (Miscellaneous points of contention include ticked-off deities and Moses's hydrophobic tendencies.) Appropriate physical and policy responses such as water-sharing agreements can make the situation better and help avoid conflict, while inappropriate responses can make the situation worse.

Water Cooperation

Humanity has so far avoided large-scale water wars. In the last few decades, water resources have in fact been a source of international cooperation rather than conflict. Given the additional stresses of climate change and growing human populations, how can we ensure this admirable track record continues? There are several technical, economic, and political ways to ensure water is available for everyone.

First, improved technology for water extraction and use can extend existing supplies. Advances in well-drilling, pumping, irrigation technology, and desalination of salt water all make water more productive. For example, the Israeli-Palestinian question has foundered on nearly every political front except water. Due to better drilling and desalination technology and greater wealth, the average water consumption inside Israel is 348 liters per person per day. By contrast, the average water consumption inside the Palestinian territories is 70 liters per person per day, 30 liters less than the 100 liters per person per day recommended for basic needs (Lein 2000, 55–56). Israel is among the world's leaders in efficient water use technology, and faced with this inequity, their answer has been to "find" more water from alternate sources such as imports or desalination. The Palestinians, on the other hand, wish to reallocate existing supplies to increase their consumption levels, a legal issue the Israelis would rather avoid (Baskin 2005).

Second, we can let the market remove the inefficiencies of water provision and distribution. Water privatization has been occurring with increasing frequency around the world, as cities and communities have entered into various sorts of partnerships with private firms to provide water and sanitation services. This has been a resounding success in some places and a frustrating failure in others. After the government of Bolivia privatized the water supply in its third-largest city Cochabamba, water rates increased 35 percent on average, pricing many poor people out of the water market. They protested and the civil security situation deteriorated into riots and arrests. Eventually the government resumed control of the water utility, but supply to the city is still intermittent and geographically incomplete (Forero 2005). On the other hand, Senegal has had success with a public-private agreement to provide water to the citizens of Dakar, its largest city. According to the World Bank, water production in Dakar has increased by 18 percent, including 81,000 new household connections since 1996 (IRIN 2005).

When does privatization work and when does it fail? Certain characteristics seem to point to success in water privatization. A robust water supply and a strong and competent government at the local level increase the chances of privatization providing an improvement in service, while scarce supplies and a weak or corrupt government spell certain failure. The Pacific Institute proposed standards and principles for privatization in 2002, and recommended that private contractors embrace the social good aspects of water by meeting basic human and ecosystem needs, undertaking conservation measures, and maintaining government oversight of privatization efforts (Gleick et al. 2002, 40–41).

Finally, ensuring the resiliency of institutions that manage water will be critically important in avoiding water-related conflict in the future. As Figure 2.3 shows, transboundary water agreements can be very flexible, covering a wide range of topics beyond merely interstate allocation of fixed amounts of water.

Previous studies on international river basins over the last 50 years identified several characteristics that put them at risk of conflict, and found that physical and environmental characteristics such as climate, water stress, population levels, and extent of hydropower were not as important in determining conflict (or lack thereof) as the institutional characteristics of the basin.

Figure 2.3 Transboundary Water Governance

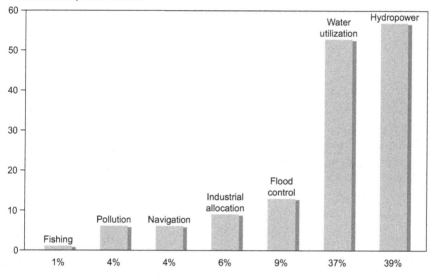

Hydropower and Quantity Dominate Issues of Transboundary Water Governance

Sectoral distribution of 145 agreements
on transboundary water resources

Source: Daoudy 2005.

(UNEP/Grid-Arendal. Available at http://www.grida.no/graphicslib/detail/transboundary-water-governance-avertingconflict_9140. Used by permission.)

In other words, if the nations sharing the water resource have signed a treaty or developed an institution for negotiating water issues, this could more than compensate for environmental stresses and help maintain peace and cooperation in the face of a changing environment (Wolf et al. 2003). Basins that contain several potentially hostile nations such as the Nile, the Jordan, the Mekong, and the Indus have been able to maintain water cooperation even when the nations involved have been in conflict over other contemporaneous political and security issues.

Diamonds, Timber, and Minerals

Resource commodities such as diamonds, timber, and minerals do not affect environmental security due to their shortage; rather it is their abundance that causes conflict and insecurity. Nations that are endowed with rich natural resources yet use these resources to further conflict instead of economic development are said to be suffering from the **resource curse**. The resource curse is the tendency for a nation's resource wealth—particularly nonrenewable resources like oil (discussed in the next section), timber, minerals, and diamonds—to support corruption and conflict rather than growth, stability, and development. This phenomenon is relatively recent in the history of conflict, since only with the emergence of a global commodity market does the possession of saleable commodities such as diamonds become sufficiently lucrative to fuel conflicts. Rather than contributing to national wealth and development, these lootable resources can be used by governments and insurgent groups to pay for internal conflicts and civil wars. These types of conflict are frequent in nations where the wealth generated from the sale of natural resources is not distributed equitably within the country.

If a nation is poor or without an educated work force, natural resources may be one of the very few sources of wealth it possesses. If the nation does not have democratic traditions or a history of democratic institutions, wealth from resources will be managed poorly. If the nation lacks infrastructure and governance to manage the resource-based wealth, it will attract predators. Lootable resources are very attractive to predators because they can be harvested with simple tools by individuals or small groups. Gaining access to them does not require an investment in heavy, expensive equipment that is difficult to obtain or transport. Illicit commodity resources can easily be smuggled because they are difficult to distinguish physically from licit resources obtained through legal channels.

Nations in Africa suffer very acutely from the resource curse. Their ecosystems are hugely wealthy and very robust, and they have extensive mineral resources of all kinds. Sixty-five percent of the world's diamonds, worth $8.5 billion per year, come from seven African nations: Angola, the Central African Republic, the Democratic Republic of the Congo, Namibia, Tanzania, Sierra Leone, and South Africa (Diamondfacts.org, n.d.). However, most African nations do not have a history of democracy, making the resource curse more likely. Most African nations gained their independence from European colonial powers only after 1945, and some like Rhodesia (now Zimbabwe) and South Africa gained independence well after that. This means that the democratic traditions of government such as equitable opportunities for wealth creation and transparent political systems are not likely to be very strong in these nations. Rather, resource wealth becomes an easy source of rent for corrupt governments. Of course, Africa is not the only continent in the world to have undemocratic nations; various states in Asia and Latin America also suffer from the resource curse.

Conflict Diamonds

Since the majority of the world's diamonds are mined in Africa, it is not surprising that much of the conflict in Africa is fueled by proceeds from legal and illegal diamond sales. Below is a map showing the world's main diamond-producing nations. Clearly, not all of these nations are prone to re-source-fueled violence. Peaceful Botswana is the world's largest producer, with 32 million carats in 2009, and Russia and Canada are close behind. However, most of the rest of the world's gem-quality diamonds come from other African nations that do have a postcolonial history of violence (for a more detailed statistical analysis, see LeBillon 2008).

The role of illicit diamond wealth in perpetuating conflict was brought to light after a horrifically brutal civil war in the West African nation of Sierra Leone beginning in 1991. Various government and rebel armies and insurgent groups fought over control of the rich alluvial diamond deposits in eastern and southern Sierra Leone for 11 years, only ending the war in 2002. Liberian warlord and sometime-president Charles Taylor backed the rebel Revolutionary United Front (RUF) in Sierra Leone, and traded dia-monds and timber for arms to continue the conflict. In 1999, UN peacekeep-ing troops were finally dispatched to Sierra Leone to stabilize the country. Taylor went into exile in 2003 in Nigeria and was arrested in 2006 while attempting to flee into neighboring Cameroon. He is now in the custody of the International Criminal Court, being tried for murder, rape, use of child soldiers, torture, and other war crimes and crimes against humanity commit-ted during his time in Liberia and Sierra Leone. During Taylor's years as the head of the RUF, his militia forced thousands of civilians to pan for diamonds in near-slavery conditions, and used brutal suppression tactics such as rape and amputation against civilians who protested. Without the use of funds from diamond and timber sales, the RUF would not have been able to supply themselves with weapons to continue fighting.

The southern African nation of Angola has also used its considerable dia-mond resources (oil as well) to fund civil conflict and corruption. Beginning with its independence from Portugal in 1975, there was civil war in Angola almost continuously until 2002. During the 1980s, the Soviet-backed An-golan government and the U.S.-backed UNITA rebel movement fought for years, and when both superpowers withdrew military and financial support for the two warring sides, they continued the conflict by supplying them-selves with arms bought via diamond and oil sales. Until 1999, diamond firm DeBeers pursued a no-questions-asked diamond buying policy, and in the late 1990s, Angolan diamonds made up approximately one-fifth of its overall purchases (Renner 2002, 33). The civil war ended with the death of rebel leader Jonas Savimbi in 2002, but the misuse of the resource wealth in Angola cost up to 1.5 million people their lives.

Collateral damage to the environment is often severe in resource-driven conflicts. In conflict zones, there is little to no sustainable management of resources because there is no management at all. Even if the government has laws about proper extraction of resources, it is almost impossible to enforce them in a war zone, and it is not uncommon to have national laws suspended in wartime. Because there is no law and order to police proper extraction methods, warring sides will attempt to extract resources in a hurry before they lose control of the territory. This means a high-risk, high-return investment strategy, enforced by armed guards and soldiers, making any on-the-ground assessment or remediation of the damage caused by such extraction methods extremely dangerous. In addition, the pollution generated from these methods is highly likely to be untreated. It can be used as a weapon to intimidate local populace or to foul enemy territory, and poaching of local wildlife can be used either for bushmeat sustenance of troops or for cash.

Resource-wealth conflict also leaves local populations traumatized. Environmental destruction means that farmland is rendered useless, or worse, mined with landmines to deny access to enemy troops, so civilians who depend on subsistence agriculture lose their livelihood. Rape, beatings, torture, kidnappings, and other human rights atrocities are deployed to force concessions from civilians, such as food, clothing, shelter, and labor (Renner 2002). Often this brutal treatment prolongs the war, because the ill-treated civilians may then be spurred to arm themselves for protection, or in retaliation.

Minerals and Timber

Diamonds are not the only lootable resource that can be used to fuel conflict and violence. Timber and strategic minerals like tin and coltan are also saleable in the global commodities market, which makes them attractive resources for criminal organizations, insurgents, and governments fighting civil wars. Timber, especially exotic hardwoods such as teak and mahogany, is in constant demand around the world for building materials and luxury goods. Tin and coltan are used for industrial applications and in every type of electronic device, from DVD players to cell phones to laptop computers. Those who control the resource extraction process also control the government apparatus that makes resource-related policy. National laws and decrees that turn resources into "state property" mean that concessions for timber and mineral extraction can be handed out to whomever the state ruler wishes to reward.

The U.S. Agency for International Development classifies conflicts over timber in one of two ways: Type I, in which conflict(s) is financed or sustained through the harvest and sale of timber, or Type II, in which conflict emerges as a result of competition over timber or other forest resources (Thompson & Kanaan 2005, 1). Often, they point out, these two types occur in the same forest. The authors identify six attributes of a conflict commodity, applying to timber, diamonds, or any other natural resource that fuels conflict. First, the resource must be accessible cheaply and easily; this makes timber more attractive as a conflict commodity than, say, oil. Second, it must be important to the livelihoods of the local people, which is why indiscriminate harvesting can engender conflict. Third, it must be lootable. Fourth, its weight-to-value ratio must be sufficiently low to make it worthwhile to seize; this makes diamonds more attractive as a conflict commodity than, say, timber. Fifth, it must be concealable, and sixth, it must be fungible, which they define as being able to be put to many uses (ibid., 6–7).

Several nations across Africa and Asia have ongoing conflicts fueled by extensive timber reserves. During the civil war in Cambodia, the Khmer Rouge regime felled large stands of timber to finance its war against the government. Similarly in Myanmar (also known as Burma), both the governing military junta and rebel groups have logged forests to pay for arms to continue their conflict. The Myanmar government is now facing sanctions from the United States and the European Union due to its refusal to accept democratic elections, so smuggling conflict timber out via Thailand is one of the few ways the government can turn timber into cash. Clear-cut deforestation in the Philippines by the Marcos regime has caused loss of livelihood and subsequent recruitment of indigenous people into resistance groups. Since the demand for wood in Asia is large and growing, participants in these conflicts are not likely to forswear conflict timber as a source of revenue. Even if the logging is illegal, meaning trees are harvested against domestic laws, governments can be helpless in preventing it, or worse, secretly complicit in criminal operations. Most recently in Latin America, Mexican cartels have been logging in the forests of Michoacan and murdering protestors, and according to the villagers, the government has done nothing to stop them. Eventually, the villagers began defending the forest with their own armed militia (*Washington Post* 2011).

Perhaps one of the worst and most persistent resource-driven conflicts in the world is now occurring in the Democratic Republic of the Congo (DRC, formerly Zaire). The DRC has one of the richest resource bases in the world, possessing diamonds, timber, cobalt, copper, tin, and up to 80 percent of the world's coltan reserves. Since its independence from Belgium in 1960, it has fought one conflict after another, the most recent civil war officially ending in 2003 at the cost of over 5 million lives. However, the eastern part of the country is still home to militias and foreign armies from neighboring Rwanda and Uganda. UN peacekeepers have been stationed in the country since 2000, but have been ineffective in halting the fighting, and occasionally have used their international military standing to enrich themselves. In 2010, the DRC government launched a military offensive to pacify the eastern part of the country, displacing thousands from the additional violence and widespread rape that is commonly used as a tool of intimidation (Al Jazeera 2009a, b). Several international human rights organizations have labeled the DRC the worst place in the world to be a woman (for greater detail, see Global Witness 2009).

As a result of the particularly brutal and long-lasting conflict in the DRC, the U.S. Senate included in the Dodd-Frank Financial Reform Act of 2010 a provision which requires that all publicly traded companies in the United States ensure that the minerals they import, such as coltan and tin, are not from conflict zones such as the eastern DRC. The objective of this provision is to forestall violence and human rights abuses in the area by denying rebel groups and militias a regular source of income through their minerals. However, it remains to be seen whether the reporting requirements contained in the Dodd-Frank Act will be tight enough to serve this objective, and if they are, whether the loss of direct access to the U.S. market will be enough to dislodge warring groups from their mines in eastern DRC.

Is the Resource Curse Inevitable?

If the theory of the resource curse is true, why do some states fall prey to the resource curse and others don't? Several factors can determine whether or not a resource-rich nation is vulnerable. First, if the nation has a democratic and transparent government in place when the resource wealth is discovered, it is less likely to suffer the curse because the profits and taxes earned from resource extraction are transparent and accountable to the citizens. If government institutions to manage wealth are not in place when it is discovered, the likelihood is greater that the wealth will be siphoned off for nondevelopment uses.

The difference between nations that get rich and try to form a government around the wealth and nations that get rich after the government is already formed appears to reside in the type of government the state has when it becomes wealthy. Some wealthy and well-governed nations like Canada and Australia have extensive natural resources: coal, oil, diamonds, timber, uranium and other minerals, as well as abundant cropland and water resources. However, they do not suffer the resource curse because they have extensively developed economies that make the sudden addition of resource-based wealth one factor among many that dictate economic and political policy.

Like Indonesia and the Philippines, Australia and Canada were colonies of Great Britain, until the Statute of Westminster granted them independence in 1931. By then, each nation already had a functioning democracy in place, and revenue from wealth-generating resource extraction was accounted for through transparent government functioning. Any increase in wealth from new resources, such as Australia's discovery of diamonds in 1969, meant an increase in the workload for the relevant natural resources ministry, not the sudden appearance of private bank accounts for the rulers of the country.

Second, nations that suffer from the resource curse don't generally invest the proceeds from the sale of resources into development that benefits all public citizens, be it infrastructure, education, or health care. Instead, the wealth is used to pay off a patronage system that props up the ruler and supplies a robust internal security apparatus to suppress challenges to the government's power, whether this is overt conflict from a rebel group or agitations from their own people. Examples will be discussed in the next section. Natural resource wealth, especially from easily extractable resources, can lead to a **kleptocracy**: a corruption of the government and theft of the country's wealth by the ruling elite.

Conversely, some poorer nations like Botswana and Costa Rica are relatively wealthy in natural resources, but have not allowed the wealth from those resources either to enrich a kleptocratic government or to beget violence and insecurity. Rather, Botswana is Africa's longest-standing multiparty democracy, and is peaceful, with an economic growth rate of 9 percent per year. Revenue from the sale of diamonds makes up 40 percent of the nation's income, but the Botswana government is attempting to diversify the economy such that it does not have to rely to such a degree on diamonds (World Bank 2010a). Likewise, Costa Rica is the development success story of Central America, with an annual growth rate of 5 percent per year and no permanent armed forces. High levels of education and political stability make Costa Rica attractive to foreign investors (World Bank 2010b).

Third, nations that are engaged in an ongoing conflict when resource wealth is discovered are very unlikely to resolve the conflict peacefully in order to then manage national wealth responsibly. On the contrary, the pillaging of resources such as oil, minerals, metals, gemstones, or timber by either the government or the insurgents allows conflicts to continue, even those conflicts that might have begun for other reasons (e.g., ethnic animosity, differences in ideology, superpower support during the Cold War; see generally Renner 2002).

Is there a way of knowing whether a nation that discovers resources has any chance of avoiding the resource curse? This depends in part on the diversity and stability of its economy. The term **Dutch disease** refers to a corresponding decline in the manufacturing sector of a nation's economy after the discovery of natural resources, as happened in the Netherlands in the 1960s and 1970s after the discovery of substantial natural gas reserves. While the Netherlands did not fall prey to resource-driven conflict, the extraction and export of new natural resources can de-diversify the economy of a previously stable state. Whether or not this puts it on the road to the resource curse depends also on its political stability and transparency.

The developing South American nation of Bolivia is home to approximately 50 percent of the world's reserves of lithium, a light metal used in a number of industrial productions, most importantly the production of batteries for electric cars and portable electronic devices like cell phones and laptops. As demand for electric cars grows, the demand for lithium carbonate for batteries will grow as well, and the Bolivian government is already planning to regulate its extraction. The socialist president Evo Morales is determined not to put his nation's economic health in the hands of foreign companies, despite pressure from auto manufacturers, and has announced a plan of industrialization to fabricate batteries in Bolivia, rather than just exporting the lithium abroad. If his plans are operationalized, including a government investment of $900 million (La Razón 2010), this could provide the country with a path for development without becoming trapped in the resource curse.

At the time of this writing, Afghanistan is the latest country to be identified as a possible candidate for the resource curse, and there the situation is not as promising as it is in Bolivia. Using data from the 1970s, American geologists have conducted recent surveys of Afghanistan and estimate that it may contain nearly $1 trillion worth of lithium and other minerals as yet unmined (Risen 2010). Given its low level of development, its history of conflict, and the repeated accusations of corruption leveled at the Karzai government, all the conditions are in place for Afghanistan's mineral wealth to be extracted by poorly paid workers, sold by multinational conglomerates, and pocketed by corrupt politicians.

Can Anything Be Done?

The conflicts discussed in this section have all been internal conflicts, cross-border violence notwithstanding. However, they affect international security in several ways. First, a nation wishing to use its natural resources to fund conflict is not going to stockpile the resource in anticipation of higher prices in a future market. If the regime is fighting for its survival, it will attempt to make as much money as it can in the short term by selling as much as possible. This can result in downward price pressure in the global commodity market not only for that particular resource, but for all downstream products that are made from that resource. This is not a given, however; global prices may not fall for one of two reasons. If demand for the resource is robust and growing, as is the demand for timber and minerals, it may keep prices high. Alternatively, a cartel buyer such as DeBeers can buy up the excess supply and sequester it off the market. Resource conflicts can also provide new markets for the small arms trade, in which every major developed nation has a presence. These conflicts often require the deployment of international food and medical aid and international peacekeeping troops, as well as for-hire private security forces.

Nations, even those fighting civil wars and conflicts, are still sovereign in an anarchic international system, and have the sovereign right to exploit the resources that lie within their territory as they see fit. This can mean using resource-based wealth for economic development or for funding a civil war. Insurgents and rebel groups fighting these wars do not have the imprimatur of the international system for their resource extraction, so they knowingly strip resources quickly and without concern for legality or environmental sustainability. The term "warlord economy" has been used to describe this type of endeavor, but it is worth asking whether the problem lies with the warlords or with the economy. There are very few options for the international community to exercise any amount of control over the exploitation of natural resources that fuel violence and conflict. However, this does not mean that they have no options at all.

Global Witness, a London-based NGO, recommends several policy options to make sales of diamonds and timber more transparent in the global market and hence less attractive to criminal organizations and insurgent groups. Their recommendations include public and competitive allocation of concessions, external monitoring units to enforce extraction laws (though who would staff and fund these units if the nation itself cannot is unclear), national resource-use legislation that embraces principles of environmental sustainability, and certificates of legality detailing the movement of goods from producer to importer to consumer, designed to improve tracking and discourage smuggling (Global Witness 2002). All of these recommendations are laudable, though some of them may not be practical to implement in countries which are engulfed in wars. But Global Witness in particular has had one notable success.

By the late 1990s, pressure from Global Witness and other NGOs with regard to the conflict diamond situation in Africa brought bad publicity to DeBeers and the diamond industry as a whole. In 1999, the UN Security Council mounted a campaign of targeted sanctions designed to exclude conflict diamonds from the legitimate diamond trade, with the cooperation of the two principal diamond industry associations. By 2002, they established a certification scheme called the Kimberley Process to ensure that all diamonds traded internationally were conflict-free. The Diamond Council claims that "more than 99% of diamonds are now from conflict-free sources and traded under the United Nations–mandated Kimberley Process." Although this claim may be optimistic (see Roberts 2003, Campbell 2002), there is no doubt that the process has brought greater transparency to the trade in diamonds and helped stem the flow of diamond-generated funds to insurgents, terrorists, and criminal organizations. Such a scheme is unique in the environmental security regime; however, there have been discussions within the EU regarding the possibility of adapting a Kimberley-like scheme for trade in conflict timber (Verifor 2006; Brack et al. 2002).

Resource abundance and its attendant wealth should be a high card in any nation's hand on the world stage. Yet the number of nations that continually suffer from the resource curse has to be considered one of the greatest development and environmental security tragedies of the 20th century. Most horribly, those who do not generally benefit from the resource wealth are those who pay the highest externality costs, in the form of political repression, polluted environments, and amputated limbs. Whether this will continue in the 21st century remains to be seen.

Petroleum

Perhaps the resource most fundamentally linked to international security in the modern era is petroleum (oil and natural gas). Petroleum is not just any commodity. It is a highly concentrated, easily movable energy source, adaptable to all sorts of energy and nonenergy uses. Energy uses include gasoline, jet fuel, diesel, and fuel oil. Nonenergy uses include plastics of all kinds, polyester fibers, food-grade paraffin wax, alcohol compounds, and of course the petroleum jelly found in cosmetics and medicines. As a natural resource commodity of significant global value, oil is unlike other natural resource commodities such as diamonds and timber. If the latter stopped flowing between markets, it could result in an economic hardship for many players, both wealthy firms and poorer miners and loggers. If oil stopped flowing, it would cause the global economy to grind to a standstill.

Oil Is Critical to the Functioning of the Modern Economy

The graphic below shows the geographical distribution of proven oil reserves, by continent or region, from 1990 to 2010.

Figure 2.4 Global Distribution of Proved Reserves by Region

Distribution of Proved Oil Reserves

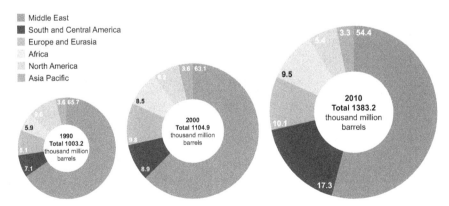

(BP Statistical Review of World Energy, June 2011, Oil, p. 7. Available at http://www.bp.com/liveassets/bp_internet/globalbp/globalbp_uk_english/reports_and_publications/statistical_energy_review_2011/STAGING/local_assets/pdf/oil_section_2011.pdf. Used by permission.)

Trade in petroleum accounts for the largest share of world trade, whether measured by volume or by value (EIA n.d.). The global petroleum market is robust and functions for the most part according to market principles. Though different crudes are graded in different ways according to weight and content of contaminants like sulfur, oil generally moves from the well to the closest refinery for further processing. Although every nation in the world uses oil to some degree or other, supplies are unevenly distributed around the world. The Middle East (Iran, Iraq, Kuwait, Oman, Qatar, Saudi Arabia, Syria, UAE, and Yemen) has 54.5 percent of the global proven reserves (BP 2011), far and away the largest region, with the Saudis holding the largest reserves within the area. This means that the Middle East will remain an area of strategic and security importance as an energy-producing region for decades.

Because petroleum is found only in some places but needed everywhere, a huge network of terminals, shippers, and routes is necessary in order to physically move oil safely and economically from exporters to importers, a network much more advanced than for any other natural resource. This can give rise to structural insecurities, as much of the over 2,144 million metric tons of oil moved in 2010 (see Figure 2.8) went through the seven chokepoints shown below.

The global energy market depends upon a smoothly functioning transport system. If oil flowing via tanker or pipeline were to get blocked at any one of these points, even for a short time, the result could well be a spike in global energy costs. Due to their physical space constraints, chokepoints also leave tankers and oil supplies vulnerable to attack by political insurgents, theft by pirates, or industrial accidents leading to catastrophic oil spills. The Strait of Hormuz connects the oil export terminals of Iraq, Iran, Kuwait, the UAE, Qatar, and Bahrain with markets around the world, and in 2009, 15.5 million barrels per day (nearly 20% of global demand) flowed through the strait, which has shipping lanes only two miles wide. The Strait of Malacca, between Indonesia and Malaysia, carries 13.6 million barrels per day, and is the key chokepoint in Asia because it is the shortest route between the Persian

Table 2.1. Proved Reserves per country in 2010 (billion barrels)

Saudi Arabia	264.5	Russia	77.4
Venezuela	211.2	Libya	46.4
Iran	137.0	Kazakhstan	39.8
Iraq	115.0	Nigeria	37.2
Kuwait	101.5	Canada	32.1
UAE	97.8	United States	30.9

[*Source:* BP 2011]

Figure 2.5 Choke Points for Global Petroleum Transit

World Oil Choke Points

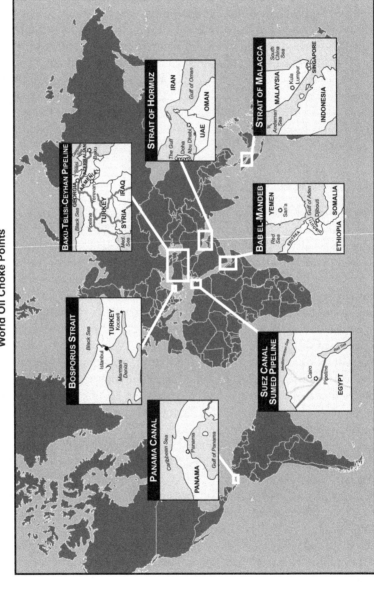

(Library of Congress.)

Gulf and Asia's energy-hungry oil markets in China, Japan, and South Korea. This and the Bab el Mandeb, which lies between Somalia and Yemen and carries 3.2 million barrels per day, are known for pirate activity (Lubin 2011; see also Cooke 2008, Al Jazeera 2008; see generally Nincic 2002).

Other than piracy and the threat of terror attacks, there is generally not much insecurity surrounding petroleum due to basic supply and demand. Like any other market commodity, changes in quantity will be reflected by changes in price. Oil-related conflicts come about due to the nonmarket aspects of oil. The types of regimes governing oil-exporting nations, the geographic locations of these nations and their geopolitical concerns, religious and cultural complications within these nations, and environmental externalities such as pollution and climate change all give rise to energy insecurity independent of the quantity of oil traded on the world market.

Oil-Exporting Nations Face Unique Security Issues

Since oil does not behave like timber, minerals, and diamonds on the global market, it stands to reason that oil-exporting nations face a type of resource curse unlike that faced by other natural resource exporters. Because oil is so critical to the world's economy, demand increases every year without significant fluctuation (the current economic recession lowered demand only temporarily). Consequently, some oil-exporting states have been able to base almost their entire treasuries on oil revenue, or petro-dollars, and very little else. Saudi Arabia, for example, gets 80 percent of its national revenue from oil, Nigeria gets 95 percent, and Venezuela 55 percent (CIA World Factbook). This can leave such states economically precarious, as the country's net worth rises or falls with the market price of oil.

States that derive their national income from economic rents rather than from taxes are called **rentier states**. Economic rents are considered unearned value on resources, so nations that merely pump oil out of the ground and sell it are engaged in rent-seeking behavior. They did not create the oil, they are only extracting a resource that happens to lie under their territory. The governments of rentier states do not have to concern themselves with the welfare of all their citizens, though some do, because their economic and hence political power is derived from extracting value from the external environment and redistributing it internally as they see fit. Consistent with our definition of the resource curse, this trend tends to limit the diversification of the state's economy away from petroleum into other areas. However, because oil is not as lootable as other, more portable resources like diamonds, the state tends to be the only entity with sufficient infrastructure to turn petroleum into petro-dollars. Hence the civil violence that can accompany the extraction of lootable resources is generally, though not always, absent in oil-producing nations.

Figure 2.6 Top Oil* Producing Countries, 1973–2010

Million barrels per day

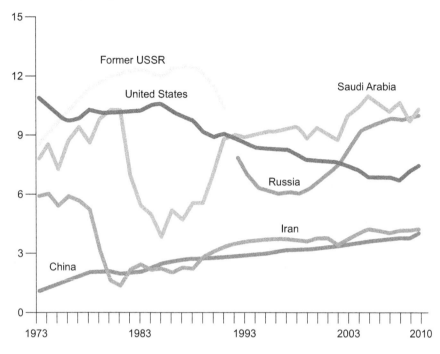

*Crude oil and natural gas plant liquids.
(U.S Energy Information Administration. Available at http://www.eia.gov/energyexplained/index.cfm?page=oil_where.)

Table 2.2. Oil Production per country in 2010 (thousand barrels daily)

Russia	10270	UAE	2849
Saudi Arabia	10007	Kuwait	2508
United States	7513	Venezuela	2471
Iran	4245	Iraq	2460
China	4071	Nigeria	2402
Canada	3336	Brazil	2137
Mexico	2958	Norway	2137

[*Source*: BP 2011]

This does not mean, however, that these nations are free of resource-related security concerns. Political scientist Terry Lynn Karl has coined the term **petro-states** to denote states that export oil and suffer from a particular form of the resource curse. More specifically, the lucrative economic characteristics of oil in the industrial era mean that governments tend to form their policies and institutions around the existence of oil.

Karl lays out four characteristics of a petro-state. First, because oil extraction is very capital-intensive and uses relatively few skilled workers who have specialized knowledge, there is very often a high level of foreign ownership and control in the petroleum sector. Second, the sector is based on extracting a depletable resource, unlike timber which can be regrown. Once the easily accessible oil is gone, the nation will be bankrupt unless there is further economic development to take its place. However, there is no internal economic or political benefit in leaving the resource in the ground, so the long-term future is traded for the short-term advantage. Third, oil-exporting countries receive extraordinary rents from their resource, which are derived from the strategic importance of oil for the global economy. As previously mentioned, oil is hugely important to international trade both by volume and by value. Demand is relatively inelastic, despite efforts to develop substitutes. This means rents received by the petro-states have very little to do with the overall productivity of the state's economy. Fourth, rents generated from oil extraction in developing countries accrue directly to the state government. Consequently, economic and ultimately political power rests on their capacity to extract oil from their environment and distribute the oil money internally (Karl 1997, 47–49; see also Karl 1999). These factors are why all petro-states tend to resemble each other in governmental structure and economic fragility despite being of different cultures, sizes, regions, and stages of development.

Not all oil-exporting nations are petro-states. Canada and Norway, for example, are not. Both nations have well-developed and diverse economies and transparent political systems, so revenue from oil is only a small fraction of their national treasury and the spending of the nation's resources is accountable to the public. Other states exhibit some of the economic markers of petro-states, but are not dependent upon petro-dollars for the majority of their revenue. Mexico is the world's seventh-largest oil producer, but its economy rests on a more diverse base than just petroleum exports. It also has a significant private sector, which feels free to engage in political dissent. The North American Free Trade Agreement also puts Mexico in an economic relationship with Canada and the United States that no other developing country has. The case of Russia is more complicated. A former military superpower, the loss of its global status after the end of the Cold War was due largely to the inability of communism to build a working economy. As the Russian economy continues to reform, revenues from oil and natural gas have the potential to aid in the country's development, but the lack of transparency and democratic tradition could leave them vulnerable to petro-statehood.

Some of the largest oil exporting nations, however, are clearly petro-states by all economic and political markers: significant oil revenue captured and distributed by the state, a government bloated with excess employees and very little revenue from taxes, a politically long-lived strong man at the helm, and a politically inactive and relatively obedient population. Saudi Arabia, which is the world's largest oil exporter, meets every one of these criteria. Eighty percent of the government's revenue comes from oil. The Al-Saud monarchy has reigned uninterrupted since 1932, and they have pacified a religiously conservative population with subsidies for cheap food and gasoline. In addition, the Saudi kingdom ranks second in the world for spending on arms and national defense, yet its only real enemies are internal dissidents who view the royal family as corrupt and un-Islamic (CIA World Factbook 2011; Kostiner 1997). Consequently it also has a strong internal security system that permits no open dissent and very little political reform.

In contrast to the Saudis' lavish subsidies, Nigeria makes no pretense of re-distributing oil wealth to its citizens. Often touted as an alternative provider to nations in the Middle East, the money from its petroleum exports goes to the country's elite, even though over 70 percent of its citizens live below the poverty line (CIA World Factbook 2011). Consequently, Nigeria is one of the very few exceptions to the trend of petro-states being generally free of internal violence. Civil unrest in Nigeria, however, has not taken the form of organized groups looking to capture and sell the oil themselves. Rather, militant groups like the Movement for the Emancipation of the Niger Delta (MEND) sabotage pipelines, platforms, refineries, and other infrastructure, and take hostages from among foreign oil workers. MEND claims to represent the interests of the local people in the Niger Delta, saying that local communities have not benefitted from the oil wealth extracted from their territory but have suffered from pollution from its production, including oil spills estimated to be around 260,000 barrels per year for the last 50 years (EIA Nigeria Country Brief 2010).

Nigeria is infamous for the case of Ken Saro-Wiwa, an Ogoni poet-turned-activist profiled in the Biography section in Part II of this volume, who protested the partnership between Royal Dutch Shell and the Nigerian government which was expatriating Nigeria's oil wealth and leaving environmental destruction behind for the Ogoni people. Saro-Wiwa was executed in 1995 on charges the human rights community says were politically motivated. While Saro-Wiwa's campaign was nonviolent, having gained a considerable amount of publicity in the foreign press, the recent actions by MEND and other local groups have cost Nigeria and its foreign partners between one-third and one-half of its oil production (ibid.; see also Hanson 2007). Some of the self-identified leaders of MEND have declared that their aim is to drive out foreign investors and redistribute oil wealth among the local communities. To this extent they have somewhat succeeded, as several foreign producers have declared *force majeur* on their oil shipments. MEND's militant techniques appear to be gaining favor in other areas; rebels in the neighboring country of Cameroon are now similarly disrupting oil production in the Gulf of Guinea (McGregor 2010).

Though very different geographically and culturally, Angola and Venezuela also fit the definition of petro-states. Angola's President Jose Eduardo Dos Santos has been in power since 1979 and promised to rebuild the country on oil and diamond revenue after the end of a 27-year civil war. Yet, as of 2010, Transparency International ranked Angola as the world's 10th most corrupt nation. Even today, Angola's oil boom continues, and the country is set to enjoy skyrocketing rates of economic growth, but most of the wealth generated from oil revenues finds its way into the hands of the ruling elite. Likewise, a national referendum in Venezuela removed all term limits for the current president, Hugo Chavez, who has been in power since 1999. Chavez has attempted to increase government control of the oil industry by nationalizing firms and assets. Since approximately 40 percent of the population lives below the poverty line, the government regularly reduces the price of gas through subsidies to between 7 and 12 cents per gallon. It cannot afford such a financial outlay, but attempts to remove or reduce the subsidy have resulted in riots and public unrest. Indeed, much of the political upheaval currently taking place across the Middle East and North African region is partially driven by the loss of government subsidies during the world financial crisis of 2007–2009.

Oil-Importing Nations Face Their Own Security Issues

It is not only petroleum-exporting nations that face national security concerns surrounding trade in oil. Importing nations have generally made energy security a key national interest, and have been willing to use hard security methods and personnel to pursue this interest. The United States alone consumes almost 20 million barrels per day, and approximately 86 million barrels per day are consumed worldwide. Of the oil consumed globally, 51.2 percent is used for transportation fuels, 5.8 percent for power generation, and the remaining 41.3 percent is feedstock for industrial and other uses (BP Energy Outlook 2030, 28).

The global economy, economic development and land use patterns in every nation, and the very way of life that most people on the earth strive for are *all* dependent upon oil that is cheap enough to use in any quantity we see

Table 2.3. Oil Consumption per country in 2010 (thousand barrels daily)

United States	19148	Germany	2441
China	9057	South Korea	2384
Japan	4451	Canada	2276
India	3319	Mexico	1994
Russia	3199	Iran	1799
Saudi Arabia	2812	France	1744
Brazil	2604	United Kingdom	1590

[*Source:* BP 2011]

fit. Unfortunately, oil is becoming more expensive now than it has ever been; the price at the time of this writing is $97 per barrel.

Current high oil prices are demand-led, unlike the supply-led shocks of 1972–73, 1979, and 1991. Previous oil crises had to do with oil exporters like OPEC restricting supplies in order to increase short-term profits. This worked for a while, but demand continued to grow and exporters eventually increased production. Now, not only is OECD demand increasing, but demand from the so-called BRICS countries (Brazil, Russia, India, China, and South Africa) is also increasing faster as they are moving toward OECD-level economic status. This means bringing down prices is not just a matter of releasing more oil into the market.

Given that the world's supply of ultimately recoverable oil is finite, though the exact amount is unknown due to uncertainties in estimating reserves, it is possible to theorize when we might reach the halfway point of extraction. In 1956, a geologist at Shell named M. King Hubbert calculated that the production of recoverable oil in the United States would reach its halfway point in 1970, and he turned out to be correct. This theory is known as Hubbert's peak, or **peak oil**. Calculating the point at which we might reach global peak oil has become somewhat of a cottage industry, with some analysts arguing that we have already passed it and others arguing that it will never arrive. Hubbert himself predicted that the world would reach peak oil in 1995, though he did not foresee the increased energy efficiency that slowed the rate of consumption in the 1970s and early 1980s. If the theory of peak oil is true, then the world must either find new supplies of petroleum or shift to nonpetroleum energy sources.

Because oil provides concentrated movable energy, securing sufficient oil supplies has always been a national economic interest since the first commercial oil wells were drilled in the late 19th century. Transportation fuel derived from oil also plays a huge role in military operations, so since World War I,

the location and control of oil supplies has been a national security imperative as well. Energy analyst Frank Verrastro, of the Center for Strategic and
International Studies, notes that demand growth in the global economy has
eroded spare capacity in the worldwide energy market, which means that any
interruption in supply can result in price spikes. As a result, the populations
of oil-importing nations that are facing higher prices for gasoline and other
goods often agitate politically for what they call "energy independence," national self-sufficiency in energy, so as to insulate the nation from supply and
price shocks. However, energy security and energy independence are not the
same thing.

There are several factors that shape energy security. First, the majority of
future demand for all types of energy is shifting from the OECD nations to
the developing world, and the types of energy in which these nations choose
to invest will determine the global energy supply landscape. There is plenty
of unconventional energy in the world, from shale oil to nuclear fusion, but
it is not always easily accessed. Second, energy prices have shown considerable variability in the 21st century, and this can place a chilling effect on
new energy investments from the for-profit sector. Third, geopolitical trends
such as resource nationalism, terror threats, and concerns about human
rights and energy equity will reduce the effectiveness of existing post–World
War II energy institutions, and may require new methods of decision making. Finally, the need to act on climate change could fundamentally transform the global energy system away from fossil fuels and toward renewables,
but this will require massive investments of time, money, and human capital
(Verrastro 2011). However, Lee Raymond, former Chairman and CEO of
ExxonMobil, opines that these very factors are the reason that energy independence is a national political pipe dream, and climate change is a fait
accompli. The global energy market is too tightly connected for any nation
to separate its own energy supplies. Energy security in his view lies in sufficient access to petroleum, and he recommends that the United States and
other energy-consuming nations "pull up our socks" and maintain relationships with oil-rich countries regardless of political or foreign policy concerns
or GHG reduction targets (Raymond 2004).

Such relationships have generally been maintained by force, by money, or
both, but some energy scholars like Michael Klare argue that following the
same path into the future will become more dangerous. Klare points out four
future trends that oil-importing nations need to realize as they search for energy security. First, energy demand is increasing globally because our consumption is increasing; we use energy for everything from development necessities
such as electricity to unnecessary luxuries. Second, oil-importing nations get
more and more of their supply from politically unstable and possibly dangerous countries. Third, and related to the second trend, Western involvement
in some of the countries provokes an anti-Western sentiment, making these

regions still more unstable. Fourth, oil-importing nations are all competing with one another, chasing the world's dwindling supply (Klare 2004).

In order to secure energy, oil-importing nations have provided military, economic, and political aid of various types to support the governments of petro-states, allowing them to continue their rentier behavior. The United States alone has enjoyed a nearly 60-year bilateral security relationship with the kingdom of Saudi Arabia, trading the kingdom's military security for uninterrupted American oil consumption. In 1980, the then U.S. president Jimmy Carter articulated in his State of the Union address the U.S. policy to attain energy security. Called the Carter Doctrine, it specifically stated that the U.S. government would use any means it deemed necessary, including armed force, to defend its national security interests in the Persian Gulf. "National interests" in this context meant only one thing: uninterrupted access to oil supplies. [The text of the president's State of the Union address generally referred to as the Carter Doctrine is found in Key Documents, Part III of this volume.] Other oil-importing states use economic aid above and beyond the price of oil to ensure energy security. Chinese national petroleum companies have been investing billions of dollars in future hydrocarbon extraction projects in petroleum-rich areas of the world, including Turkmenistan, Kazakhstan, and Ecuador (EIA China Country Brief 2010).

Energy is such a critical national security need that states will buy oil and natural gas from whomever they can, regardless of the behavior of the nation selling it. This largesse from energy-hungry nations has gone to support some morally questionable regimes. Coming back to our discussion of morality in international relations, it is worth considering if appearing to condone objectionable behavior on the part of oil-rich governments is germane to the pursuit of energy security. Both Hans Morgenthau and Lee Raymond would say no. The hunger for energy means that nations who say they support democracy might matter-of-factly sign contracts with, and supply weapons to, regimes that have questionable human rights records, like the United States has done with Saudi Arabia. Nations that advocate noninterference in the internal affairs of other nations might import energy from undemocratic and brutal regimes, like China has done with Sudan, Libya, and now Myanmar.

On the other hand, do oil- and gas-exporting nations have any responsibility beyond that of a commercial contract to keep energy flowing to importing nations? In 2006, Russia cut off exports of natural gas to Ukraine and Belarus, citing contract provisions over prices. Most Western analysts, however, thought that the timing of this cutoff was designed to deprive millions of people in Eastern Europe of heat in the coldest part of winter. Western governments accused Russia of attempting to suppress the new, Western-leaning foreign policy initiatives of their former SSRs, such as Ukraine's desire to join the EU, a charge Prime Minister Vladimir Putin denies. This natural gas supply shock, not unlike the OPEC-led oil supply shock of 1973, impressed upon the importing countries both Russia's willingness to use the "energy weapon" and the need to diversify their sources of natural gas.

The OECD now consumes 53 percent of the world's oil. However, between 2000 and 2010, oil demand rose by 40 percent in non-OECD countries. If the global economy had not been in recession from 2007 to 2009, demand would likely have risen further (EIA 2011). Since oil demand is growing in non-OECD countries faster than in OECD countries, the oil-importing security concerns will shift to them as well, making this a global problem. The national and international security concerns that surround oil, climate change issues, and other environmental externalities like oil spills all mean that a substitute for oil would be very valuable and very welcome. Unfortunately, there is none right now.

Future Issues

How do we know if resource shortage or abundance has become a security issue to the point where it will become less of a problem if the resources are left in the ground? Is there a point at which resources should simply not be developed? Some economists say no, and that we should not worry about resource

Figure 2.7 Mike Luckovich cartoon

(By permission of Mike Luckovich and Creators Syndicate Inc.)

security or about environmental security in general. By all environmental indicators, their argument goes, we are better off than we have ever been.

How to Lie with Economics

The most visible proponent of this argument is Danish statistician Bjørn Lomborg. In his widely read 2001 book, *The Skeptical Environmentalist*, and in several related articles, Lomborg examines the environmental problems of the day and concludes that not only are they not security problems, they are not even really problems. In response to what he calls the doom-saying environmental movement, Lomborg argues that the examination of present-day data shows that human well-being is better than it has ever been. Contrary to Malthus's warning of population growth and mass starvation (discussed further in Chapter 3), population has gone up but there has not been a mass famine because agricultural production has gone up further. This means that globally there are fewer people starving than at any point in the past. Lomborg also argues that erosion and degradation of cropland will not be a problem in the future, because increases in agricultural technology will allow humans to get more food from the remaining arable land in order to keep pace with growing populations, as we did during the Green Revolution. He goes on to say that discovery of oil reserves has also kept pace with demand, so we are facing no energy shortage. Finally, he argues that we are far from exhausting our nonrenewable resources like minerals (Lomborg 2001).

Writing in 2001, it is not surprising that his statistical predictions of low oil prices and falling hunger levels did not turn out to be correct 10 years later. However, the backbone of his argument appears to be that the future will look like the past, which critics view as logically inconsistent and statistically unsound. Lester Brown, in arguing that Lomborg's treatment of environmental scarcity and abundance is facile at best, concludes that "[a]nalyzing environmental issues requires examining the interactions between the global economy, the earth's ecosystems, and world political arrangements" (Brown 2001). Leaving aside the fact that Lomborg only looks at human benefit within this triad of complicated systems and leaves out gains for other species and ecosystem robustness as a whole, all his optimism is predicated on the "certainty" (i.e., hoping) that continued technological development will extend present gains into the future ad infinitum.

Lomborg is right in pointing out that our ingenuity has helped us make enormous strides in human well-being, from food to medical care to energy to technology. But the evidence to support his argument that this trend will continue forever is solely economic. One of his favorite metrics is commodity prices, which indicate the relative value of a commodity in a known market. Assuming commodities are priced correctly, higher prices can move demand away from a scarce commodity and toward a more abundant one.

Unfortunately, ecologists know that the environmental resources that under-lie economic progress do have real, physical limits, and that these resources are not infinitely substitutable. For example, there is only so much water you can pump from an underground aquifer before you empty it. Then you cannot pump faster than it naturally recharges, and there is no substitute for water you can invent to use in the meantime. Consequently, the price for water skyrockets. If you can pay to import water, you have put off your problem into the future, but what if you can't pay, or there is no water to import? Many of the environmental security issues related to resources must take into account the reality that the market does not solve all resource allocation problems, and that for populations without critical resources, violence and conflict can become the most attractive alternative.

Morality in the Search for Resources—A Fool's Errand?

Economics aside, conflicts over resources engender the same ethical questions and concerns that all conflicts do: how can we stop fighting and use the resources for the greatest general good? This brings us back to the discussion of morality in international security. The realists say that morality has no place in the anarchic international arena, and any nation that has the ability to exploit its resources has the sovereign right to use them in any way it wishes. If water supplies in the Middle East are sparse, should they not be hoarded by whichever nation can corral them? If Angola has oil and diamonds, should they not be sold to help arm the government against whomever it perceives as its enemies? In other words, does morality play a role in extracting, selling, or obtaining critical natural resources? Should it play a role?

This is a complicated question, both in academic theory and in real world international relations. In an anarchic world, it is every nation—or subna-tional group—for itself, and the notion of sovereignty seems to underline this assumption. Yet we do have international regimes designed to apply moral standards to international affairs. The human rights violations that were attendant to the diamond-mining regime in Africa were so repugnant that they became the rationale behind the Kimberley Process. Despite the eco-nomic argument for extracting resources quickly and cheaply, Global Witness and other NGOs reasoned, not without justification, that if consumers were aware of the horrible conditions under which the diamonds they valued so much were extracted and traded, they would not be so keen to pay "three month's salary" for crystallized carbon, beautiful though it is. It can be argued that because the diamond market is small, the players are few, and diamonds are noncritical luxury goods, an international regime of governance based on shared morality and concern for human rights is both tolerable and doable. Even the forestry industry has begun to examine similar types of regimes for international trade in conflict-free timber. Hopefully, conflict-free tin and coltan are not far behind.

Could we build a similar regime for oil? Not likely, though we could add an element of morality and human rights to the pursuit of renewable energy. Ideally, all resource extraction industries would be fair to workers, humane, and environmentally sound. But rentier theory works against that ideal, as does mundane human greed. To the government of a rentier state, there is no economic benefit in leaving resources untapped because that is the only wealth the state creates. Without that wealth to pacify the population, it can grow restive and begin to pressure the government for economic and eventually political change, perhaps even driving out its leaders from office. In this instance, human rights reforms are the last thing any regime will be inclined to implement.

Perhaps we are already there with water. Some water scholars have argued that access to adequate quantities of clean and safe water is a human right (McCaffrey 1992, Gleick 1998), much the same as the right to food or the right to education. In March of 2009, the 5th World Water Forum met in Istanbul. This was a gathering of over 24,000 people from 182 countries to discuss water issues such as the effects of climate change, pollution, economic development, and equal access. At this summit, it was proposed that water be included in the UN Universal Declaration of Human Rights, and by 2010 it was official: the UN General Assembly declared that "safe and clean drinking water and sanitation is a human right essential to the full enjoyment of life and all other human rights" (UN News Centre 2010). Of course, many of the rights explicitly guaranteed to humanity in theory are in no way provided in practice, so it remains to be seen if and how the new enshrinement of water in the pantheon of human rights translates into better water security.

Even if morality is not involved, surely there must be a way for wealth in natural resources to translate into peace rather than conflict? Many scholars of environmental security are considering these very questions from a variety of standpoints and theoretical approaches. Geoff Dabelko and Ken Conca have conceptualized the idea of "environmental peacemaking" that,

> environmental cooperation can generate movement along the pace continuum, rendering violent conflict less likely or less imaginable . . . environmental cooperation can be an effective general catalyst for reducing tensions, broadening cooperation, fostering demilitarization, and promoting peace. (Conca & Dabelko 2002, 9)

This is an ambitious research agenda for the field of environmental security but it is not one we have the luxury of ignoring or abandoning because it is too difficult, too far in the future, or too idealistic.

Figure 2.8 Imports and Exports of Oil in 2010 (million metric tons)

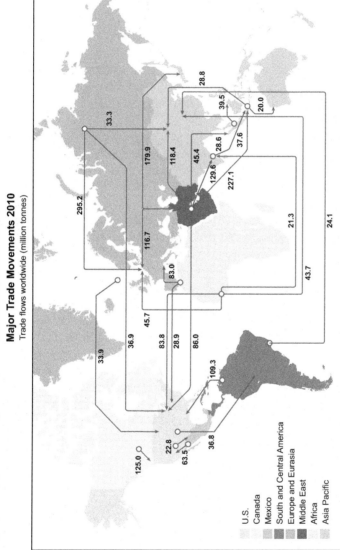

Major Trade Movements 2010
Trade flows worldwide (million tonnes)

U.S.
Canada
Mexico
South and Central America
Europe and Eurasia
Middle East
Africa
Asia Pacific

(BP Statistical Review of World Energy, June 2011, Oil, p. 19. Available at: http://www.bp.com/liveassets/bp_internet/globalbp/globalbp_uk_english/reports_and_publications/statistical_energy_review_2011/STAGING/local_assets/pdf/oil_section_2011.pdf. Used by permission.)

References

Al Jazeera. 2008. "Africa: Piracy in the Gulf of Aden." November 19, 2008. http:// english.aljazeera.net/news/africa/2008/11/2008111971844162942.html

Al Jazeera. 2009a. "UN mission 'failing' in DR Congo." November 25, 2009. http:// english.aljazeera.net/news/africa/2009/11/2009112512426135762.html

Al Jazeera. 2009b. "Rape used as a weapon in DR Congo." October 23, 2009. http:// english.aljazeera.net/news/africa/2009/10/2009102282534764573.html

Al Jazeera. 2010. "Civilians suffer in DRC conflict." January 8, 2010. http://english. aljazeera.net/news/africa/2010/01/201018628273118.html

Baskin, Gershon. 2005. "The Israeli-Palestinian Conflict—Overview for Discussion on Conflict and Cooperation." Water as a Source of Conflict and Cooperation: Exploring the Potential. Conference proceedings, Tufts University, February 2005.

Bates, Bryson, Zbigniew Kundzewicz, Shaohong Wu, and Jean Palutikof. 2008. "Climate Change and Water." Technical Paper of the Intergovernmental Panel on Climate Change, June 2008. http://www.ipcc.ch/pdf/technical-papers/ climate-change-water-en.pdf

Binningsbø, Helga Malmin, Indra de Soysa, and Nils Petter Gleditsch. 2007. "Green Giant or Straw Man? Environmental Pressure and Civil Conflict, 1961–99." *Population and Environment.* Vol. 28, No. 6, July 2007, pp. 337–353.

"Bolivia inicia sola el proceso para industrializar el litio." *La Razón.* October 22, 2010. http://www.la-razon.com/version.php?ArticleId=119958&EditionId=2322

Brack, Duncan, Chantal Marijnissen, and Saskia Ozinga. 2002. "Controlling Imports of Illegal Timber: Options for Europe." London: Royal Institute of International Affairs, trade.ec.europa.eu/doclib/html/122298.htm.

British Petroleum. 2011a. *BP Statistical Review of World Energy June 2011.* Section 6: Oil. www.bp.com/statisticalreview

British Petroleum. 2011b. *BP Energy Outlook 2030.* January 2011, 80 pp. http:// www.bp.com/liveassets/bp_internet/globalbp/globalbp_uk_english/reports_ and_publications/statistical_energy_review_2011/STAGING/local_assets/ pdf/2030_energy_outlook_booklet.pdf

Brown, Lester. 2001. "On Bjorn Lomborg and Population." *Grist.org,* December 12, 2001. http://www.grist.org/article/bjorn

Brown, Oli, and Alec Crawford. 2009. "Rising Temperatures, Rising Tensions: Climate Change and the Risk of Violence Conflict in the Middle East." Winnipeg: IISD, 42 pp.

Carius, Alexander, Geoffrey D. Dabelko, and Aaron T. Wolf. 2004. "Water, Conflict, and Cooperation." *ECSP Report.* No. 10, 2004, pp. 60–66.

Conca, Ken, and Geoffrey D. Dabelko. 2002. *Environmental Peacemaking.* Washington: Woodrow Wilson Center Press, 244 pp.

Cooke, Jennifer G. 2008. "Piracy in the Gulf of Aden." Washington: Center for Strategic and International Studies. http://csis.org/files/media/csis/pubs/081002_cq_cooke_pirates.pdf

Darimani, Abdulai. 2005. "Mineral Resource Capture and Conflicts in Africa." MAC: Mines and Communities, February 2005, http://www.minesandcommunities.org/article.php?a=1537

Diamondfacts.org. n.d. "Fact #9" http://www.diamondfacts.org/index.php?option=com_content&view=article&id=107&Itemid=150&lang=en

EIA, Energy Information Administration. 2011. Annual Energy Outlook 2011. Washington: U.S. Department of Energy. http://www.eia.gov/forecasts/aeo/pdf/0383(2011).pdf

EIA, Energy Information Administration. n.d. "Trade." http://www.eia.gov/pub/oil_gas/petroleum/analysis_publications/oil_market_basics/trade_text.htm

Falkenmark, Malin, and Carl Widstrand. 1992. "Population and Water Resources: A Delicate Balance." *Population Bulletin*. Vol. 47, No. 3. Washington: Population Reference Bureau.

Forero, Juan. 2005. "Bolivia Regrets IMF Experiment." *New York Times*. December 14, 2005. http://www.nytimes.com/2005/12/14/business/worldbusiness/14iht-water.html?pagewanted=all

Gleick, Peter H. 1998. "The Human Right to Water." *Water Policy*. Vol. 1, pp. 487–503.

Gleick, Peter H., Gary Wolff, Elizabeth L. Chalecki, and Rachel Reyes. 2002. *The New Economy of Water: The Risks and Benefits of Globalization and Privatization of Fresh Water*. Oakland, CA: Pacific Institute, 48 pp.

Global Forest Watch. n.d. "Indonesia: Overview." http://www.globalforestwatch.org/english/indonesia/overview.htm

Global Witness. 2002. "The Logs of War: The Timber Trade and Armed Conflict." Programme for International Cooperation and Conflict Resolution, FAFO Report 3769. http://www.globalwitness.org/library/logs-war

Global Witness. 2009. *Faced with a Gun, What Can You Do? War and the Militarization of Mining in Eastern Congo*. London, July 2009.

Hanson, Stephanie. 2007. "MEND: The Niger Delta's Umbrella Militant Group." Washington: Council on Foreign Relations, March 22, 2007. http://www.cfr.org/nigeria/mend-niger-deltas-umbrella-militant-group/p12920

Homer-Dixon, Thomas. 1994. "Environmental Scarcities and Violent Conflict: Evidence from Cases." *International Security*. Vol. 19, No. 1, Summer 1994, pp. 5–40.

Humphreys, Macartan. 2005. "Natural Resources, Conflict, and Conflict Resolution." *Journal of Conflict Resolution*. Vol. 49, No. 4, August 2005, pp. 508–537.

IPCC. 2007. *Climate Change 2007: Impacts, Adaptation, and Vulnerability*. Contribution of Working Group II to the Fourth Assessment Report of the Intergovernmental Panel on Climate Change. New York: Cambridge University Press.

IRIN. 2005. "Senegal: A Model for Water Provision in Urban Africa?" IRIN News, March 22, 2005, http://www.irinnews.org/report.aspx?reportid=53542

Karl, Terry Lynn. 1997. *The Paradox of Plenty: Oil Booms and Petro-States*. Berkeley, CA: University of California Press, 342 pp.

Karl, Terry Lynn. 1999. "The Perils of the Petro-State: Reflections on the Paradox of Plenty." *Journal of International Affairs*. Vol. 53, No. 1, Fall 1999, pp. 31–48.

Klare, Michael T. 2004. *Blood and Oil: The Dangers and Consequences of America's Growing Dependency on Imported Petroleum*. New York: Metropolitan Books, 265 pp.

Kostiner, Joseph. 1997. "State, Islam, and Opposition in Saudi Arabia: The Post-Desert Storm Phase." *Middle East Review of International Affairs*. Vol. 1, No. 2, July 1997. http://meria.idc.ac.il/journal/1997/issue2/jv1n2a8.html

LeBillon, Philippe. 2008. "Diamond Wars? Conflict Diamonds and Geographies of Resource Wars." *Annals of the Association of American Geographers*. Vol. 98, No. 2, pp. 345–372.

Lein, Yehezkel. 2000. "Thirsty for a Solution: The Water Crisis in the Occupied Territories and its Resolution in the Final-Status Agreement." Jerusalem: B'Tselem, July 2000. http://www.btselem.org/Download/200007_Thirsty_for_a_Solution_Eng.doc

Lomborg, Bjørn. 2001. "Resource Constraints or Abundance?" In *Environmental Conflict*. Paul F. Diehl and Nils Petter Gleditsch, eds. Boulder, CO: Westview Press, pp. 125–152.

Lubin, Gus. 2011. "A Brief Tour of the 7 Oil Chokepoints That Are Crucial to the World Economy." *Business Insider*. February 5, 2011. http://www.businessinsider.com/oil-chokepoints-suez-canal-2011-1#

Lujala, Päivi, Nils Petter Gleditsch, and Elisabeth Gilmore. 2005. "A Diamond Curse?" *Journal of Conflict Resolution*. Vol. 49, No. 4, August 2005, pp. 538–562.

McCaffrey, Stephen C. 1992. "A Human Right to Water: Domestic and International Implications." *Georgetown International Environmental Law Review*. Vol. 5, pp. 1–24.

McGregor, Andrew. 2010. "Cameroon Rebels Threaten Security in Oil-Rich Gulf of Guinea." *Terrorism Monitor*. Vol. 8, No. 3, http://www.jamestown.org/programs/gta/single/?tx_ttnews%5Btt_news%5D=37208&tx_ttnews%5BbackPid%5D=457&no_cache=1

National Research Council. 2010. *Advancing the Science of Climate Change*. Washington: National Academies Press.

Nincic, Donna J. 2002. "Sea Lane Security and U.S. Maritime Trade: Chokepoints as Scarce Resources." In *Globalization and Maritime Power*. Sam J. Tangredi, ed. Washington: National Defense University.

O'Connor, Anne-Marie, and William Booth. 2011. "Taking a Stand for Timber." *Washington Post*, July 7, 2011, p. A6.

Pacific Institute Water Conflict Chronology. http://www.worldwater.org/conflict/map/

Raymond, Lee R. 2004. "Facing Some of the Hard Truths about Energy." Remarks to the Woodrow Wilson International Center for Scholars, Washington, D.C., June 7, 2004.

Renner, Michael. 2002. *Anatomy of Resource Wars.* Washington: Worldwatch Institute.

Risen, James. 2010. "U.S. Identifies Vast Mineral Riches in Afghanistan." *New York Times,* June 13, 2010.

Shiklomanov, Igor A. 1999. State Hydrological Institute (SHL. St. Petersburg) and United Nations Educational, Scientific and Cultural Organisation (UNESCO, Paris), 1999.

Snyder, Richard, and Ravi Bhavnani. 2005. "Diamonds, Blood, and Taxes." *Journal of Conflict Resolution.* Vol. 49, No. 4, August 2005, pp. 563–597.

Thompson, Jamie, and Ramzy Kanaan. 2005. "Conflict Timber: Dimensions of the Problem in Asia and Africa. Volume 1. Synthesis Report." Final Report submitted to the U.S. Agency for International Development. February 24, 2005.

"The Transboundary Freshwater Dispute Database." Updated 2008. Oregon State University. http://www.transboundarywaters.orst.edu/database/

UN News Centre. 2010. "General Assembly declares access to clean water and sanitation is a human right." July 28, 2010. http://www.un.org/apps/news/story.asp?NewsID=35456&Cr=SANITATION

USAID. 2005. "Forests & Conflict: A Toolkit for Intervention." Washington: USAID. http://www.usaid.gov/our_work/cross-cutting_programs/conflict/publications/docs/CMM_Forests_and_Conflict_2005.pdf

USGS. 2009. "Summary of Estimated Water Use in the United States in 2005." Fact Sheet 2009–3098, October 2009, http://pubs.usgs.gov/fs/2009/3098/.

van Midwoud, Pieter, and Arend Jan van Bodegom. 2006. "Independent Monitoring of the FLEGT Timber Legality Assurance System: Thinking Outside the Box." Verifor Briefing Paper. London: Overseas Development Institute, December 2006.

Verrastro, Frank A. 2011. "Security Implications of the Changing Energy Landscape." *Global Forecast 2011.* Washington: CSIS, pp. 42–45.

Vörösmarty, C. J., P. B. McIntyre, M. O. Gessner, D. Dudgeon, A. Prusevich, P. Green, S. Glidden, S. E. Bunn, C. A. Sullivan, C. Reidy Liermann, and P. M. Davies. 2010. "Global Threats to Human Water Security and River Biodiversity." *Nature.* Vol. 467, September 30, 2010, pp. 555–561.

"Water Conflict Chronology." Updated 2009. Pacific Institute. http://www.worldwater.org/conflict/index.html

Wolf, Aaron T., Annika Kramer, Alexander Carius, and Geoffrey D. Dabelko. 2005. "Managing Water Conflict and Cooperation." In Worldwatch Institute, *State of the World 2005: Redefining Global Security.* New York: W.W. Norton & Company, pp. 80–95.

Wolf, Aaron T., Shira B. Yoffe, and Mark Giordano. 2003. "International Waters: Identifying Basins at Risk." *Water Policy.* Vol. 5, pp. 29–60.

World Bank. 2010a. *Botswana: Country Brief.* September 2010. http://web.worldbank. org/WBSITE/EXTERNAL/COUNTRIES/AFRICAEXT/BOTSWANAEXT N/0,,menuPK:322821~pagePK:141132~piPK:141107~theSitePK:322804,00. html

World Bank. 2010b. *Costa Rica: Country Brief.* May 2010. http://web.worldbank. org/WBSITE/EXTERNAL/COUNTRIES/LACEXT/COSTARICAEXT N/0,,contentMDK:20232979~pagePK:141137~piPK:141127~theSitePK: 295413,00.html

CHAPTER 3

Food Security

Economists talk about the 'subsistence margin': for the Hassans there is no margin left. Mr. Hassan recently suffered a fever, leaving him unable to work for five days. Now the family must borrow money or sell assets, perhaps even their land, to make ends meet. Poor nutrition makes them easily sickened, reduces their ability to work, and affects the children's physical development. We cannot measure what hunger does to their mental state
> —from "The Hassans: A Portrait of Hunger" in *Ending Hunger in Our Lifetime: Food Security and Globalization*

The United Nations defines **food security** as people having access to sufficient stocks and supplies of food to provide a nutritionally adequate diet. Out of a current world population of 6.8 billion people, approximately 925 million are chronically undernourished (FAO Global Hunger Index).

Food Security

Food security encompasses the simple idea of freedom from hunger, and can be defined in many different ways. In addition to the United Nations' definition above, the World Food Summit on Food Security defined food security as existing "when all people at all times have physical, social, and economic access to sufficient, safe, and nutritious food to meet their dietary needs and food preferences for an active and healthy life" (FAO 2009). In a world that has seen increasing food production, it may seem surprising that there are still hungry people in the world today, but ensuring food security for all peoples is more than just a matter of producing enough foodstuff.

There are other definitions of food security. "National food security" is often thought to mean food self-sufficiency on the part of a country, meaning the country can produce all of the food it needs itself. Similarly, "national food sovereignty" is used to measure the degree to which a country can acquire the food it needs either through domestic production or through imports from a stable source. A nation that cannot produce all its own food and cannot afford to import food is not food secure (Pinstrup-Andersen 2009). Given the complexity and interconnectedness of the global food market, few nations rely solely on food they produce themselves.

The Food and Agricultural Organization identifies four pillars of food security (FAO 2009):

1. **Availability**—good-quality and safe food must be grown and harvested in sufficient quantity, and/or imported if necessary.
2. **Access**—food must be made available to all citizens locally at reasonable cost.
3. **Utilization**—food must be consumed in appropriate amounts and combinations to maximize nutrition.
4. **Stability**—any system that provides food security must be robust over time, so that the nutritional needs of the population are met each year.

A nation must rely on all four of these pillars to maintain food security. If one or more of the pillars should be imperiled in some way, through environmental factors, a recession, natural disasters, wars, and the like, countries that were previously food secure might suddenly find themselves closer to shortages or famine than they were prepared for. What happens to a nation facing food insecurity? And what types of actions and responses are available to them?

Effects of Famine and Chronic Hunger on Development

Food security is a fundamental aspect of human development, and is enshrined in the UN Universal Declaration of Human Rights. Yet all over the world, millions of people live without sufficient food every day.

Undernourishment, or simple hunger, occurs when a person regularly does not get enough calories to sustain his or her body's energy requirements, which is approximately 1,800 kcal per day. This is not the same type of hunger that occurs when an otherwise well-fed person misses a meal. Chronic hunger is a permanent state of low energy and lethargy. Malnutrition, on the other hand, occurs when a person does not get sufficient nutrients in the right amounts from the food eaten. Most people who are undernourished are also malnourished, but it is possible for a person to be obese and yet malnourished. This would be the nutritional equivalent of living on nothing but french fries. However, most food security issues stem from too little or unevenly distributed food rather than too much.

Figure 3.1 FAO Hunger Map 2011

Where Are the Hungry?

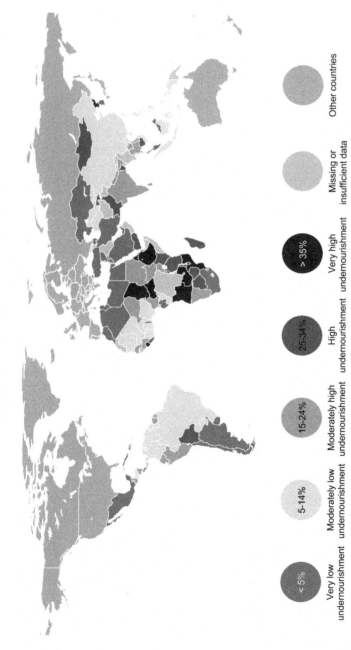

(Food and Agriculture Organization of the United Nations. Available at http://www.fao.org/docrep/014/i2330e/i2330e00a.pdf)

Per the FAO's 2010 estimate, the majority of food insecure people live in the developing world: 239 million in sub-Saharan Africa, 578 million in Asia and the Pacific, 53 million in Latin America and the Caribbean, 37 million in the Middle East and North Africa, and 19 million in the developed world (FAO 2010).

The medical and developmental consequences of undernourishment and malnutrition are acute and dangerous, particularly for children. Nutrition and development experts have identified a "1,000-day window" between a child's conception and its second birthday when a child is in the greatest need of adequate amounts of nutrition for healthy development. Beyond this point in time, the developmental effects of undernourishment are largely irreversible (IFPRI 2010, 21). More than one-third of child deaths worldwide are attributable to undernourishment and poverty. In addition, undernourishment can lead to stunted growth (when children are too short for their age), which in turn leads to slowed brain development, resulting in lowered IQ and poor learning. Approximately 178 million children around the world suffer from undernourishment-related stunted growth. Malnutrition in vital nutrients such as Vitamin A, zinc, iron, and iodide can negatively affect immunity and healthy development, leading to a host of health problems and vulnerabilities later in life (WHO Facts). In 2000, the UN collected micronutrient data indicating that 56 percent of pregnant women, 44 percent of nonpregnant women, and 53 percent of school-age children suffer from iron-deficient anemia. Goiter, a disease of the thyroid caused by iodine deficiency, affects about 740 million people, and more than 2 billion people worldwide have diets deficient in iodine. Deficiency in Vitamin A damages the eyesight and weakens the immune systems of an estimated 225–250 million preschool-age children globally (Runge et al. 2003, 19).

Developmental deficiencies resulting from food insecurity can manifest themselves as economic deficiencies for a nation over the long term. Children who have been exposed to famine or undernourishment see its negative effects on school performance, educational attainment, employment, and earnings when they reach working age, though even the promise of a meal provided by their school can sharply increase children's attendance (Victoria et al. 2008; see also Umaña-Aponte 2011). The World Bank determined that malnutrition is costing poor countries up to 3 percent of their yearly GDP, while malnourished children are at risk of losing more than 10 percent of their lifetime earnings potential (World Bank 2006).

Since the first of the Millennium Development Goals, agreed to by all 192 UN member nations in 2000, is to reduce by half the number of people who suffer from hunger by the year 2015, it is helpful to have a snapshot each year of how close the world's governments are to achieving this goal. The International Food Policy Research Institute, along with various partner institutions, began calculating the Global Hunger Index in 2006 as a way to provide a global overview of severe hunger and determine how nations rank in measures of food insecurity. The 2011 GHI was calculated for each country as a function of three factors: the proportion of those undernourished, the prevalence of underweight children, and the under-five child mortality rate.

Globally, there has been improvement between the 1990 base year GHI of 19.8 and the 2011 GHI of 14.6. This means that all 122 nations for which the GHI was calculated have, on average, reduced hunger (a lower score is a better performance). Regionally, however, the results differ considerably. Sub-Saharan Africa and South Asia have the highest scores, indicating that they suffer the greatest amount of hunger. However, the main causes of hunger differ in each region. In sub-Saharan Africa, political instability and ineffective governance, war and conflict, and high HIV/AIDS rates raise the proportion of the general population that is undernourished. In South Asia, by contrast, the low nutritional, educational, and social status of women raises the proportion of underweight children and under-five child mortality. Some individual nations like Malaysia have improved their GHI scores by reducing the number of underweight children through targeted government intervention. Other nations have experienced a falling GHI due to high HIV/AIDS rates—like Swaziland—or hyperinflation and economic collapse—like Zimbabwe. The Democratic Republic of the Congo, with three-quarters of its population undernourished, suffered the largest increase in GHI; this is due to poor infrastructure, economic instability, and loss of food production made worse by a protracted civil war (IFPRI 2010).

Factors that Affect Food Production and Availability

In the past, humans have dealt with long-term food insecurity in only one way—by increasing food production. Whether by converting new land to agriculture, raising more livestock, and/or exploiting new fisheries, more food meant less hunger. Now, however, hunger and famine can occur even when there is plenty of food, though food shortages push countries that much closer to food insecurity. Below, we will examine the various factors that affect the production and availability of food. Environmental factors that affect food production include climate change and the reallocation of arable land to production of crops for biofuels. Distributional and social systems that affect both food production and availability include the functioning and failures of markets, the recent economic recession, the ongoing rise in oil prices, the problem of food waste, and the roles of caste, status, and gender in societies. Political factors that affect the availability of food include wars and insurgencies, economic sanctions, and the weaknesses of fledgling democracies.

Environmental Factors

Climate Change

Of all the environmental factors that could impact food production, climate change is the most wide-ranging and long-lasting. Our entire global food production and distribution system has been built on certain assumptions about temperature and rainfall in certain places and at certain times of the year. As humans alter the global climate through emissions of greenhouse gases and changes in land use, including loss of carbon sinks such as forests, these assumptions may no longer hold true.

The Intergovernmental Panel on Climate Change (IPCC) released its Fourth Assessment Report in 2008, and painted a stark picture of global warming's effects on agriculture and livestock production. At mid to high latitudes (from 30 degrees latitude N and S to the poles), a moderate warming of 1–3°C, along with associated CO_2 and rainfall changes, is expected to increase crop yields slightly. At low latitudes (between 30 degrees N and S), however, moderate warming is expected to decrease crop yields. While it may seem like these two findings balance each other out, resulting in a mere shift in crop production from one geographical area to another, it is important to note that low-latitude regions support over half of the world's population, and this percentage is growing, as most of the population increase in this century is expected to occur in the developing world. Assuming that enough food can be grown, such a shift will require more transportation of food crops from North to South. Should warming increase beyond 3°C, crop output models predict a global decline in production (IPCC AR4 WGII 2007, 275). This raises the specter of a worldwide food shortage.

Crops also need regular precipitation to grow, and most global climate models do a poor job of representing precipitation changes over land. Read at the regional scale, however, several trouble spots for possible rain-induced crop failure can be identified. Warming temperatures across the Indian Ocean have disrupted transport of atmospheric moisture into eastern and southern Africa, reducing rainfall (Funk & Brown 2009, 275). This could contribute to a possible 30 percent reduction in regional cereal crop production between 2007 and 2030 (ibid., 277). Coupled with a growing population, this predicts a significant shortfall in per capita food availability. The growing population in South Asia could face a similarly insecure situation, as cereal crop production there could drop by as much as 38 percent (ibid., 278). Lowered soil moisture generally may cause some areas to become unsuitable for farming (Schmidhuber & Tubiello 2007, 19704; see also CGIAR 2011).

In addition, it is not just gradual changes in temperature and precipitation that will affect production of food. Climate change is also expected to increase the occurrence of extreme weather events such as droughts, wildfires, storms, and flooding. More frequent extreme events can lower long-term food yield by damaging crops at particular critical stages of growth. Excessive soil moisture, increased flood frequency, soil erosion, heat stress, frost occurrence, and saline intrusion can affect crops during their growing season (IPCC AR4 WGII 2007, 284). Warmer ambient temperatures may also increase demands for irrigation, further stressing freshwater resources (ibid.), and increased climate variability and droughts can lead to loss of livestock (ibid., 287), on which many rural poor depend. Aside from changes in precipitation, elevated CO_2 levels and temperatures and a longer growing season are likely to result in negative effects such as weeds and pests (NRC 2010, 295; see also Schmidhuber & Tubiello 2007).

The **CO_2 fertilization effect** is something of an "x-factor" in determining food plant production trends under climate change. Generally, increased levels of CO_2 will increase plant output by increasing biomass, but preliminary research shows that crops such as wheat, rice, and soybeans will fare better under an atmosphere with twice the preindustrial carbon dioxide level than corn and sorghum. However, these predictions are dependent both on temperature and water stress, and on region. At higher atmospheric CO_2 concentrations, crop output falls across the board (Schmidhuber & Tubiello 2007, 19704; see also AR4 WGII 2007, 479–80).

Using temperature data from 1995–2010, climate change appears to be statistically significant to the 95 percent level (Black 2011), and there is evidence that this is already affecting food production. A recent study found that temperature trends for the 1980–2008 period have shown statistically significantly warmer temperatures than can be accounted for by natural variability. Linking this input to a crop output model for rice, soybean, wheat, and maize which account for 75 percent of the calories that humans consume, the authors determined that wheat production fell 5.5 percent and maize production 3.8 percent below what they would have been without this artificial warming. The effects on rice and soybean were less significant (Lobell et al. 2011), though the authors admit the models did not capture all identifiable climate inputs. However, since warming trends are predicted only to increase, this means that multifaceted adaptation policies will be necessary to prevent climate change from eroding food production and hence food security (see Howden et al. 2007).

Production of Biofuels

Since the burning of fossil-based fuels for transportation is one of the key contributing factors to anthropogenic climate change, many nations such as Brazil, India, and the United States have begun to produce biofuels as a cleaner alternative. Biofuels are liquid fuels derived from biomass and are used to produce ethanol or biodiesel to either supplement or replace gasoline. Corn/maize, soybean, jatropha, and switchgrass are commonly used for biofuel production. While there are few studies specifically on the effects of climate change on production of biofuel crops, their reaction to climate stress is expected to be similar to that of food crops (IPCC AR4 WGII 2007, 288).

Figure 3.2 Biofuels, World Annual Production

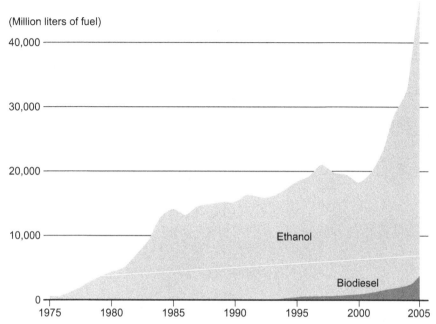

World Biofuels Annual Production

(Million liters of fuel)

(Data from Earth Policy Institute. 2006. Data files for Supermarkets and Service Stations Now Competing for Grain. http://www.earth-policy.org/Updates/2006/Update55_data. htm (Accessed November 17, 2008). Graphic by Hugo Ahlenius, UNEP/GRID-Arendal, http://www.grida.no/graphicslib/detail/biofuels-production-1975-2005-ethanol-and-biodiesel_f58b. Used by permission.)

More relevant to food security, however, is the amount of arable land used to produce biofuel crops that would or could otherwise be used to produce food crops. Lester Brown, from the Worldwatch Institute, points out that the grain required to fill a 25-gallon SUV tank with ethanol could feed one person for a year (Brown 2009, 53). Thus, biofuels can represent a significant diversion of crops away from food uses. The IPCC predicts the need for a 55 percent increase in global food crop production by 2030, and an 80 percent increase by 2050, just to keep pace with growing populations worldwide. In order to achieve this, another 185 million hectares (+19%) of rain-fed cropland and another 60 million hectares (+30%) of irrigated cropland will have to be brought into production (ibid., 280–281). While many industrialized states see the production of biofuels as an important step to mitigate greenhouse gas emissions, a combination of growing populations and increasing environmental degradation in sub-Saharan Africa, Asia, and Latin America will decrease food security.

Soil Degradation

A third factor that will decrease agricultural output and imperil food security is degradation of soils. This can occur through erosion, compaction, loss of nutrients, oversalinity, or most likely, some combination of these.

Soil can be eroded by wind or by water, and this erosion can be exacerbated by poor tillage techniques. Topsoil erosion causes long-lasting ecological damage because it can take hundreds of years to form a soil layer an inch thick. Gradual erosion occurs when wind and rain blow or wash away a small amount of soil over a long period of time, whereas a large amount of soil can be moved suddenly by a storm or an extreme weather event. Some degree

Figure 3.3 The Vicious Cycle of Land Degradation

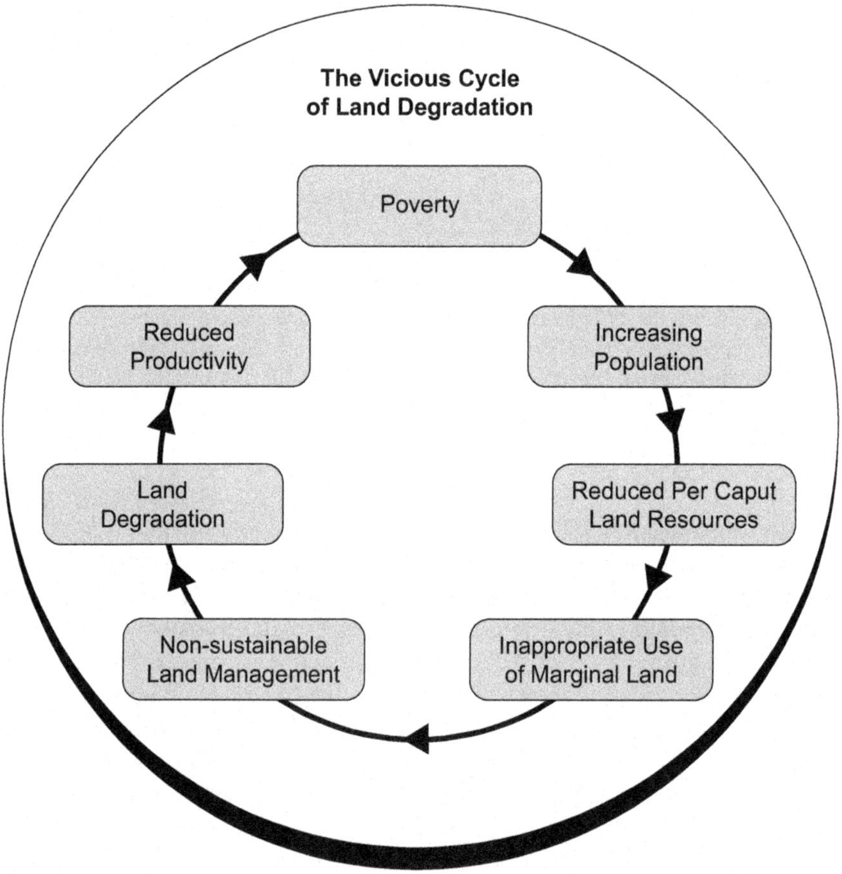

(The Conservation of Lands in Asia and the Pacific. National Resources and the Environment Department, Food and Agriculture Organization of the United Nations. 2000. Available at http://www.fao.org/docrep/v9909e/v9909e00.htm.)

of erosion is normal, but the loss of too much soil relative to its capacity to regenerate can render previously arable land barren. For example, in the 1930s, soil desiccated by drought and eroded by wind caused the famous Dust Bowl in the Great Plains area of the United States and Canada, prompting 2.5 million people to migrate west in search of work. Not until windbreaks were planted and farmers educated about soil conservation did the fertility of the land return. During the mid-1950s, the Soviet government turned approximately 330,000 km^2 of land from steppe to agriculture as part of their national development plan. Initially a success, the Virgin Lands Program eventually failed due to erosion of soil and lack of infrastructure to transport crops and fertilizers to and from populated areas. Currently, China's extraordinary efforts at agricultural development are resulting in deforestation and soil erosion on an immense scale. How immense is currently anyone's guess, as the government of China is withholding data on erosion under the label of state secrecy.

Compaction of soil occurs when pressure is applied, usually by traffic, to reduce the space for water and air within the soil; this can negatively affect root growth and metabolism, especially in wet years, and decrease soil fertility (DeJong-Hughes et al. 2001). Salination occurs when salts from irrigation water or saline groundwater build up in the topsoil, rendering it infertile to plants. Soil can also lose nutrients in various ways, by overuse of fertilizers and pesticides, by growing the same crop in the same place for an extended period of time, and by chemical contamination. For example, the Soviet government used land across Central Asia in the 1960s and 1970s to grow cotton for export. Forced to yield the same crop over and over again, the land required large amounts of agricultural chemicals, which polluted the water and soil. The current Karimov government continues the same practice.

Distributional factors

Increasing Global Wealth
Wealthy and middle-class lifestyles have, for most of the modern era, been confined to the developed world, along with a small number of government and social elites in developing nations. However, according to the OECD, the world population will shift from being mostly poor to mostly middle class by 2022. Brazil has seen 24 million of its citizens leave poverty, China alone may have as many as 800 million middle class citizens, and India's middle class is predicted to grow to 267 million in five years (Bryant 2011).

Rising global affluence puts more wealth in the hands of more people. Overall, this contributes to development, and is a desirable trend. When considering food security, greater wealth generally results in a shift in diet, as newly wealthier people eat higher on the food chain. They consume a larger portion of their daily calories from meat and dairy products and a smaller portion from grains and beans. As they get richer, they may shift their eating habits away from food cooked at home, and toward packaged and convenience foods and eating out at restaurants.

Eating higher on the food chain can have a significant impact on global food productivity, since ecologically each increase in trophic level web decreases caloric energy by a factor of 10. This means that 90 percent of the energy at each level is lost to metabolic processes at that level, and only 10 percent is passed up to the next level. By eating lower on the food chain, energy transfer is maximized from producer (food) to consumer (eater), and this ensures that the same amount of food calories feeds more people. However, the move from a plant-based diet to a meat-based diet that has traditionally accompanied an economic shift to the middle class means that a fixed amount of food calories feeds fewer people. At a time when the global population is set to increase, this will increase food insecurity.

Global Markets

With growing populations that wish to eat higher on the food chain and agricultural production being curtailed by climate change, loss of topsoil, and demand for biofuels, nations that are facing food insecurity will usually attempt to make up for any shortfall in crop supply by buying surplus food on the global market. Increasing global food production and increased trade means that most nations have not faced significant systemic difficulty when importing or exporting food. However, the economic recession of 2007–2009 caused a 12 percent drop in international trade, and prices of basic foodstuff in the open market have reached record highs. The FAO Food Price Index is a measure of the monthly change in international prices of a basket of food commodities. The average prices of these commodities from the period 2002–2004 are assigned a value of 100, and the relative prices each year from 2008 through the first month of 2012 are shown below.

Agriculture is the most contentious realm for international trade. Nations are traditionally protective of their farmers for political reasons, and may either subsidize domestic agricultural production for export, or protect domestic food markets from imported goods through tariffs, quotas, and other protective measures. The recent actions of nations, large corporations, and trading firms on the global food market have had a wide-ranging effect on prices, though the purpose of free trade is to stabilize global markets, not perturb them. At the conclusion of the Uruguay round of the WTO trade talks in 1994, developed nations agreed to drop tariffs on agricultural goods and open their markets to imports from developing nations. However, this has not happened, and after the recently collapsed Doha round, the impasse between the developed nations and the developing nations over financial protection for poor farmers is likely to remain a significant barrier to trade in agriculture.

Figure 3.4 Global Food Price Index, February 2012

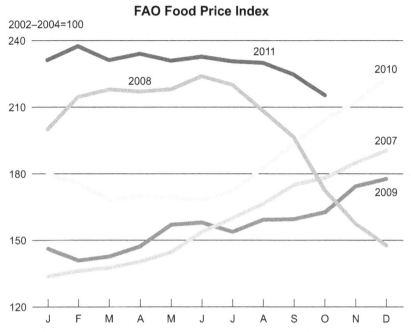

FAO Food Price Index

2002–2004=100

(Food and Agriculture Organization of the United Nations. Available at http://www.fao. org/worldfoodsituation/wfs-home/foodpricesindex/en/)

The recent recession caused food prices to rise considerably. The World Food Program predicted that at least 60 of 107 developing nations would suffer declining per capita income, and an additional 40 million people would be driven into hunger (de Schutter 2010). By 2009, Afghanistan, Mozambique, Sri Lanka, Sudan, Uganda, and Zambia, among other nations, were all facing stubbornly high food prices (WFP 2009), and these are likely to stay high over the coming decade due to increasing demand from a growing global population; diversion of maize, soy, and other crops away from food and into biofuels production; and higher oil prices, which translates into increased prices for petroleum-based fertilizers and higher costs to transport crops from field to market.

There has been some debate in financial circles over the role that financial speculation plays in food price volatility. In 2000, commodities markets in the United States were deregulated, and between 2003 and 2008, when food prices peaked during the recession, the amount of money invested in commodity index funds increased from $13 billion to $317 billion (Lawrence 2011). The UN special rapporteur on the right to food concluded that the emergence of large institutional investors in the food commodities market played a significant role in the volatility of food prices, and that supply and demand fundamentals could not have accounted for the wild swings in basic commodities such as rice and wheat (de Schutter 2010; see also IATP 2008). However, a report prepared for the OECD concluded that there was no causal relationship between speculation on the global financial markets and rising food prices (Irwin and Sanders 2010). If the commodities market is not re-regulated, as some food aid groups are asking for, then this connection could be made more explicit in the future, should global food stocks continue to contract.

In addition to financial manipulations, event-driven market shocks such as the loss or interruption of supply can cause prices to rise. Environmental factors such as droughts, floods, and wildfires can cause nations to suspend food exports, thereby keeping supply off the global market. In times of food insecurity, suspending exports can keep domestic food prices low and shore up political support at home. This has happened three times in the past few years, with devastating consequences for global food prices. In response to market fluctuations and rising domestic prices, Russia and Argentina implemented restrictions on wheat exports in 2007; Egypt followed with restrictions on rice. In 2008, Vietnam and India, the second- and third-largest exporters of rice respectively, banned exports temporarily to keep domestic prices low. In 2010, suffering from droughts, wildfires, and the worst heat wave in 130 years, Russia took the controversial step of banning wheat, barley, corn, and rye exports completely for nearly a year, causing a run-up in food prices and panic in food-importing states, and further exacerbating an ongoing drawdown of global grain stockpiles.

Event-driven price shocks can upset the food commodity market not only due to a direct shortage, but an indirect one as well, since nations that are dependent upon imports often resort to hoarding food or buying large quantities at rapidly rising prices to ensure their domestic food security. This then takes further supplies off the market and causes prices to rise even faster. In the face of high food prices and continually rising transportation costs, locally produced food becomes far preferable—from both an environmental standpoint and a security standpoint—to either imported food or food aid (Funk & Brown 2009, 272).

Food Waste

With food stocks in short supply, wasting food would seem to be the most nonsensical action for preventing food insecurity. Yet a shocking amount of food is wasted in both developed countries and developing countries at different points in the agricultural system. Approximately 80 percent of food wastage in developing countries occurs in the farm, storage, and transportation sectors, wherein the food spoils before it can be used. This is known as PHL, or postharvest losses, and this lost food is wasted before it even reaches the end user. A lack of labor to harvest crops, improper storage and handling, poor roads and other agricultural infrastructure, vulnerability of food stocks

Figure 3.5 Per Capita Food Losses and Waste (kg/year)

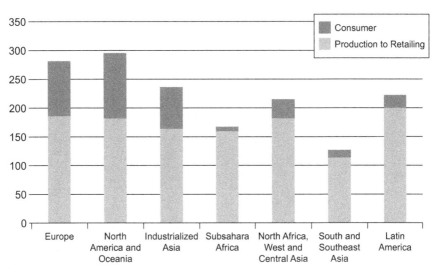

Per Capita Food Losses and Waste (kg/year)

(Gustavsson, Jenny, Christel Cederberg, Ulf Sonesson, Robert van Otterdijk, and Alexandre Meybeck. 2011. Global Food Losses and Food Waste: Extent, Causes and Prevention. Rome: FAO, 29 pp.)

to extreme weather events and pests, and outright mismanagement or malfeasance in food procurement can increase PHL and reduce food security. A recent study from the FAO/World Bank estimated that between 10 percent and 20 percent of the grain harvested in sub-Saharan Africa is lost prior to processing, and calculated the value of this loss at approximately $4 billion per year, or 15 percent of the area's estimated $27 billion annual grain production. This exceeds the total amount of food aid that sub-Saharan African nations have received over the last decade (World Bank 2011).

In contrast, the farm, storage, and transportation sectors only account for approximately 30 percent of food wastage in developed countries. The rest occurs in the retail and prepared food sector, and in the home, as the figure above indicates. Relatively wealthy customers in the developed world often prefer to buy perfect-looking food, and will discard even slightly blemished or imperfect items. In addition, restaurants that serve super-sized portions and supermarkets that offer customers a "buy one, get one free" deal encourage consumers to buy more than they can use, because food is perceived as cheap (Godfray et al. 2010). This rejected food is wasted after it has gotten to the end user.

The farm-to-fork chart below shows the amount of energy in kilocalories that is produced, converted, lost, and consumed at different points of the agricultural system, across a global average. The drop from 4,600 kcal on the farm to 2,000 kcal available for human consumption represents a loss of 57 percent

Figure 3.6 Loss of Food Energy between Farm and End User (kcal)

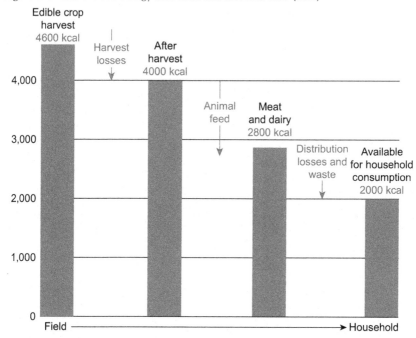

(Data from SIWI. 2008. Saving Water: From Field to Fork; Curbing Losses and Wastage in the Food Chain. http://www.siwi.org/documents/Resources/Policy_Briefs/PB_From_Filed_to_Fork_2008.pdf [Accessed November 17, 2008]. Graphic by Hugo Ahlenius, UNEP/GRID-Arendal. Available at http://www.grida.no/graphicslib/detail/losses-in-the-food-chain-from-field-to-household-consumption_1099. Used by permission.)

of the energy potential of what is grown. This lost and wasted food increases food insecurity by removing supply from the market. Wasted food also means wasted human and environmental inputs such as water, fertilizer, soil, and labor, and unwanted environmental outputs such as methane from landfills.

There is a certain anger associated with seeing food go waste, especially in such astonishing quantities: a quarter of the food wasted in the United States would provide three meals a day for 43 million people (Hall, cited in Bloom 2010, 47). Given that many small farmers in the developing world live on the margins of food insecurity, even a small reduction in food loss and wastage could improve their nutritional and developmental status considerably. The sense of injustice contained in food wastage statistics reflects the inequity of poverty; people who are hungry in the presence of food abundance are angry, and they have every right to be.

There are a variety of options that can reduce food wastage, both in the developed world and in the developing world. Within the former, food wastage can be reduced by making consumers aware of just how much food is wasted and the impact of this lost food on the environment and the climate. Leftover processed food can be rescued and sent to charitable organizations. In the developing world, better infrastructure such as roads, electricity, and storage and processing facilities will help to keep crops viable until they reach the point of sale.

Political, Social, and Health Factors

There are also some nonenvironmental and nondistributional factors that affect food availability, and hence food security. Political factors include wars and conflicts, sanctions imposed by other nations, and the transition to democratic forms of government. Socioeconomic factors include gender and caste considerations. Health factors include contamination and food-borne diseases.

Political Factors

Two of the four horsemen of the end-time are war and famine. The collateral damage to the environment from war is discussed in greater length in Chapter 5, but it is worth noting here that war and conflict wreak unparalleled destruction on arable land. Not only do acts of war destroy topsoil, water resources, and crops and seedlings, but munitions can poison land and water, landmines can render millions of hectares dangerous and unfarmable, and armed groups can conscript farmers involuntarily to fight.

If a regime behaves badly enough on the international stage, other nations may impose economic sanctions on it as an incentive to address the grievance by forcing the offending nation to change its behavior. Short of an outright declaration of war, there is not much that one nation can do to force another to act differently, so sanctions that restrict or prohibit trade are a commonly used tool. However, their usefulness is debatable, since ruling elites are somewhat insulated against the hardships resulting from sanctions. Instead, the common people are often the unintended targets, losing access to food in their markets. A well-known example of sanctions not resulting in the intended regime change is the UN Security Council's imposition of a trade embargo on Saddam Hussein's Iraq in 1990. In retaliation to Saddam's invasion of Kuwait, the Security Council embargoed all imports of Iraqi oil and forbade export of goods to Iraq except for medicines, and in certain circumstances, food. When the country began to suffer high rates of malnutrition resulting from a lack of food, the UN created the Oil-for-Food Program in 1996, allowing Iraq to resume export of oil in exchange for food. However, the sanctions did not result in either Saddam's departure or a change in his regime's policies. Amid investigations of corruption by highly placed UN officials, the Oil-for-Food Program was terminated after the Second Gulf War.

Nations that are transitioning into democratic forms of government or that have received development aid from the World Bank or IMF may also face food security issues, as their agricultural production is not necessarily responding to domestic food demand. Nations that accrue large amounts of debt due to borrowing can be required by the World Bank or the IMF to produce food for export, in order to provide earnings to pay off debt. Compounding interest can make this obligation never-ending (Devereux 2009, 29; see also Stanford 2007). This means that even as nations have increased their agricultural output, a combination of increasing population and increasing indebtedness will combine to perpetuate food insecurity.

Social Factors

Even where food is available on an aggregate basis, not all members of society may have equal access to it. In particular, women are often at a food security disadvantage relative to men, and lower caste or lower status groups in society are at a disadvantage relative to high caste or high status groups. In a globalized food market, famine has been redefined from being a geographic event like a poor regional harvest to being an economic class event; those who have wealth have food, and it is the economically and socially marginalized who suffer.

Women account for more than half the agricultural output in Africa and Asia (IFPRI 2008), and are often primarily responsible for buying and preparing food at the household level. Yet they often do not have the same access to food and the means to ensure continued food security that men do. Legal and social restrictions often prevent many women from owning land, borrowing money or having access to credit, or making decisions regarding family assets, and this reduces their ability to provide food security for their households (PAHO n.d.). Women's time and mobility may be constrained due to housekeeping or child care duties. They may even fear for their safety, since women are often the targets of sexual violence, especially in conflict and postconflict environments. Individual country studies in Nigeria and Bangladesh, and cross-country analyses from sub-Saharan Africa and South Asia have concluded that food security is directly related to the status of women in a society, and even modest gains in women's education can translate to significant increases in household-level food security (Smith and Haddad 2000, Ajani 2008, Quisumbing et al. 2008).

Low caste or low status segments of society are also disadvantaged in the competition for food. Lower classes are usually poorer and more dependent upon agriculture or other natural resources for their livelihoods. The upper levels of society may not see lower classes as deserving of scarce food in a crisis, or they may make it difficult for lower classes to have access to food. For example, only the socially privileged castes can own land in parts of South Asia such as Nepal and India; others must lease land from the owners. In addition, they may not have rights to irrigation water, rendering their labor less productive, and they may not have easy access to markets to buy and sell food (Bk 2010). Even government feeding programs that serve school-age children are haphazardly administered, often based on caste. This means that low-caste children do not get fed, or members of the low-caste community are not hired to cook or serve meals (Thorat & Lee 2005; see also Asian Human Rights Commission). When one part of the local community or society is food insecure and another is not by design, this engenders resentment and possibly conflict.

Health Factors

Food-borne diseases affect how populations utilize the food they do have. Recalls of contaminated food, whether due to improper storage or cross-contamination with pathogens such as *E. coli,* can affect food security by depleting food supply (McDonald 2010, 126). In addition, infectious diseases, some of which can be vectored by climate change–induced ecological shifts, can make hunger and malnutrition worse by impeding an individual's ability to extract nutrients from food. This nutritional deficit then makes an individual more susceptible to disease by weakening his or her immune system (Guerrant et al. 2008; Schmidhuber & Tubiello 2007).

Fisheries

Food security as it relates to fisheries merits special consideration. Exploitation of fisheries is expected to rise as the global population increases and nutritional authorities promote fish consumption as part of a healthy diet. Fisheries, like water, forests, and oil, is another example of a cross-border natural resource, but unlike trees and oil wells, fish stocks move from one territory to another, potentially placing nations in conflict. Arguments over fisheries do not necessarily result in violent conflict, but political posturing and point-making can tie up military resources and strain alliances.

Caught Fish

In 2008, ocean and freshwater fisheries and aquaculture (fish farming) together accounted for 142 million tons of fish, approximately 115 million tons (81%) of which was destined for human consumption. Of this 142 million, approximately 80 million came from marine stocks, 10 million from inland stocks, and 52 million from aquaculture. In the same year, the value of capture fisheries equaled $93.9 billion, and aquaculture another $98.4 billion (FAO 2010b, 5–6). Countries that are developing and acquiring wealth are demanding more animal protein, fish as well as meat; in 2007, fish accounted for approximately 16 percent of animal protein intake globally (ibid., 64), and the whole of the primary fishing industry and secondary fish-processing industry accounted for more than 180 million jobs (ibid., 6).

Legal and Security Concerns

Unlike crops, oceanic fish stocks are migratory. A highly migratory stock is one with a geographically wide-ranging distribution, and can often be found on the high seas, outside any nation's Exclusive Economic Zone (EEZ, a 200–nautical mile zone off a nation's coast to which it has exclusive access to economic resources). A straddling stock is one that migrates from one nation's EEZ to another. This division of the ocean into exclusive zones encourages free rider behavior, since each nation is economically motivated to catch as many fish as it can while the stock is in its EEZ before it moves into another nation's purview. Hence there is no economic advantage to preserving a straddling stock and letting it repopulate. In addition, fish stocks in international waters are vulnerable to predation by any nation. This is a classic example of what is known as the Tragedy of the Commons, in which publicly shared resources become overused and depleted because the individual's desire to acquire them outweighs the common desire to preserve them. The UN Fish Stock Agreement came into force in 2001 to govern migratory, straddling, and other high seas fishery resources, but its terms are upheld by regional fisheries management organizations whose enforcement records are inconsistent.

Nations will argue over fish stocks, especially if fishing accounts for a major part of their national economy, and even allies have threatened each other with military force. Iceland and the United Kingdom, both NATO members, clashed repeatedly over fishing grounds in the North Atlantic. Beginning in 1958, Iceland began unilaterally expanding its fishing rights, first from 4 miles to 12 miles, then to 50 miles, and then to 200 miles off its coast, on the grounds that fishing was critical to the Icelandic economy and that over-fishing by foreign vessels had caused stocks to decline. The United Kingdom objected to this expansion, and when Iceland's Coast Guard cut the nets of British fishing vessels, the Royal Navy was sent to protect them. After a number of violent clashes, Iceland threatened to close the NATO base at Keflavik, whose radar was critical to the Soviet submarine detection net in the North Atlantic. Eventually, the dispute was settled by negotiation, and the 200-mile Exclusive Economic Zone was recognized by the United Nations as customary international law.

A similar though less serious incident occurred in 1995, when Canada and Spain clashed over turbot fisheries off the Canadian Grand Banks. The Canadian Coast Guard cut the nets of Spanish fishing vessels, which then returned with the Spanish Navy to protect them. With the Canadian armed forces prepared to fire upon the Spanish fleet, the EU and the Canadian government eventually agreed to mutual fishing limits, and the dispute was resolved without further conflict. Such competition does not make military action inevitable, though other, nonsecurity factors like national pride, economic stability, and domestic politics often interfere with rational policymaking. The continued prospect of resource wars may convince nations that they should cooperate over scarce resources rather than resort to conflict, since ultimately a show of military force will not save a stock from crashing if it is overfished.

Factors that Affect Fisheries

Technology has given humans a decisive advantage over fish. Approximately 59 percent of the 4.3 million fishing vessels in the world are motorized (the rest are powered by oars and sails; FAO 2010b, 30), which allows them to go wherever fish go, unrestrained by winds or tides. As of 2008, the most recent data from the FAO, only 15 percent of global fish stocks are underexploited. Fifty percent are fully exploited, and 32 percent are overexploited, depleted, or recovering (FAO 2010b, 8).

Climate change will affect fish stocks just as it affects crop and livestock production, though the nature and extent of these effects are not yet well known. Marine fishery stocks fluctuate naturally in response to a number of factors, both climatic and nonclimatic. Climatic factors include rising ocean temperatures, which will shift the range of certain temperature-sensitive stocks northward, and can cause local extinctions of fish that are already at the southern edge of their current ranges. Cold-water species like salmon and trout are particularly vulnerable to temperature changes. Warming may also reduce nutrient availability in the surface layer of the ocean (FAO 2010, 115). Inland fisheries and aquaculture are at particularly high risk for changes in precipitation and sudden inputs in land runoff from storms and other extreme weather events. Sudden temperature spikes can cause localized mortality of stocks, and bleaching of coral reefs is likely to lower the complexity of reef-based fisheries. The effects of increasing ocean acidification through CO_2 absorption on fish and plankton is highly uncertain (Brander 2007; NRC 2010).

Ramifications for National and International Security

Food insecurity can stem from a multitude of causal factors. Undernourishment is a form of chronic food insecurity in which the society or parts of it regularly do not get enough calories. By contrast, famine is a form of acute food insecurity in which a sudden interruption in supply or spike in demand causes widespread and severe hunger over a relatively short period of time. Both undernourishment and famine can chip away at a nation's development, its social cohesion, and even its very existence.

Lester Brown, founder of the Worldwatch Institute and long-time scholar of food security, points out that "our global civilization depends on a functioning network of politically healthy nation-states to control the spread of infectious disease, to manage the international monetary system, to control international terrorism, and to reach scores of other common goals" (2009). National security and stability are often threatened by changes in food prices and availability. If enough states fail due to food insecurity, Brown posits that it could cause the entire international system to founder.

Power Shifts between Food-Producing Regions

If food scarcity is event-driven, then a nation can usually make up for the shortfall by buying food on the global market. Prices rise temporarily and then return to normal after the causal event. In this case, the market does exactly what it is supposed to, redirect food supplies toward those who need them and can pay for them. However, larger trends than these isolated events are affecting food security, including climate change, rising populations, and the increasing demand for biofuels. Consequently, these trends could signal a shift in the relative power between nations that trade in food. Climate change–induced shifts in production regions means that nations that have exported grain in the past may become importers, and nations that have produced enough for their own needs, and perhaps exported a little, may find themselves in the enviable position of being able to export a lot. Along with shifts in export capacity come shifts in international political power in an increasingly food-insecure world.

As shown in the map above, most of the world's exported grain presently comes from countries well north of the equator: the United States, Russia, Canada, Ukraine, and the EU. The United States is by far the world's largest grain exporter, predominantly corn and wheat. Most of the world's grain is imported by countries in the arid global south: Mexico, Saudi Arabia, and Egypt; Japan and South Korea are the exceptions—developed countries with little arable land. As temperatures increase, the northernmost grain exporters, Canada and Russia, stand to benefit from an increased growing season, while the United States, the EU, and Ukraine are likely to find their yields constrained. A shift in relative power between Canada and the United States, for example, might have significant ramifications for NATO and its future role in international security. Concurrent with increased Canadian presence in the Arctic, Canada's profile as a regional power and its influence within NATO would increase relative to that of the United States, which is used to setting the terms of NATO involvement overseas. Alternatively, Russia, which has in the past shown no compunction about using energy as a tool of foreign policy, might now be able to use food the same way, dictating the actions of its grain customers on the world stage more to its liking.

Figure 3.7 World Grain Exporters and Importers

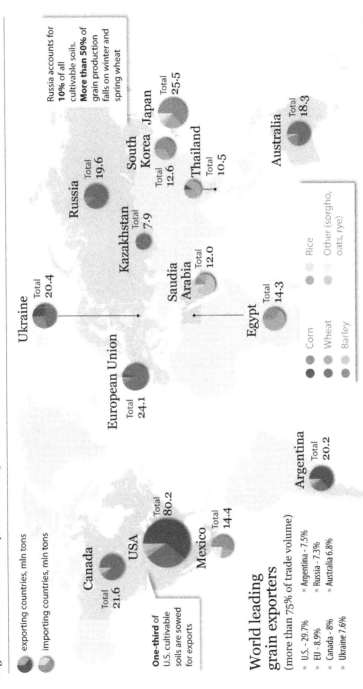

exporting countries, mln tons
importing countries, mln tons

Russia accounts for **10%** of all cultivable soils. **More than 50%** of grain production falls on winter and spring wheat

Canada
Total 21.6

USA
Total 80.2

Mexico
Total 14.4

One-third of U.S. cultivable soils are sowed for exports

European Union
Total 24.1

Ukraine
Total 20.4

Russia
Total 19.6

Kazakhstan
Total 7.9

Saudia Arabia
Total 12.0

Egypt
Total 14.3

Argentina
Total 20.2

South Korea
Total 12.6

Japan
Total 25.5

Thailand
Total 10.5

Australia
Total 18.3

Corn
Wheat
Barley
Rice
Other (sorgho, oats, rye)

World leading grain exporters
(more than 75% of trade volume)

- U.S. - 29.7%
- EU - 8.9%
- Canada - 8%
- Ukraine 7.6%
- Argentina - 7.5%
- Russia - 7.3%
- Australia 6.8%

Statistics from the U.S. Department of Agriculture for 2009-2010

RIANOVOSTI © 2010

www.rian.ru

(Ria Novosti. Used by permission.)

Figure 3.8 World Grain Production and Stock to Use Ratio, 2011

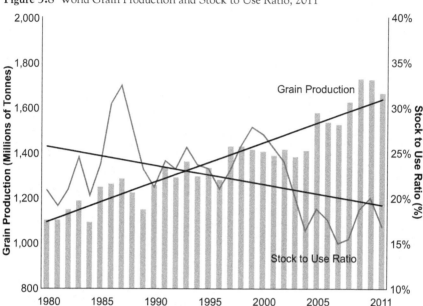

(Trostle, R. Why Another Food Commodity Price Spike? *Amber Waves*, 9[3], p 24. Published by the USDA Economic Research Service. Available at http://www.ers.usda.gov/media/206383/commoditypricespike_1_.pdf)

If the trends driving food scarcity are large or long-lasting enough, the global food market may not be able to provide sufficient supply from any source to meet demand. In this case, governments will look to nonmarket solutions. If they cannot rely on regular imports, nations may have to draw down their grain stocks in order to ensure that sufficient food supplies remain in their domestic markets. Global grain stocks at the end of 2011 are estimated to be 341 million tons, a three-year low, and further drawdowns are expected in 2012 to meet growing demand (Reuters 2011). While this solution is acceptable on a temporary basis, nations are unwise to lower grain stocks to a minimal level. Strategic reserves of grain (or oil) are designed to protect domestic markets against exogenous supply shocks. Between price fluctuations in the short term and the advancement of global climate change in the medium and long term, nations wishing to ensure food security should be building up strategic grain stocks, not drawing them down. Doing the latter shortens their margin of survival.

Food Riots

Subsidizing food purchases for one or more classes of society is a long-established economic policy tool. Whether changes in food costs are event-driven (driven by an extreme weather event or other short-term factor) or trend-driven (driven by increasing demand or environmental change), rising prices strain the nation's treasury. If poorer sectors of society depend on subsidized food, especially staple crops, rising food prices can put basic food out of financial reach for a significant number of people and result in unrest and food riots. The recession of 2007–2009 caused violent and deadly food riots in over 60 countries, including Egypt, Niger, Ethiopia, Indonesia, Cameroon, Somalia, Malaysia, Peru, Bolivia, Egypt, Haiti, Mexico, Yemen, and Mozambique (von Braun 2009).

Authoritarian nations often use food subsidies as a way to pacify large populations and undercut possible political unrest. The current public protests in the Middle East against long-established governments are the result of many factors, not the least of which is the anger among citizens over the rising price of food. One of the basic duties of governments is to provide affordable food, and those that fail to do so will see their legitimacy to rule questioned. To avoid further unrest, nations across the Middle East are plying their citizens with food and food subsidies. Recently, Algeria, Jordan, Libya, and Syria have cut taxes on food, Tunisia and Yemen have increased food subsidies, and Kuwait is outright giving each citizen 14 months of free food (Economist 2011). Whether these handouts will buy Middle Eastern nations enough time to make economic and political changes remains to be seen, but authoritarian regimes do not tolerate threats to their rule with grace. Food insecurity might be the political and economic tipping point that results in long-sought regime change.

Food as a Weapon

Often a casualty of war, food can also be a weapon of war. The provision or withholding of food is viewed as a legitimate tactic of war, stemming from the traditional use of blockade or siege tactics during conflict (Marcus 2003, 265–266). Food can be withheld by preventing it from being grown and harvested, destroying it after harvest, preventing its transportation, or by purposefully contaminating it or otherwise rendering it unfit for human consumption (Saltveit n.d.). However, since the adoption of the 1949 Geneva Conventions, sometimes informally referred to as the "rules of war," international humanitarian law has moved toward prohibiting deliberate starvation of civilian populations. Alternatively, exhortations by governments at war to avoid food wastage as a means of contributing to the war effort were commonplace by mid-century (Stuart 2009).

Mere lack of food is not enough to cause famine; a famine is usually exacerbated by political intent. There have been several significant famines created specifically as a tool for destabilizing rebellious populations. Stalin used mass hunger to subdue Ukrainian nationalism. In 1929, he decreed that all agriculture in the USSR would be collectivized, by force if necessary. After a lower-than-expected wheat harvest, and to quell Ukrainian nationalism, he imposed high production quotas on Ukrainian farms and seized not only wheat but all food when they failed to meet them. Anyone resisting or attempting to hoard food was arrested, and this artificially generated famine resulted in the starvation death of as many as 11 million Ukrainian peasants who were forbidden to leave the country in search of food (Marcus 2003, 252–255). Likewise, in the early 1980s, the recurring famine in Ethiopia was not felt equally across the country. The government withheld donated food aid from insurgents in the northern areas near Eritrea in order to starve out opposition to the government (ibid., 255–259). The recent tragedy in western Sudan includes the withholding of food and the expulsion of aid groups from the Darfur region by Sudanese president Omar al-Bashir, and the International Criminal Court issued a warrant for his arrest in 2009 for war crimes. The case of North Korea is addressed in detail later in the chapter.

Food is a weapon that is not only deployed in times of conflict. The United States passed Public Law 480 in 1956 with the objective of taking surplus American grain off the public market when it would otherwise drive down commodity prices, repackaging it as aid, and distributing it around the world in accordance with U.S. foreign policy goals. During the Cold War, it was reasoned that food aid to poorer developing nations would accomplish a number of goals, such as providing high-profile humanitarian relief on the world stage and reducing the number of other food options available to nonaligned foreign governments. The withholding of food aid could be viewed as a disincentive for hungry nations to conduct their own foreign policy against American objectives, though this tactic met with limited success (Wallensteen 1976).

It is not just governments that deploy or withhold food as a weapon. In January 2010, the World Food Program was forced to discontinue its emergency food aid operations in southern Somalia because food aid had been seized, offices had been attacked, and workers had been threatened or killed by an Islamist militia group called Al Shabaab. Claiming to be linked to Al Qaeda, Al Shabaab demanded that women be excluded from working in food aid in Somalia, and that the WFP pay them approximately $20,000 every six months for "security" during their operations. Unwilling to meet these requirements, the WFP was forced to suspend food aid to over one million recipients. Food aid continues in northern and central Somalia (WFP 2011a).

While besieging a city or other locality has traditionally been an accepted method of warfare, by the 20th century, international law had progressed to the point where intentional starvation of civilians was no longer a morally and ethically acceptable means of prosecuting a conflict. The four Geneva Conventions, informally referred to as the "rules of war," address among other things the treatment of civilians during war. In 1977, two additional protocols were negotiated relating to the protections to which victims of war were entitled. Article 54 of Protocol I (see Appendix II) deals with the conduct toward and protection of victims of international conflicts, while Article 14 of Protocol II deals with the protection of victims of noninternational, or civil, conflicts (see the boxed text). In either case, attacks on foodstuff, arable land or irrigation works, and the deliberate starvation of civilians are directly prohibited, and violations of these conventions are considered to be war crimes.

Military Power and Food

Food does not have to be a weapon directly; food can also be the means to finance a conflict. If a particular commodity crop is in high demand globally—such as coffee, cotton, or cocoa—its production can be used to fund civil or international conflict. In this way, agricultural products can contribute to the resource curse in much the same way oil, diamonds, and timber do. Ivory Coast, for example, is the world's largest supplier of cocoa beans, and this commodity has for long enriched the military supporters of outgoing ruler Laurent Gbagbo. When Gbagbo refused to step down in favor of the elected Alassane Ouattara, Ouattara called for an export ban on cocoa in January 2011 in an effort to shut off Gbagbo's lucrative revenue stream. In March 2011, Gbagbo attempted to nationalize Ivory Coast's entire cocoa crop, mandating that growers sell only to the state government. In response, a significant portion of the nation's bumper crop was smuggled over the borders into neighboring Ghana and Liberia and sold from there.

The military power of a state does not always correlate inversely with food security. If a state has reached a level of development significant enough for it to have a strong and professional military, it is probably developed enough to have workable markets and an economy that relies on more complex goods than just primary commodities. In this case, the participation of a significant portion of the population in the armed forces and the production and export of arms correlates positively with food security. However, if the military is used to settle political conflicts against internal enemies or a large portion of the national budget goes to pay the military, then the state is more likely to suffer from famines (Scanlan & Jenkins 2001).

Food insecurity is generally higher during and after civil wars rather than international wars. During a civil war, the very government structures that contribute to food security can come under attack and collapse. If this happens, governments cannot exert stability or control over the provision or cost of food, assuming they are attempting to provide food to the entire population and are not selectively withholding it as a means of intimidation (Ali & Lin 2010). Should relief forces be sent to promote peace within the country, they must make the restoration of food security one of their primary missions. If they are not seen by both sides in the conflict as acting impartially and with the primary purpose of saving lives, they will be viewed not as peacekeepers but as combatants and legitimate military targets, and this would complicate the food insecurity situation further (Natsios 1994, 137).

Even after conflict ends, food insecurity remains. Wars take a huge toll on agricultural production capacity, food markets, and national infrastructure, and unexploded ordnance and landmines can render agricultural land too dangerous to farm (Messer & Cohen 2006, 11). Consequently, nations that have emerged from an international or more likely civil war may find themselves struggling with food insecurity and undernutrition for many years.

Food Aid

Is food aid the answer to food insecurity? Aid, in the form of emergency food supplies, has often been sent from nations with surplus to nations that are facing acute food insecurity on a temporary basis due to extreme weather events, political crises, or violent conflict. Provision of food aid under these circumstances is usually viewed as a humanitarian effort, but the key word is "temporary." Food aid is not designed to supplant a nation's own agricultural production capability, and most donor nations that will supply aid for emergency purposes are reluctant to keep supplying it on a long-term basis.

Additionally, the recent global financial crisis has cut into wealthier nations' ability to provide aid. Global food aid supplies are at a 20-year low, according to the World Food Program. Only 6.3 million tons of food aid was delivered globally in 2008, compared to 13.2 million tons in 1990 (WFP 2009; see chart below). This means that food-insecure nations should not rely on regular aid as a means of achieving long-term food security. Donors of food aid can also be spooked into withholding donations after receiving bad information about harvests and food demand, or by accusations of cronyism and corruption within the recipient nation (Devereux 2009, 30–31).

Some nations have refused food aid if it contains genetically modified crops. In 2002, Zimbabwe, Mozambique, and Zambia rejected food aid from the United States despite suffering drought and failed harvests. Under pressure from UN relief agencies, Mozambique and Zimbabwe eventually relented and accepted U.S. aid in the form of milled GM corn. Despite three million people facing famine, however, the Zambian government would not relent, citing environmental, health, and regulatory concerns surrounding transgenic food. Whether this was a wise application of the precautionary principle or a rash decision condemning millions of people to hunger is not known in full, even today.

The Lifeboat Ethic

There are scholars who argue that long-term food aid can in fact strip a country of food security, not provide it. In 1974, Garrett Hardin, the

Figure 3.9 Global Food Aid (delivered quantities, MT)

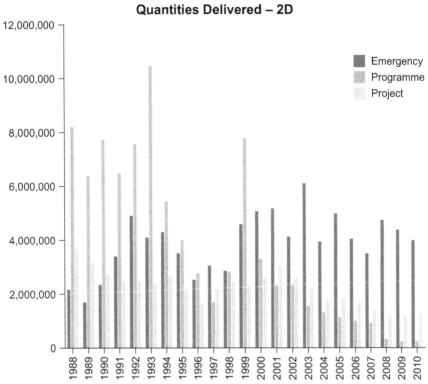

(World Food Program. Available at http://www.wfp.org/fais/reports/quantities-delivered-two-dimensional-report/chart/year/All/cat/All/recipient/All/donor/All/code/All/mode/All/basis/0/order/0)

ecologist who first articulated the tragedy of the commons, argued through a concept he called the "lifeboat ethic" that providing food aid to a food-insecure nation actually prolongs famine and poverty. A nation becomes chronically food-insecure, he argued, because the size of the population has outstripped the ecological carrying capacity of the nation supporting it. As populations in nature grow, food becomes their limiting factor, and humans are no different.

In his analogy, each wealthy nation is akin to a lifeboat holding 50 people, with capacity for 10 more. In the sea outside are the poor nations (100 people) that are asking the 50 people in the lifeboat for help. Hardin saw three possible options. First, take all 100 aboard. The lifeboat would swamp and everyone would drown. Second, take 10 more aboard. This fills the lifeboat to capacity, and the safety margin is gone. In addition, how do the people in the lifeboat choose which 10 to accept? Third, take no more people aboard.

This preserves the lives of those in the boat and their safety margin. The third option is Hardin's recommended solution. The poor nations have swamped their own lifeboats with overpopulation, and now must live within the carrying capacity of their ecosystems. This means controlling their population. Food aid, Hardin held, did more harm than good in the long run because it allowed nations to grow their populations unsustainably.

Yet people, children especially, continue to starve around the world, as a near-constant stream of pictures and news reports attests. Hardin's argument strikes many people as cruel and inhumane: how can nations that have excess food justify withholding it if other nations are in crisis? This is consigning millions around the world to the long-term physical and developmental effects of undernutrition, discussed previously. But because ecological limits are real, his supporters argue that his option is the kindest of the three in the long run. Avoiding some deaths now by providing food aid means more deaths later when the population continues to reproduce and the food aid is discontinued.

The best compromise would seem to be food aid in the short term and food capacity building in the long term, a sort of macro-level variation on the "teach a man to fish" axiom. However, it is worth keeping in mind that long-term capacity building requires long-term investment, and each nation faces different ecological, economic, cultural, social, and political realities. The Zambian case above and the North Korean case below highlight the predicament that both food aid donors and recipients find themselves in, one of mismatched donor and recipient values and priorities. Unless a nation can grow or trade its own food, its security and sovereignty will be subject to the whims of other nations. This means that food aid is not an investment in long-term security and stability for either the recipient nation or the donor nation.

Political, Ethical, and Moral Issues of Hunger: The Case of North Korea

The Democratic People's Republic of Korea (DPRK, or North Korea) is a Stalinist dictatorship and has been under almost constant threat of famine and humanitarian emergency since the mid-1990s. Kim Jong Un, the current ruler, has only been in power since the December 2011 death of his father Kim Jong Il, himself the son of the country's founder Kim Il Sung. Agriculture in North Korea is collectivized and centrally planned, and suffers from a lack of inputs and capital investment. Most food within the country is distributed by the Public Distribution System, the government-run food agency, though the government occasionally permits private "farmers markets" in order to encourage increased food production. However, if these markets become too attractive, the Communist Party has been known to step in and shut them down.

Perversely, the North Korean government has spent considerable money to develop and test nuclear missiles, which it insists it needs to defend itself from its enemies, particularly South Korea and the United States. The government probably views this nascent nuclear capability as a matter of national pride, tinged with a certain amount of totalitarian paranoia. However, the DPRK's pursuit of nuclear capability redirects scarce funds away from food production, and those who suffer from this aid-based, whim-of-the-government system of food availability are the North Korean people.

At the beginning of 2011, the UN warned that due to flooding and an exceptionally harsh winter, approximately 6 million of North Korea's 24 million people could face starvation that year if the nation was not provided with an additional 434,000 MT of food aid (WFP 2011b). However, donor countries, of which South Korea and the United States are by far the largest, have balked at providing further food aid for two reasons. First, the North Korean ruling party often fails to get the food to the most needy people, often diverting aid into private markets for sale at steep prices, or redistributing it as gifts to members of the North Korean military. Yet the DPRK has one of the highest malnutrition rates in the world. According to a recent FAO/WFP report on food security in North Korea, 25 percent of reproductive-age women are undernourished, and 32 percent of children are stunted (FAO 2011). Second, the ruling regime has played cat-and-mouse for years with the rest of the international community over its nuclear weapons development program. It originally ratified the Nuclear Nonproliferation Treaty, then withdrew in 2003 and began constructing its own uranium enrichment program. On October 9, 2006, the DPRK tested its first nuclear weapon underground. Despite efforts by neighboring China and other states to negotiate some sort of food-for-weapons arrangement, Kim Jong Il had repeatedly refused to give up North Korea's nuclear weapons capability.

What is the best way to improve food security for North Korea? It seems clear that the anti-international behavior of the ruling regime is responsible for the poor state of the country's citizens, but because the party permits no opposition, the citizens are not able to protest. They cannot afford to buy much of the food in the markets, and because they are not permitted to leave the country, they cannot emigrate in search of a better life elsewhere. South Korea, on the other hand, is one of the richest countries in Asia on a per capita basis. From a climate perspective, South Korea suffers the same droughts, floods, and poor weather conditions that affect North Korean food production, and South Korea also imports much of its food. Why, then, does South Korea not suffer the same degree of food insecurity?

Economist Amartya Sen argues that famines do not occur in multiparty democracies. This is because a true democracy like South Korea has something that regimes like North Korea do not: a free and independent press, an educated electorate, and freely elected politicians who will intervene to alleviate hunger in the face of a food shortage (Sen 1999). In a democracy, power doesn't result from internal repression but rather from internal support, and providing a working domestic food market generates that support. While there is evidence that these conditions are not sufficient to prevent famines, as Sen would attest, they help to explain why South Korea does not face starvation on a regular basis and North Korea does.

The scope and length of food insecurity in North Korea is unparalleled anywhere in the world. Does the international community have any obligation to alleviate this disastrous situation? Legally, the answer is no; there is no international law or custom that requires any nation to provide food aid to any other nation, no matter how severe the famine may be. Politically, providing food aid could even be dangerous to donor countries from an international security standpoint. In the case of the DPRK, not only does the food go to the nuclear-armed regime and its political and military supporters, but continually receiving aid in response to uncooperative and seemingly irrational behavior proves to the Kim family regime that their preferred method of brinksmanship in dealing with the outside world is the correct one. If Kim Jong Un continues to make belligerent pronouncements about North Korean nuclear capability, the rest of the world may very well balk at providing further aid to his country.

Ethically, however, the question becomes a bit murkier. The citizens of North Korea do not have any say in the actions of their government, and in fact are subject to harassment and arrest if they question the regime's policies or even ask where the food is. Nor are they permitted to emigrate voluntarily, effectively making them prisoners in their own country. Finally, since all agricultural planning is done by the government, North Korean farmers do not have access to modern technologies or financial instruments that would allow them to maximize food yield. By every humanitarian indicator, the general North Korean population is in the direst of straits, and far from helping them, their own nuclear-armed government stands in their way. Whether the rest of the world wishes to watch this tragedy unfold and take no steps to ameliorate it is a question that arises each year that the North Korean government appeals for food aid. Now, Kim Jong Un has a new opportunity, as he assumes power, to increase North Korea's food security by assuring donor nations that their aid will reach the neediest citizens. However, torn between openness and international cooperation, and the prevailing suspicion and paranoia of his government, he may follow the country's traditional path of brinksmanship, thereby condemning his citizens to decades of famine.

Future Issues

Addressing food security, much less guaranteeing it for their citizens, is a tricky proposition for governments. Food security sits at the intersection of a number of difficult and contentious issues: growing world population, stagnant or declining agricultural output, market access policies for agricultural goods, new technologies like GMOs designed to modify food at the genetic level, and global climate change. It is impossible to improve food security without addressing these underlying causes and variables, which makes it a true interdisciplinary problem for future scholars and policy makers.

Traditional discussions of national and international security relegate food to the realm of low politics, along with environmental, demographic, and gender issues, as it supposedly lacks the gravitas of high politics security issues like nuclear weapons and military readiness (discussed in chapter 1). However, there are some scholars who point out that oil and other forms of energy have been a high politics security issue since the middle of the last century, while the food that is "fuel for humans" has not been viewed through the same lens (Fullbrook 2009). But food is a security good like any other, and while there are substitutes for oil, there are no substitutes for food. At its root, food security is an environmental problem, which, high and low politics notwithstanding, makes it no less of a security problem.

Agro-Imperialism

Some nations, in their desire to secure adequate food supplies, have turned to a somewhat radical alternative. Rather than rely on technological improvement to increase crop yield or on imported food purchased from the global market, some nations are outsourcing food production altogether in an effort to lock in food supplies in the face of growing populations and environmental perturbations. This means that, in a deal made between sovereign governments and backed up by private funds, agriculturally rich land in one country can be sold or leased to provide crops exclusively for hungry people in another country.

In the past four or five years, several of these deals have been negotiated by cash-rich but food-insecure nations. Consider the example of Saudi Arabia, whose population is growing by 1.5 percent each year. A desert country with only 1.67 percent arable land, it imports approximately 73 percent of its food. Dwindling supplies of fresh water point to food insecurity and attendant political unrest unless the kingdom can secure additional food supplies free from the volatility of the international market. In 2009, the Saudis announced a $250 million joint venture investment in Ethiopia and Sudan for agricultural land to be planted with crops for export (Rice 2009).

The idea behind these arrangements is that the investing nation will control the means of production and make use of the crop however it sees fit. Supporters say that this will bring foreign investment, technological know-how, and a guaranteed export market to agriculturally underdeveloped and underproducing countries. Critics have called the practice "agro-imperialism" and argue that exporting food from already food-insecure nations is not only ludicrous and ill-advised, but guaranteed to lock in fundamental economic and developmental inequality between nations for decades to come.

From the food security perspective of a cash-rich nation, this type of sovereign commercial arrangement allows it to control the production of food from farm to fork, a smart move in the face of climate change and rising global food prices. This is completely legal international commerce, with an added benefit of spreading agricultural knowledge to underdeveloped nations. However, outsourcing food production in such a manner brings the "private good" aspects of food in direct conflict with its "public good" aspects. If Saudi Arabia pays for the land, the seed, and the labor, why aren't they entitled to reap the benefits of a contract deal agreed to by the recognized authority, the Ethiopian government? To this extent, food is being treated as a private good, a commodity like oil, timber, or anything else traded on the international market. But Ethiopia is one of the most food-insecure nations on the earth. With a growth rate of 3.2 percent per year, Ethiopia's own population will double in approximately 20 years. Does the government of Ethiopia have the right to trade away the agricultural capability of the country to a foreign nation when 47 percent of its own children are underweight, and 4.5 million Ethiopians receive food aid from the World Food Program? A nation whose citizens are starving is widely viewed as entitled to surplus food in the form of food aid. To this extent, food is being treated as a public good, and it is this dual view of food and the responsibilities of a government and the world toward feeding the hungry that make such deals ethically questionable, if not legally so.

Can Food Security Be Achieved Collectively?

The assumption inherent in this example is that if the government of Ethiopia does not provide for the food security of its own citizens, then the global community will either be forced to step in and provide aid, or watch a human tragedy of immense proportions unfold. In the end, agro-imperialism takes food security from being a collective endeavor to being a my-nation-against-yours endeavor, and from being guaranteed through collective means like global markets to being guaranteed through exclusive means, like fences around cropland, armed soldiers to guard crop shipments, and nontransparent back-door deals signed by a government that cannot or will not provide for its own citizens.

Addressing food security by leasing foreign agricultural land and producing crops for export would seem to indicate that food security is a zero-sum game. When push comes to shove (push being climate change and growing populations, shove being failing harvests and food riots), the private good and public good aspects of food are brought into direct conflict. Is security itself a public good or a private good? Is it possible at an international level, or is it possible at a national level only? Food aid would seem to be an indication that food security has been pursued at the international level, but land grabs and dedicated food exports are a way of pursuing food security at the national, zero-sum level only. The provision of security by collective means is not appropriate in every case (e.g., nuclear weapons), but for an agricultural system that relies directly on the cross-border nature of ecosystem services such as rain and pollination, successful food production in one nation can presage security within the entire region.

There are other security aspects of such food sovereignty contracts that need to be considered. Africa's agricultural capacity is predicted to be hard-hit by climate change. If its agricultural output is below estimates and it is unable to fulfill its export obligations, then (a) the food-importing nation may find the food is not worth what was paid for it, and (b) the food destined for export might be repossessed by a native population "double-exposed" to the effects of both climate change and increasingly globalized trade. The history of colonialism and resource plunder in Africa by foreign powers leaves many Africans suspicious of development offers from wealthier nations. Displacing agricultural production from one nation to another for food security reasons could also be problematic from an environmental perspective. The economic pressure to increase land productivity to ensure contract crops for export means that fewer hectares will be left fallow to let nutrients regenerate or preserve the soil. Land will be farmed more intensively and could rely more on fossil water for irrigation and agrochemicals like fertilizers and pesticides, and the importing party would be under no restraint to limit use of these chemicals since they would not suffer the direct effects within their own nation.

The scientific journal *Nature* posits that agricultural output can be increased and 9.1 billion people can be "easily" fed if the world puts more money and time into research ("How to feed a hungry world" 2010, 531). It should come as no surprise then that wealthy nations and agro-businesses favor technological fixes to the problem of food security, but what if we don't have the technology or the problem goes beyond technology? Sustainability, and hence security, is not merely a matter of finding the right technological fix. It is the result of a complicated interplay of a number of scientific and social/political/cultural factors, placing food security squarely within the realm of environmental security.

Important Articles

See Appendix II of this book for Article 54 of "Protocol Additional to the Geneva Conventions of 12 August 1949, and Relating to the Protection of Victims of International Armed Conflict (Protocol I)".

Protocol Additional to the Geneva Conventions of 12 August 1949, and relating to the Protection of Victims of Non-International Armed Conflict (Protocol II)

Article 14. Protection of objects indispensable to the survival of the civilian population
Starvation of civilians as a method of combat is prohibited. It is therefore prohibited to attack, destroy, remove or render useless for that purpose, objects indispensable to the survival of the civilian population such as foodstuffs, agricultural areas for the production of food-stuffs, crops, livestock, drinking water installations and supplies and irrigation works.

Source: *Protocol Additional to the Geneva Conventions of 12 August 1949, and relating to the Protection of Victims of Non-International Armed Conflicts (Protocol II)*, 8 June 1977, 1125 UNTS 609, available at: http://www.unhcr.org/refworld/docid/3ae6b37f40.html. Used by permission of the United Nations.

References

Ajani, Olubunmi Idowu Yetunde. 2008. "Gender Dimensions of Agriculture, Poverty, Nutrition, and Food Security in Nigeria." Nigeria Strategy Support Program, Background Paper No. NSSP 005, May 16, 2008. IFPRI.

Ali, Hamid E., and Eric S. Lin. 2010. "Wars, Foodcost and Countervailing Policies: A Panel Data Approach." *Food Policy.* Vol. 35, pp. 378–390.

Bk, Nirmal Kumar. 2010. "Climate Change and Livelihoods: Implications of Social Exclusion on Vulnerability to Food Security of Women and Low-Caste Groups in Nepal." Paper presented at "Environmental Change and Migration: From Vulnerabilities to Capabilities" conference, Bad Salzuflen, Germany, December 5–9, 2010.

Black, Richard. 2011. "Global Warming since 1995 now 'Significant'." *BBC News.* June 10, 2011. http://www.bbc.co.uk/news/science-environment-13719510

Brander, K.M. 2007. "Global Fish Production and Climate Change." *PNAS.* Vol. 104, No. 50, December 11, 2004, pp. 19709–19714.

Brown, Lester R. 2004. *Outgrowing the Earth: The Food Security Challenge in an Age of Falling Water Tables and Rising Temperatures.* New York: W.W. Norton & Co., 239 pp.

Brown, Lester R. 2009. "Could Food Shortages Bring Down Civilization?" *Scientific American*. Vol. 300, No. 5, May 2009, pp. 50–57.

Bryant, Christina Case. 2011. "Surging BRIC Middle Classes Are Eclipsing Global Poverty." *Christian Science Monitor*. May 17, 2011. http://www.csmonitor. com/World/2011/0517/Surging-BRIC-middle-classes-are-eclipsing-global-poverty.

CGIAR, Consultative Group on International Agricultural Research. 2011. *Mapping Hotspots of Climate Change and Food Insecurity in the Global Tropics*. A report by the CGIAR Research Program on Climate Change, Agriculture, and Food Security. CCAFS Report No. 5. http://www.ccafs.cgiar.org.

DeJong-Hughes, J., J. F. Moncrief, W. B. Voorhees, and J. B. Swan. 2001. "Soil Compaction: Causes, Effects, and Control." University of Minnesota—Extension. http://www.extension.umn.edu/distribution/cropsystems/DC3115.html

De Schutter, Olivier. 2010. *Food Commodities Speculation and Food Price Crises: Regulation to Reduce the Risks of Price Volatility*. Briefing Note 02, UN Special Rapporteur on the Right to Food. September 2010, 14 pp.

Devereux, Stephen. 2009. "Why Does Famine Persist in Africa?" *Food Security*. Vol. 1, pp. 25–35.

Easterly, William, and Laura Freschi. 2010. "Why Are We Supporting Repression in Ethiopia?" *New York Review of Books*, November 15, 2010.

FAO, Food & Agricultural Organization. 2009. "Declaration of the World Summit on Food Security." Rome, November 16–18, 2009.

FAO, Food & Agricultural Organization. 2010a. *The State of Food Insecurity in the World: Addressing Food Insecurity in Protracted Crises*. Rome: FAO, 57 pp.

FAO, Food & Agricultural Organization. 2010b. *The State of the World Fisheries and Aquaculture*. Rome: FAO, 197 pp.

FAO, Food & Agricultural Organization. 2011. *Special Report: FAO/WFP Crop and Food Security Assessment Mission to the Democratic People's Republic of Korea*. November 25, 2011. Rome: FAO, 34 pp. http://www.fao.org/docrep/014/al982e/al982e00.pdf

Fullbrook, David. 2010. "Food as Security." *Food Security*. Vol. 2, pp. 5–20.

Funk, Chris C., and Molly E. Brown. 2009. "Declining Global Per Capita Agricultural Production and Warming Oceans Threaten Food Security." *Food Security*. Vol. 1, pp. 271–289.

Garber, Kent. 2008. "How Countries Worsen the Food Price Crisis." *U.S. News & World Report*. April 9, 2008.

Godfray, H., Charles J., John R. Beddington, Ian R. Crute, Lawrence Haddad, David Lawrence, James F. Muir, Jules Pretty, Sherman Robinson, Sandy M. Thomas, and Camilla Toulmin. 2010. "Food Security: The Challenge of Feeding 9 Billion People." *Science*. Vol. 327, February 12, 2010, pp. 812–818.

GRAIN.org. 2008. "Seized! The 2008 Land Grab for Food and Financial Security." GRAIN Briefing, October 2008. http://www.grain.org/go/landgrab.

Guerrant, R. L., R. B. Oriá, S. R. Moore, M. O. Oriá, and A. A. Lima. 2008. "Malnutrition As an Enteric Infectious Disease with Long-term Effects on Child Development." *Nutrition Reviews.* Vol. 66, No. 9, September 2008, pp. 487–505.

Gustavsson, Jenny, Christel Cederberg, Ulf Sonesson, Robert van Otterdijk, and Alexandre Meybeck. 2011. *Global Food Losses and Food Waste: Extent, Causes and Prevention.* Rome: FAO, 29 pp.

Hall, Kevin D., Juen Guo, Michael Dore, and Carson C. Chow. 2009. "The Progressive Increase of Food Waste in America and Its Environmental Impact." PLos ONE. Vol. 4, No. 11, November 2009, e7940. http://www.plosone.org/article/info%3Adoi%2F10.1371%2Fjournal.pone.0007940

Hardin, Garrett. 1974. "Lifeboat Ethics: The Case against Helping the Poor." *Psychology Today,* September 1974.

Harlan, Chico. 2011. "Starving N. Korea Begs for Food, but U.S. Has Concerns about Resuming Aid." *Washington Post.* February 22, 2011.

Headey, Derek. 2010. "Rethinking the Global Food Crisis: The Role of Trade Shocks." *Food Policy.* Vol. 36, pp. 136–146.

"How to Feed a Hungry World." *Nature.* Vol. 466, No. 7306, July 29, 2010, pp. 531–532.

Howden, S. Mark, Jean-Francois Soussana, Francesco N. Tubiello, Netra Chhetri, Michael Dunlop, and Holder Meinke. 2007. "Adapting Agriculture to Climate Change." *PNAS,* Vol. 104, No. 50, December 11, 2007, pp. 19691–19696.

IATP, Institute for Agriculture and Trade Policy. 2008. "Commodities Market Speculation: The Risk to Food Security and Agriculture." Minneapolis, MN: IATP, 16 pp.

IFPRI. 2008. "Strengthening Women's Control of Assets for Better Development Outcomes." Washington: IFPRI.

IFPRI, International Food Policy Research Institute. 2010. *Global Hunger Index: The Challenge of Hunger: Focus on the Crisis of Child Undernutrition.* Washington: IFPRI, 56 pp.

Irwin, Scott S., and Dwight R. Sanders. 2010. "The Impact of Index and Swap Funds on Commodity Futures Markets: Preliminary Results." OECD Food Agriculture and Fisheries Working Papers, No. 27, OECD Publishing. http://www.oecd.org/dataoecd/16/59/45534528.pdf

Lacey, Marc. 2008. "Across Globe, Empty Bellies Bring Rising Anger." *New York Times,* April 18, 2008.

Lawrence, Felicity. 2011. "Global Food Crisis: The Speculators Playing with Our Daily Bread." *The Guardian.* June 2, 2011.

Lim, Louisa. 2011. "North Korea's Pleas for Food Aid Draw Suspicion." NPR, April 12, 2011.

Lobell, David B., Wolfram Schlenker, and Justin Costa-Roberts. 2011. "Climate Trends and Global Crop Production since 1980." *Sciencexpress.* 10.1126/science.1204351, May 5, 2011, pp. 1–3.

Marcus, David. 2003. "Famine Crimes in International Law." *American Journal of International Law*. Vol. 97, pp. 245–281.

McDonald, Bryan L. 2010. *Food Security*. Malden, MA: Polity, 205 pp.

Messer, Ellen, and Marc J. Cohen. 2006. *Conflict, Food Insecurity, and Globalization*. FCND Discussion Paper 206. Washington: IFPRI, 45 pp.

National Research Council. 2010. *Advancing the Science of Climate Change*. Washington: National Academy of Sciences, 503 pp.

Natsios, Andrew. 1993. "Food through Force: Humanitarian Intervention and U.S. Policy." *The Washington Quarterly*. Vol. 17, No. 1, Winter 1994, pp. 129–144.

Pinstrup-Andersen, Per. 2009. "Food Security: Definition and Measurement." *Food Security*. Vol. 1, pp. 5–7.

Powledge, Fred. 2010. "Food, Hunger, and Insecurity." *BioScience*. Vol. 60, No. 4, April 2010, pp. 260–265.

Quisumbing, Agnes, Ruth Meinzen-Dick, and Lucy Bassett, with contributions by Michael Usnick, Lauren Pandolfelli, Cheryl Morden, and Harold Alderman. 2008. "Helping Women Respond to the Global Food Crisis." IFPRI Policy Brief 7, October 2008. Washington: IFPRI, 4 pp.

Reuters. 2011. "Record Crop Seen But Grain Stocks May Fall Further." Reuters, March 24, 2011, http://in.reuters.com/article/2011/03/24/idINIndia-55857920110324.

Rice, Andrew. 2009. "Is There Such a Thing as Agro-Imperialism?" *New York Times*. November 22, 2009.

Runge, C. Ford, Benjamin Senauer, Philip G. Pardey, and Mark W. Rosegrant. 2003. *Ending Hunger in Our Lifetime: Food Security and Globalization*. Published for the International Food Policy Research Institute. Baltimore, MD: Johns Hopkins University Press, 288 pp.

Saltveit, Mikal E. n.d. "Food as a Weapon of War." Encyclopedia of Food and Culture. http://www.enotes.com/food-encyclopedia/food-weapon.war.

Scanlan, Stephen J., and J. Craig Jenkins. 2001. "Military Power and Food Security: A Cross-National Analysis of Less-Developed Countries, 1970–1990." *International Studies Quarterly*. Vol. 45, pp. 159–187.

Schmidhuber, Josef, and Francesco N. Tubiello. 2007. "Global Food Security under Climate Change." *PNAS*, Vol. 104, No. 50, December 11, 2007, pp. 19703–19708.

Sen, Amartya. 1999. *Development as Freedom*. New York: Knopf, 384 pp.

Stanford, Claire, ed. 2007. *World Hunger*. New York: H.W. Wilson Company, 198 pp.

Stuart, Tristram. 2009. *Waste: Uncovering the Global Food Scandal*. New York: W.W. Norton & Co., 451 pp.

Thorat, Sukhdeo, and Joel Lee. 2005. "Caste Discrimination and Food Security Programs." *Economic and Political Weekly*. Vol. 40, No. 39, September 24, 2005, pp. 4198–4201.

"Throwing Money at the Street." *The Economist*. Vol. 398, No. 8724, March 12, 2011, p. 32.

Umaña-Aponte, Marcela. 2011. "Long-Term Effects of a Nutritional Shock: The 1980 Famine of Karamoja, Uganda." Working Paper No. 11/258. Centre for Market and Public Organization, University of Bristol, April 2011. http://www. bristol.ac.uk/cmpo/publications/papers/2011/wp258.pdf

UNEP. 2009. *The Environmental Food Crisis: The Environment's Role in Averting Future Food Crises*. A UNEP Rapid Response Assessment. Norway: Birkeland Trykkeri AS, 101 pp.

Victoria, Cesar G., Linda Adair, Caroline Fall, Pedro C. Hallal, Reynaldo Martorelli, Linda Richter, and Harshpal Singh Sachdev, for the Maternal and Child Undernutrition Study Group. 2008. "Maternal and Child Undernutrition: Consequences for Adult Health and Human Capital." *The Lancet*. Vol. 371, No. 9609, January 26, 2008, pp. 340–357.

Von Braun, Joachim. 2009. "Threats to Security Related to Food, Agriculture, and Natural Resources—What to Do?" Presented at "Strategic Discussion Circle," EADS, Berlin. March 26, 2009.

Wallensteen, Peter. 1976. "Scarce Goods as Political Weapons: The Case of Food." *Journal of Peace Research*. Vol. 13, No. 4, pp. 277–298.

WHO Nutrition Facts. http://www.who.int/features/factfiles/nutrition/facts/en/index. html

World Bank. 2006. *Repositioning Nutrition as Central to Development*. Washington: The International Bank for Reconstruction and Development/The World Bank, 246 pp.

World Bank. 2010. *World Development Report 2010: Development and Climate Change*. Washington: The International Bank for Reconstruction and Development/ The World Bank, 417 pp.

World Bank. 2011. *Missing Food: The Case of Post-Harvest Grain Losses in Sub-Saharan Africa*. Washington: The International Bank for Reconstruction and Development/The World Bank.

World Food Program. 2009. "Financial Crisis and High Food Prices." Media Backgrounder. July 8, 2009.

World Food Program. 2011a. "Somalia: WFP Activities." http://www.wfp.org/coun tries/Somalia/Operations

World Food Program. 2011b. "WFP/FAO/UNICEF Rapid Food Security Assessment Mission to the Democratic People's Republic of Korea." Special Report, March 24, 2011. http://documents.wfp.org/stellent/groups/public/documents/ena/ wfp233442.pdf

World Food Program/Food & Agricultural Organization. 2010. *State of Food Insecurity in the World 2010*.

CHAPTER 4

Climate Change

Every effect from a destabilized society washes up on our shores sooner or later.
—Gen. Anthony Zinni (USMC ret.), 2007

I have not seen Al Gore's movie.
—U.S. vice president Dick Cheney, February 2007

Our discussion of environmental security so far has focused mostly on the security implications of the environment as it is now. However, with our growing realization that human peacetime activities are changing the climate, we have to ask ourselves if it is still reasonable to assume that the future will look like the past. As we learn more about the way the earth's very complicated climate system works, we begin to realize that the entire future of our development, including our security, may fall along a different path than the one we currently envision.

Climate change, also referred to as global warming, is driven by the enhanced greenhouse effect. Ultraviolet light from the sun passes through earth's atmosphere; some of it is reflected back from clouds and other surfaces, and some is absorbed by land and water. This latter portion is then reradiated from the earth's surface as infrared heat. Some of the heat escapes the atmosphere and some is trapped by the atmosphere, resulting in a warmer planetary surface. The earth's atmosphere acts like the glass in a greenhouse, letting in most of the light but trapping much of the heat. Without this atmospheric phenomenon, life would not exist on earth, but as humans emit increasing amounts of greenhouse gases like carbon dioxide (CO_2) and methane (CH_4), the "glass" in the atmosphere is getting thicker and is holding in more heat than it has in the last 10,000 years (IPCC AR4 WGI

SPM 2007, 3). The IPCC's Fourth Assessment Report was unequivocal in 2007, stating that,

> The understanding of anthropogenic warming and cooling influences on climate has improved since [2001], leading to a *very high confidence* [at least a 9 out of 10 chance of being correct] that the global average net effect of human activities since 1750 has been one of warming. . . . (IPCC AR4 WGI SPM 2007, 3)

This additional heat energy results in increasing ambient air temperatures, increasing water vapor content in the atmosphere, rising sea levels, declining snow and ice cover, thawing permafrost, changing precipitation levels, longer and more intense droughts, and changes in extreme temperatures, with fewer very cold days and nights and more very hot days and nights (IPCC AR4 WGI SPM 2007; see also NRC 2010). The chart below shows the increase in both mean and variation of temperatures expected in a globally warmed world.

The changes in temperature predicted for the 21st century are frightening in many aspects. Temperatures increase further over land than over water, and furthest of all over the Arctic. As discussed previously, this will lead to other, higher-order effects, such as sea level rise, precipitation and water quality changes, and lowered agricultural output. Such an altered world will certainly face new challenges in terms of international security, because the climate assumptions upon which we base so many of our economic, political, and social systems will themselves be challenged.

There are only a few studies (see Further Resources) that examine the links between global climate change and international security, for several reasons. First, security studies do not generally take environmental drivers into account, as discussed in Chapter 1. Because security has traditionally dealt with immediate threats and the effects of climate change will be felt over the next century, there is a timescale mismatch between them, which can lead security scholars and practitioners to leave climate change off their agendas when planning threat assessments. Second, it is difficult conceptually to link two complicated systems such as the earth's climate system and our current system of international relations because they themselves are linked by a number of intermediate variables. However, this is a task that scholars and policy analysts have a responsibility to shoulder, and the intersection of climate change and security is a rich area for future research. As climate change progresses, policy makers and students of environmental security will need to understand how it affects national and international security interests. This chapter will examine the Arctic as the bellwether of climate change and what the strategic implications of a warming Arctic might be; it will also examine the effects of climate change on infectious diseases and international public health,

Figure 4.1 Effects of Greenhouse Warming on Extreme Temperatures

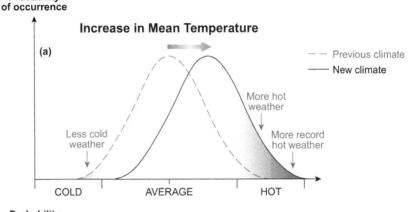

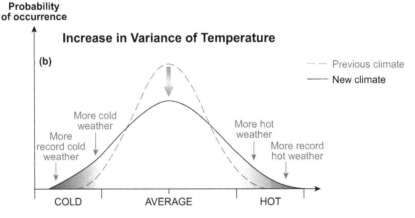

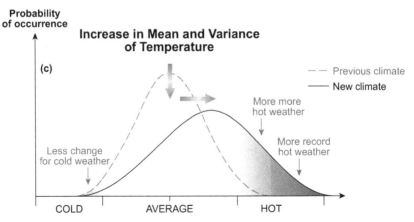

(IPCC Third Assessment Report, Climate Change 2001. Synthesis report, figure 4-1. Available at http://www.grida.no/publications/other/ipcc_tar/)

both of which are connected to security; it will conclude with a discussion climate-related push factors for human migration, and the implications of climate refugees on security.

The Warming Arctic

Arctic Thaw

There is no larger or more insistent red flag for planet-wide climate change than the thaw currently occurring in the Arctic. The IPCC's Fourth Assessment Report (2007) predicts that the Arctic is *very likely* (>90% probability) to warm this century in most areas, the annual mean warming is *very likely* to exceed the global mean warming, and Arctic sea ice is *very*

Figure 4.2 Projected Winter Surface Temperature Increase, 2090 (°C)

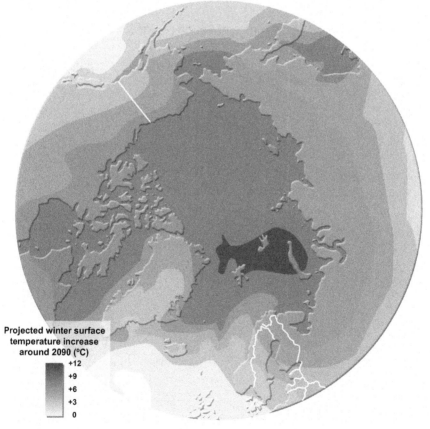

(Arctic Climate Impact Assessment [ACIA], 2004. Impacts of a Warming Arctic. Available online at http://www.acia.uaf.edu/)

likely to decrease in extent and thickness (IPCC AR4 WGI 2007, 902). Since the Fourth Assessment Report has been released, more recent scientific studies have confirmed this trend. Warming across the Arctic Ocean basin has been "particularly pronounced since 1995, and especially since 2000; summer 2007 [sea surface temperature] anomalies are up to 5°C." (Steele et al. 2008).

Average temperatures in the Arctic have risen at almost twice the global average rate in the past 100 years (IPCC AR4 WGI SPM 2007, 7), and the warming trend is accelerating. The map above shows one estimate of increasing surface temperatures predicted for the end of this century in the Arctic Basin, with projected surface temperatures rising to almost 12°C (21.6°F) in some areas near the Barents Sea. Even the apparent mean warming of around 7–8 °C (12.6–14.4 °F) is astonishingly high. Loss of ice and snow in the Arctic serves as a positive feedback loop for climate change by accelerating the rate of warming: light-colored snow and ice reflect sunlight, but as they melt and give way to dark-colored land and water, the sunlight is absorbed and returned to the atmosphere as heat. More heat in turn accelerates the rate of melt, and as the Arctic gets warmer, sea ice disappears, as shown in Figure 4.3. The mass of sea ice lost in the Arctic has been decreasing since 1987, and 2007 saw 1.2 million km² of sea ice lost since the previous low of 2005, beyond the IPCC's worst case predictions (Markus et al. 2009; see also Kwok & Rothrock 2009, Lindsay et al. 2009). If current trends continue, the Arctic sea could be ice-free in the summer by 2040 (Kerr 2007).

Climate change effects are not limited to the Arctic Ocean. High latitude land masses are also predicted to warm significantly, with the largest temperature increase coming in winter (IPCC AR4 WGI 2007, 905). This means that permafrost, soil in which the water is perpetually frozen under normal conditions, will melt and become squishy, which reduces the stability and bearing capacity of the land. In addition, increasing temperature correlates strongly with increased precipitation (ibid., 906), and rainfall across Arctic landmasses has increased by 8 percent over the past century (ACIA 2004, 22). Increasing rainfall results in faster snowmelt and flash flooding in some areas where infrastructure is not designed to withstand heavy precipitation.

Security Impacts of Increased Arctic Transit

What are the security implications of a thawed Arctic? More open sea in the Arctic means that oceangoing nations will have greater opportunities for surface transit, since ice-free surface routes will become more attractive for both commercial shippers and naval and coast guard vessels. There are two main routes across the Arctic Ocean, the Northern Sea Route above Norway and Russia, and the Northwest Passage above Canada and the American state of Alaska. Of the two, shown in Figure 4.4, the Northern Sea Route is the one that is ice-free more often, since it lies on the shallower side of the Arctic Ocean basin.

Figure 4.3 Loss of Summer Sea Ice, Arctic

NOAA GFDL CM2.1 Model Simulation

Aug Sept Oct Average Sea Ice Concentration

(NOAA Geophysical Fluid Dynamics Laboratory. Available at http://www.gfdl.noaa.gov/
the-shrinking-arctic-ice-cap-ar4)

Figure 4.4 Arctic Transit Routes

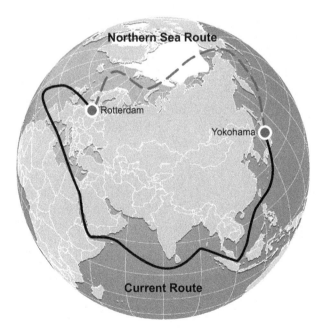

A thawing Arctic means an increase in civilian ship and container traffic. With shipping companies facing high fuel prices, Arctic transit can become more economical in terms of both money and time. Compared to more southerly routes via the Suez or Panama canals, transit through the Arctic can shave weeks off travel time and thousands of miles off journeys from Asia to Europe and North America; it can also allow shippers to avoid piracy and terrorism concerns that are prevalent in more heavily traveled straits like Malacca and the Gulf of Aden.

The Northwest Passage as a shipping route is 9,000 km shorter than the Panama Canal route, and 17,000 km shorter than the longer route around Cape Horn which many larger vessels that can no longer fit through the Panama Canal must take. However, ships transiting the passage require icebreaker assistance, as there is still significant multiyear ice for much of the year. A current lack of fueling or resupply stations along the Canadian Arctic coast can add significant risk to commercial Arctic passage (NRC 2007, 35).

With less sea ice cover on its side of the Arctic Ocean, Russia opened the Northern Sea Route to commercial shipping in 1991. Transiting the NSR saves approximately 7,000 km on the journey from Europe and the eastern coast of North America to Asia. So far it has not been used significantly by non-Russian vessels, but the Russian government wishes to make the NSR a regularized commercial passage. The sea level in the Russian Arctic has risen in recent decades by 1.85 mm per year, greater than the global average (IPCC AR4 WGI 2007, 413), and climate change is expected to increase the navigation season for the NSR from the current 20–30 days per year to 90–100 days per year by 2080 (ACIA 2004, 83). If this occurs, Arctic shipping could become a lucrative revenue stream for Russia, necessitating a regular Arctic presence to escort ships safely through the NSR. Interestingly, should polar transit become more common, the Bering Strait could become a new oceanic chokepoint for sea traffic (Ellis 2007).

More commercial shipping will necessitate a stronger military presence by the circumpolar nations to ensure security. Yet, for a nation that has significant military presence elsewhere in the world, the United States lags behind its Arctic neighbors; Canada and Russia are already increasing their military facilities and capabilities in the Far North. Since 2002, Canada has had plans to station six to eight Arctic offshore patrol vessels in Halifax, and build a refueling station at Nanisivik and a personnel training base for Arctic operations at Resolute Bay. Such plans have been on the drawing board for years, but now that existing scientific evidence increasingly points to accelerating ice melt, the Canadian government is operationalizing these plans with the expectation that the Arctic will soon be a much busier place. Russia is also increasing its visible military presence in and around the Arctic, particularly in areas that provide direct Arctic access. It has strengthened its forces on the Kola Peninsula, and in 2007, Russian aircraft overflew Iceland and the GIUK

Gap repeatedly. Icelandic minister of justice Björn Bjarnason lamented in 2007 that NATO closed its military base at Keflavik in October of 2006, and recommended that Western nations should have a military presence in the Arctic, because the lack of such could be interpreted by Russia as a lack of national interest in the area (Bjarnason 2007).

The U.S. Coast Guard is currently planning its first permanent Arctic base near the Alaskan town of Barrow. Starting off as a seasonal helicopter base, it would expand as the Arctic warms into a full-time response base for search and rescue, and environmental protection. However, a strong U.S. presence in the Arctic will depend almost entirely upon American icebreaking capability, of which it currently has very little. By contrast, Russia has 4 active nuclear-powered icebreakers and another 12 diesel-powered icebreakers; Canada has 6 heavy icebreakers and another 10 light icebreakers. Sweden, Finland, Norway and other circumpolar nations also have icebreaking capability.

Past military operations in the Arctic have generally been confined to submarine operations, search and rescue, and the occasional icebreaker escort, but any nation wishing to ply the Arctic waters with an eye toward security will face climate change–induced technical issues. Under normal conditions, Arctic sea ice has two important sonar characteristics useful for submarines. First, low frequencies carry much further under the ice cap, and with abnormally low signal loss. This allows messages to travel with greater accuracy. Second, ambient noise can be very high in marginal ice zones, where the sea ice meets open water. This can mask the noise signature of a submarine. In addition, strong sonar signals could be either submarines or ice keels, created when sea ice is compacted by wind and current. This uncertain sonar signature means that submarines can hide undetected under the polar ice cap. Climate change alters the sonar signature of the Arctic by changing both ambient noise and acoustic propagation. Lessened sea ice means a reduction in marginal ice zones, reducing submarine hiding places. Warmer temperatures and wind-generated mixing of surface water will increase signal loss at low frequencies. As a result, the U.S. Navy may need a new sonar algorithm to take into account the altered polar conditions (USARC 2002).

Security Impact of Oil/Gas Exploration

The Arctic is not only a transit route but also a significant national security destination in its own right. Particularly valuable are the mineral and petroleum reserves believed to lie under the Arctic Ocean. In 2008, the U.S. Geological Survey estimated that basins within or near the Arctic could contain approximately 22 percent of the world's undiscovered oil and gas reserves. According to Mead Treadwell, Chair of the U.S. Arctic Research Commission, there are also considerable mineral resources located in the North. In addition to a possible 10 billion barrels of hydrocarbons, there could be as much as 182 million tons of manganese, 12 million tons of nickel, 9 million tons of copper, and 5,000 tons of cobalt. These are strategic minerals, necessary for key industrial and defense applications.

Of course, the United States is not the only nation interested in petroleum and minerals from the Arctic. In October 2007, Norway's Snohvit field began producing natural gas for the U.S. market, the first petroleum project north of the Arctic Circle. Exxon Mobil Canada and Imperial Oil have begun to explore 205,000 hectares of Arctic floor beneath the Beaufort Sea for oil and gas (CBC 2007). In anticipation of an Arctic oil boom, the Russians currently have three 70,000-ton Arctic Shuttle Tankers being built by Samsung Heavy Industries in Korea for 2009–2010. These double-acting tankers can break moderate ice up to 1.5 m thick without an icebreaker escort and are designed to transport oil from Arctic fields to land ports (PortNews 2007). Increasing Asian demand for LNG will provide the Russians with an opportunity not only to expand the use of NSR but also to sign commercial energy contracts in China, Japan, and South Korea.

In the face of all these potential economic windfalls, it is still uncertain whether the world will see a willy-nilly rush to start drilling in the Arctic. The cost of doing so is significant due to the cold, the still-dangerous shifting ice, the depth of the water, and the uncertainty of the legal regime governing the Arctic. However, the resulting pressure to secure any available petroleum resources could push nations into the Arctic sooner rather than later, especially since land operations in places like Iraq and Nigeria have become money-losing ventures due to the constant threat of militancy and in-country sabotage.

Legal Status of the Arctic

Unlike land, which is expected to be claimed by one nation or another, the traditional legal principle of *mare liberum* (free seas) has been extended to the Arctic. Even though it is frozen for most of the year, it is still regarded by law and by tradition as open seas. No specific legal regime has been developed to govern the Arctic because its frozen state made access all but impossible for surface ships and irregular for submarines. Such territory and resource claims as were made were not adjudicated with any haste, since near-constant sea ice made free ocean access at the top of the world moot. Now that climate change is transforming the Arctic into a new Mediterranean, there are significant international concerns regarding borders, transit rights, and legal claims in this area. The eight circumpolar nations (the United States, Canada, Russia, Denmark, Norway, Finland, Iceland, and Sweden) each govern their own slice of the ocean and are now eyeing the seabed underneath.

The 1982 UN Convention on the Law of the Sea (UNCLOS) lays out specific rules for how much adjacent undersea territory a nation can claim. Article 56 allows coastal states to claim an exclusive economic zone 200 nautical miles out from their coastline, giving them sovereign jurisdiction over all resources therein. However, if a nation can demonstrate in accordance with Article 76 that an undersea formation is an extension of its continental shelf, that area can be claimed as well. All of the circumpolar nations except the United States are parties to UNCLOS, though the United States has accepted most of its terms as customary international law.

As allowed by the terms of UNCLOS, Russia has begun to claim vast swaths of the seabed under the Arctic Ocean based on the presumed territorial extension of an undersea geographic feature known as the Lomonosov Ridge. Russia claims that, under Article 76, the Lomonosov Ridge is an extension of its continental shelf. If its claim were to be approved, the terms of UNCLOS could give Russia legal control of approximately 40 percent of the Arctic sea floor and more importantly, the petroleum reserves believed to lie underneath. On August 2, 2007, a Russian submersible planted a titanium replica of the Russian flag on the sea floor directly beneath the North Pole. Decried as a publicity stunt by the United States, Canada, and other Western nations, the action was designed to enhance the Russian government's territorial claim. Every other circumpolar nation has also begun the bathymetric surveys necessary to submit similar claims regarding its continental shelf to the UNCLOS secretariat.

The ocean floor is not the only area of the Arctic that is open to competing legal claims. Complicating transit is the fact that the Canadian government asserts that the Northwest Passage which passes through the Canadian archipelago is internal Canadian waters, since it was originally explored by the British prior to Canada's independence, and also since the land on either side is inhabited by people from the First Nations of Canada. This will allow Canada to exert a certain measure of legal control over any vessel in the passage. However, both the United States and the EU maintain the position that the route is an international strait (a narrow body of water that connects two expanses of high seas and is used for international navigation) under the terms of UNCLOS, and as such, ships and submarines should be allowed to transit the strait without Canada's permission or even notification. This legal difference of opinion has largely been moot due to the persistence of sea ice blocking the passage. Now, however, the question of Canadian legal control of the passage may be weakened every time a non-Canadian ship transits the passage, forcing the Canadian government to defend its claim by stepping up its enforcement capabilities.

The positive feedback loop between increasing ambient air temperature and Arctic snow and ice melt means that the Arctic thaw will not slow down or reverse itself within the next few centuries. Once made, Arctic change will be permanent unless some type of global cooling occurs, a phenomenon that seems virtually impossible given the current levels of warming to which we are already committed. However, the security of the Arctic does not rest with any one nation. The circumpolar nations can benefit significantly from some sort of trans-Arctic security regime. Currently, the United States already has several international security arrangements specifically focused on the Arctic, such as a bilateral agreement with Denmark regarding air bases in Greenland, and the multilateral North Atlantic Ice Patrol. Reciprocal support with Canada is commonplace (NRC 2007, 23). These types of arrangements can build confidence among states. In addition, an increased commitment toward scientific exploration of the Arctic can help guide states in their legal and political claims based upon a clear understanding of the terrain. The link between a warming Arctic and cooperative security could be positive, but only with sufficient foresight and planning.

Migration

We seek your leadership. But if for some reason you are not willing to lead, leave it to the rest of us. Please get out of the way.

—Papua New Guinea to the United States,
Bali Climate Conference, 2007

Migration is a complex phenomenon, just like environmental security generally, and when all other environmental coping mechanisms have been exhausted, migration is a last-resort option. The UN defines refugees as "people who are outside their own country, owing to a well-founded fear of persecution, for reasons of race, religion, nationality, membership of a particular social group, or political opinion." The UN High Commission for Refugees estimated that there were approximately 37.5 million refugees, including internally displaced persons (IDPs), at the start of 2010 (CIA World Factbook 2011). Since the definition of refugees mentioned above was rendered during the Cold War, it was aimed specifically at political refugees; anyone fleeing political persecution was eligible for refugee status. Anyone fleeing degraded environmental conditions was not. The definition of **environmental refugees** did not come about until 1985, when Essam El-Hinnawi of the UN called them "people who have been forced to leave their traditional habitat, temporarily or permanently, because of a marked environmental disruption (natural or anthropogenic) that jeopardized their existence and/or seriously affected the quality of their life." This is a much more wide-ranging definition, and could possibly include tens or even hundreds of millions of people, though estimates vary widely.

Protected by the legal concept of **non-refoulement**, which states that a refugee may not be expelled back into conditions under which his or her life would be threatened, refugees generally flee to a nearby country, called a country of first asylum. They are often extremely vulnerable, generally arriving without formal documentation or formal authorization from the host country, which may be reluctant to provide legal protection. Two-thirds of the world's refugees live in developing countries. Many refugees are confined to remote refugee camps, segregated settlements, and urban slums for years without effective protection or basic rights such as the right to work, move freely, and have a basic education. Expanding the definition of refugee to include people displaced for environmental reasons would increase the burden of asylum on most countries, as these countries could then be required to take in refugees from neighboring nations that are dealing with environmental conditions only marginally worse than they themselves are facing.

Determinants of Migration

The forces that create refugees, that cause them to leave their home countries, are called **push factors** (as opposed to **pull factors**, which may draw refugees to a certain country or region; see generally Abell 1996). These factors usually work in combination rather than singly, and at a quick glance it is easy to see why. Ecological degradation can erode the environmental conditions on which the population depends to earn a living or grow sufficient food. Political persecution, whether due to membership in a different ethnic or social group, religion, or race, can generate large numbers of refugees fleeing an unfriendly government. Civil war will disrupt the entire structure of the society and the government, including its ability to provide security. Exacerbating any climate-related push factor is population growth. The earth currently supports more than 7 billion people, with a population growth rate of 1.09 percent per year (CIA World Factbook 2011). Population growth alone does not automatically generate refugees, but if a nation's population begins to outstrip its ecological carrying capacity or if that same capacity is foreshortened in some way, as is hypothesized to happen under climate change, migration becomes a more attractive option than staying put.

The intersection of environmental degradation, migration, and conflict does not reside merely in theory. Several conflicts in the last few decades can trace their roots at least partially to environmental drivers. In the 1960s, for example, land erosion and soil depletion compounded by high population growth rates and inequitable land distribution forced poor farmers in El Salvador over the border into Honduras. As the number of migrants grew, sentiment from local Hondurans changed from acceptance to hostility, culminating in the 1969 Soccer War which claimed almost 2,000 lives and disrupted economic relations between the two nations for nearly a decade (Homer-Dixon & Percival 1996; see also Robins & Pye-Smith 1997).

The India-Bangladesh border provides another example of migration-induced conflict. Moving away from floods, soil erosion, and silting of rivers due to dam construction, Bengalis have settled illegally in the Indian states of

Assam and Tripura by the millions. Since the 1950s, population has doubled in Bangladesh and the population density as measured in terms of people per square kilometer is one of the highest in the world. So many refugees entered Tripura that the original Buddhist and Christian majority quickly became a minority in its own state. By 1980, refugees were being targeted for violence by the local Tripuris. Regular flooding also sent the Bengalis over the border into Assam, and by the early 1980s, they too had become targets of violence, with one five-hour incident resulting in the deaths of more than 1,700 people (Reuveny 2008; see also Homer-Dixon & Percival 1996).

In the Philippines, the connection between environmental degradation and conflict was more roundabout. Colonial-era land distribution policies left good arable land in the hands of elite families and agricultural corporations, forcing subsistence farmers onto marginal lands. Unable to grow sufficient food, farmers and agricultural laborers migrated in large numbers to the major cities, where they were attracted to political insurgency (Homer-Dixon & Percival 1996, 49; see also Slack 2003).

Despite clear examples, there is a certain level of academic dissatisfaction among some environmental security scholars with the term "climate refugees," which they feel implies mono-causality with regard to the refugee phenomenon, as though people were forced to flee from their homes because of climate change alone. They are also concerned about the inexactitude of the wildly varying estimates of climate refugees, which range from a few million to up to 250 million. However, as mentioned previously, migration is a complex phenomenon, and the value of the term climate refugees lies in its explicit recognition that environmental degradation from anthropogenic climate change is now one driving factor in the causal chain of factors that can generate refugees. Similarly, the lack of an exact number of climate refugees should not become a barrier to consideration of policies and remedial measures that would reduce their security impact. Even the lower bounds of most estimates place the number of possible climate refugees in the millions, a number large enough to merit serious consideration of the problem on humanitarian grounds, if nothing else (see Norwegian Refugee Council 2008 and Docherty & Giannini 2009 for further discussion of the term).

Climatic Push Factors for Refugees

While climate change can affect pull factors by making one destination more or less environmentally attractive than another, it will have the largest effect on the push factors of ecosystem health and stability. Millions of people could be forced to relocate due to environmental pressures such as rising sea levels, stronger storms and hurricanes, loss of soil moisture due to drying from higher temperatures, droughts, and loss of water from shrinking glaciers (Sachs 2007). Disease, discussed further below, also plays an interlocking role with climate-related

refugees. Whether the outbreak of disease may cause people to flee a region is unclear, and logically would vary with the virulence of the disease, but it is certain
that as refugees are evacuated from disease-prone areas, they are more likely to
serve as carriers and introduce the disease into new areas (Bryan et al. 1996, 346).

Climate change and other environmental drivers can generate refugees in
a number of ways. Sea level rise displaces people directly through flooding or
indirectly through saline intrusion into groundwater. Changes in precipitation patterns lead to drought, flooding, desertification and soil erosion, rendering farmland useless. Changes in weather patterns lead to evacuation of
areas suffering increased extreme events such as storms and cyclones.

Sea Level Rise

The link between sea level rise and refugees is particularly strong, since over
half of the world's population lives within 200 km of a coastline. There are two
different mechanisms by which climate change can cause rising sea levels. As
ambient air temperatures increase, land-based ice such as glaciers, ice caps, and
ice sheets will melt and run off into the ocean, adding to the overall volume of
water and altering its salinity. In addition, because the ocean has been absorb-
ing so much heat, thermal expansion of sea water contributes to sea level rise.
The IPCC estimated in 2007 that sea levels could rise between 0.2 meters and
0.6 meters by the end of the 21st century (IPCC AR4 WGII TS 2007, 40), but
new research indicates that sea levels could in fact rise faster over the same time
frame, to levels somewhere between 0.75 meters and 1.9 meters higher than
at present (Vermeer & Rahmstorf 2009; see also Overpeck & Weiss 2009). Of
all the geophysical and environmental ramifications of anthropogenic climate
change, sea level is the most permanent because it is the most difficult to reverse. Depending on the rate of temperature rise, we are committed to sea level
rise through the year 3000 (IPCC AR4 WGI 2007, 828–831)

Low-lying countries are particularly vulnerable to climate-related sea level
rise, extreme storm surges, and subsequent outmigration. Approximately
158 million people live in Bangladesh, a country slightly smaller than Iowa,
and over one-third of the country floods annually during the summer monsoon season, June through October; risk for infectious diseases remains high.
Dhaka, the capital, is located just north of the confluence of the Ganges
and Meghna rivers and floods yearly, while the upland areas often face water
shortages due to aquifer drawdown and fluctuations in glacial melting. By
2070, Dhaka is expected to see a 1200 percent increase in the population
exposed to climate change-driven sea level rise and port flooding (Nicholls et al. 2008, 26), so the possibility of up to 20 million climate-driven
refugees from Bangladesh is very high (Simms 2005, 30). Large numbers of
Bangladeshi refugees have moved into India in the past. The Indian government has already built roughly half of a 2,550 mile border fence and covered it with barbed wire (Reuters 2007). If more refugees were to attempt to

circumvent the border controls, and especially if Muslim refugees moved into largely Hindu areas, it could result in India taking further military action to secure border areas. Muslim refugees could get moral or financial assistance from volatile Pakistan on India's other border, putting India and Pakistan in conflict yet again. With two nuclear armed nations facing each other over a large-scale refugee issue, the rest of the world would be highly motivated to ensure that the situation remained stable.

Small island nations, such as Fiji, Vanuatu, and others in the Pacific and the Caribbean where more than 50 percent of the population lives within 1.5 km of the shore are also extremely vulnerable to sea level rise–induced migration. The elevation of many of the small islands is only a few meters above sea level, and they may lose significant amounts of their territories due to sea level rise. In addition, fresh water resources on ocean islands will be severely compromised due to intrusion of salt water into the freshwater lens from which most island populations draw their water for drinking and agriculture (IPCC AR4 WGII, 689–690). The particular vulnerability of island nations to climate change raises an interesting ethical question regarding the right of asylum: If anthropogenic climate change driven historically by the actions of developed nations erodes the territory and/or livability of developing island nations, do the wealthy nations have any responsibility to provide refuge to those forced out of their homes? Legally, the answer is no, since environmental refugees are not a recognized category of forced refugees. Ethically and morally, however, the answer is less clear.

Sea level rise and an increase in intensity (and possibly duration) of extreme weather events will cause coastal inundation (IPCC AR4 WGII 2007, 324). A recent study from the OECD found that approximately 40 million people are currently threatened by coastal flooding, and that climate change could more than triple this number to approximately 150 million people by 2070 (Nicholls et al. 2008). The majority of these areas are located in the developing world, and they have minimal flood defenses or other protection against extreme events. Areas vulnerable to coastal flooding include not only cities, but also ports and coastal aquifers.

Climate change–induced sea level rise will have a particularly strong effect on wide, flat deltas of large rivers, known as megadeltas. Due to the confluence of factors such as dense population, natural land subsidence, sea level rise, and decreased sediment delivery from upstream dams, these megadeltas are highly vulnerable areas. The map above shows the megadeltas that will face medium to extreme levels of population displacement by the 2050s, and notably, most of them are in Asia. The Nile, the Mekong, and the Ganges-Brahmaputra all face potential population displacement upwards of one million people. Megadeltas are generally highly settled, due to the possibility of riverine farming and offshore fishing. Should these areas require evacuation

Figure 4.5 Relative Vulnerability of Coastal Deltas in 2050 to Sea Level Rise

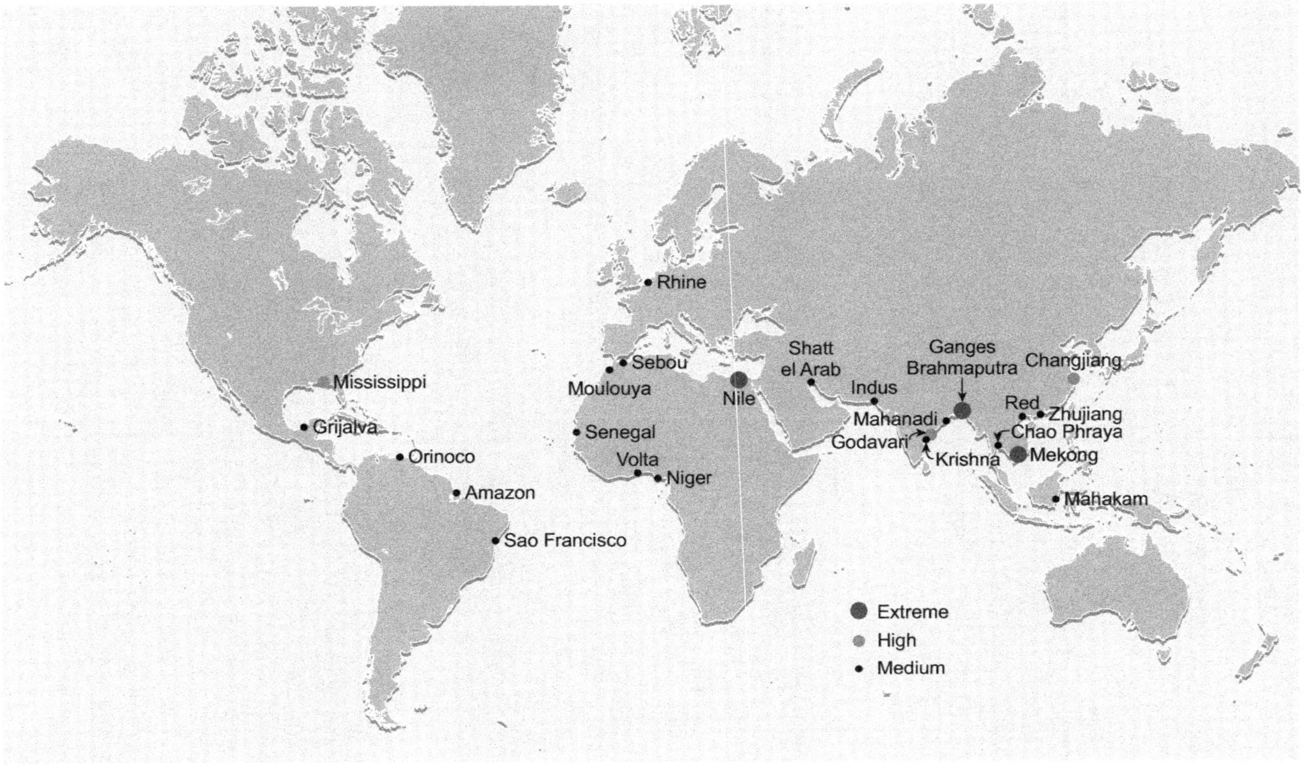

Extreme
High
Medium

Changjiang
Zhujiang
Red
Chao Phraya
Mekong
Mahakam
Ganges
Brahmaputra
Krishna
Mahanadi
Godavari
Indus
Shatt
el Arab
Nile
Rhine
Sebou
Moulouya
Senegal
Volta
Niger
Mississippi
Grijalva
Orinoco
Amazon
Sao Francisco

(IPCC Fourth Assessment Report, Working Group II, Climate Change 2007.)

due to direct sea level rise or climate-induced storm surges, the large-scale human misery would be memorable.

Sea level rise does not only threaten territory. Saline intrusion into freshwater aquifers can contaminate the water that coastal communities use for drinking and irrigation. As mentioned previously, island nations with freshwater lenses are particularly vulnerable, but any nation with a coastal aquifer can find its fresh water supply contaminated with salt. Saline intrusion into the aquifer beneath Maputo has already driven Mozambican farmers away from formerly arable land (allAfrica.com 2011) and a future 50 centimeter rise in sea level along the Gaza/Israel coast could result in the aquifer that lies under the area losing up to 12.5 million cubic meters of freshwater permanently (Melloul & Collin 2006; see also Moreaux & Reynaud 2001).

Extreme Events

The IPCC states that impacts of more frequent and more intense extreme weather events, such as storms and hurricanes, floods, heat waves, and droughts are very likely to increase (IPCC AR4 WGII TS 2007, 64). Table 4.1 contains the IPCC summary table of possible impacts due to extreme weather and climate events. The cumulative effect of all these events is greater climate instability, which leads to deterioration of the ecological carrying capacity of a region, which in turn leads to instability in the economic, social, and political systems that depend on the environment. As a result, people suffering under a changed climate are more likely to migrate away from disaster and toward better opportunities.

Hurricanes and storms are predicted to become more intense in a globally warmed world, though it is uncertain if they will become more frequent. Such storms carry an immense human cost. Take the example of Cyclone Nargis, which struck Myanmar in May 2010. It is estimated that 22,500 people were killed, and possibly millions were made homeless, but exact figures are difficult to get and could be much higher. The military junta government did not request foreign aid for three days after the cyclone struck and would not allow foreign aid workers to disburse the aid it finally did accept. Instead, it seized the food aid sent by the World Food Programme, causing the WFP to suspend shipments. Both the United States and France considered air dropping aid without permission, reasoning that it fell under the UN's "responsibility to protect" mandate and was therefore allowable under international law, but ultimately decided against it as they felt it would be inefficient (CBC 2010).

Floods will also become more severe as precipitation intensity increases. With more than one-sixth of the earth's population dependent on meltwater from glaciers and seasonal snow packs, projected changes in water availability under climate change will be "adverse and severe" (IPCC AR4 WGII 2007, 187). In 2010, Pakistan suffered from heavy precipitation in the upper Indus River valley which resulted in severe flooding. Roads, bridges, markets, fields full of crops, and whole villages were swept away. What came to be referred to as "Pakistan's Katrina" cost upwards of $9.7 billion in a country with an average per capita income of $980. The floods killed 2,000 people, and displaced more than 11 million, more people than any other natural catastrophe in history (ICRC 2011), leaving them as internally displaced persons, or IDPs, within their own country.

The devastation left in the wake of the floods gave antigovernment militants an opportunity to recruit among the IDPs. When the government could not reach all the affected people in a timely fashion, some Islamic militant groups were there with camps, medical aid, food, and transportation for the flood victims, and the government either could not or would not get to these areas with aid of its own. Such as situation both engenders allegiance to the militants and calls the legitimacy of the government into question (Ahmed 2010). A spokesman for one of the militant groups contacted the media in India and Pakistan to say that the floods were divine retribution for those who had supported the government against the militants (Channel4News 2010).

Increasing global temperatures and altered precipitation levels can result in droughts and drying of soils, which degrade otherwise arable land. Approximately half of the subhumid and semi-arid parts of Africa are at moderate to high risk of desertification (IPCC AR4 WGII 2007, 439). In 2011, a severe drought across the Horn of Africa caused the death of tens of thousands of people and the displacement of more than 78,000 people from Somalia, 439). In 2011, a severe drought across the Horn of Africa caused the death of tens of thousands of people and the displacement of more than 78,000 people from Somalia alone, who have fled to the neighboring states of Kenya and Ethiopia (Pflanz 2011). The Dadaab refugee camps, which were designed to hold up to 90,000 people from the East African drought two decades ago, now house more than 350,000 people with 10,000 new arrivals every week. The executive director of UNICEF called the combination of continuing drought, conflict, rising food and fuel prices, and a succession of poor harvests "the perfect storm" of issues to spark a flood of refugees (Jones 2011).

Migration and International Security

Migration scholar Nazli Choucri posits that a state's security is a function of three factors: First and most traditionally, the state's military capability to secure its borders or use its military power to pursue state objectives; second, the ability of the government to discharge its duties and protect itself from corruption, revolt, or disorder; and third, its ability to meet the demands of the population given the available resources (Choucri 2002). Of these three factors, migration affects the third most directly by changing the population levels that are dependent upon the carrying capacity of any particular ecosystem or by changing the relative proportions of ethnic groups within a state.

States that are faced with an influx of refugees will ask themselves certain questions to determine if they present a security problem. For example, are the migrants useful or desirable to the host society? Nations like Canada that welcome immigrants of different nationalities and cultures can benefit from migration. Nations like Japan or Saudi Arabia that prefer to maintain a certain amount of cultural or religious homogeneity are more likely to view refugees as an alien set of people. What is their motivation and volition? Were they forced to flee a disaster or untenable environmental change, or are they coming voluntarily? How long will the refugees be there? Most refugees are viewed as temporary occupants, but their presence is not always temporary; for example, there are second generation Palestinian refugees in Israel. If they are fleeing a disaster or environmental crisis, they often come without the proper papers, visas, or identification. The outcome of this decision-making process is that the host government must decide if the refugees are to be confined or assimilated. (N.B.: It is not a foregone conclusion that an influx of environmental refugees will cause conflict. If refugee resources can be leveraged by the host community, an influx of migrants can be a beneficial occurrence [Jacobsen 2002].)

Jacobsen outlines a number of ways in which refugees can create new security problems or exacerbate old ones. If refugees are fleeing from a political or military conflict, the host government may fear that the refugee camps are harboring guerillas. Refugees can create a power imbalance between the sending and receiving governments, especially if the sending government sees refugee camps as a haven for the enemy. Refugees who bring arms with them can create a violent or dangerous atmosphere in the camps. Often refugees are of a different race, ethnicity, language, or religion from the host population, and this can change the cultural makeup of the receiving community (Jacobsen 2002). Finally, a large influx of refugees into a confined area like a camp can be disastrous for the local environment (Martin 2005).

Because climate change is expected to produce rapid environmental changes in the future, the corresponding migration flows may be too large for a host country to assimilate (Reuveny 2007, 60). Even if quantity estimates are uncertain, the mere possibility of climate refugees numbering in the millions is daunting to security scholars and policy makers, since the scope of climate change effects that can drive migration is only set to increase. Traditional push factors for refugees such as ethnic violence or political changes are limited in scope and reversible on human timescales, so their displacement effects are less compared to climate push factors like sea level rise or desertification that are irreversible on human timescales and likely to render lands permanently unusable. The legal concepts of asylum and non-refoulement are generally held to apply to individuals and small groups; they have not been applied as a legal concept to possibly millions of climate refugees.

If the changes that provoke migration are gradual and linear, such as those that begin with incremental increases in ambient air temperature, changes in precipitation, or sea level rise, then societies and states can adapt to a steady influx of refugees with a minimum of cost and unrest by implementing forward-thinking adaptation policies. If the changes are nonlinear, such as those that begin with extreme events, then the potential for conflict and violence is much greater because societies and states don't have time to adapt. If large enough movements of environmental refugees occur, it would cause major social and political disruptions all over the world.

Many of the traditional calculations and considerations regarding the security implications of refugees do not apply to those forced from their homes and lands due to climate change and environmental degradation. For example, states or coalitions have used military force to affect the behavior of governments whose actions produce refugees, as NATO did against the Serbs in Bosnia and Kosovo (see Posen 2004 on military causes of displacement). However, the enforcement of a truce or the creation of safe havens is applicable only to political disputes. There is no safe haven from an environmental disaster. The refugees from Somalia fleeing hunger in the Horn of Africa are now finding that Kenya and Ethiopia are facing the same catastrophic levels of drought. Consequently, there is little that these two states can provide in the way of aid to Somalian refugees, as all three states are dependent on the UN World Food Programme for food aid. Similarly, states have sent refugee push-outs as a foreign policy tool, such as the Russification of Central Asia and the Baltics, and the 1980 Mariel boatlift from Cuba. This has traditionally been done to control a territory or to destabilize or pressure a neighboring state (Loescher 1992). However, such push-outs are motivated by political or cultural reasons, not environmental ones, although push-outs of a particular group are not difficult to imagine if land, water, and food become scarce or degraded. Governments might even see this as a rational response to climate change within their territory. Finally, the international community's traditional practice of waiting until an emergency unfolds and then providing aid will become increasingly unsustainable as climate change–induced disasters and degradation increase.

Future Issues: Timescale Mismatch and Nonlinearity

The climate change–driven trends affecting migration are years or even decades away, according to the best predictions of the IPCC. Because it is impossible—or at least scientifically inadvisable and incorrect—to say that climate change *caused* a specific event like Hurricane Katrina, trends caused by the anthropogenic climate change signal are only distinguishable in retrospect, when separated from the noise of natural climate variation. Security concerns, however, are generally based on the politics, circumstances, or personalities of the day. In as little as 10 years time, regimes, policies, and alliances can all change, rendering a security threat of today moot tomorrow, and vice versa. Scientists, on the other hand, generally refuse to make climate predictions before 2030 at the earliest, and the IPCC projections made for AR4 are for the target period 2090–2099 (IPCC AR4 WGI SPM 2007, 14, note 15).

Consequently, policy makers who consider the effects of climate change on this government or that political policy need to be very circumspect because the uncertainty threshold is so high that far out, more so on the political side than on the scientific side. Even looking at what may appear now to be long-term security trends, such as radical Islamism, the "war on terror," or American economic hegemony is a step to take with caution, especially with regard to phenomena like migration which have a long time horizon. Other long-term trends such as geopolitics, the hunger-migration link, and the developed world/developing world dichotomy seem safe to consider for 2030 and beyond.

In addition, our consideration of the effects of climate change is, for the most part, linear. We expect that if the global average ambient air temperature increases by three degrees between 2000 and 2100, then it will be one degree higher than the present by 2033, and two degrees higher than the present by 2067. Certainly this sort of linear projection allows climate models to run smoothly, and in the absence of data to the contrary, does not appear to be an unreasonable assumption. But the possibility, however unquantifiable, of a nonlinear event cannot be discounted.

Climatic "tipping elements" can be defined as "subsystems of the Earth system that are at least subcontinental in scale and can be switched—under certain circumstances—into a qualitatively different state by small perturbations" (Lenton et al. 2008, 1786; see also IPCC AR4 WGI 2007, 775–777). Lenton and his colleagues evaluated potential tipping elements to identify the ones which pose the greatest concern based on current knowledge. At the top of their list of 10 were Arctic summer ice melt and the loss of the Greenland ice sheet, followed by the loss of the West Antarctic ice sheet, loss of boreal and rainforests, and intensification of both ENSO events and the West African monsoon. While the study does not go further to examine the downstream socioeconomic effects of these tipping elements, it is not hard to surmise that these events can be significant drivers of migration. An increase in monsoons and the loss of forests can potentially displace millions of people, while the loss of Arctic summer sea ice creates a positive feedback loop that reinforces the entire climate change cycle. Most interestingly, the study authors draw a parallel conclusion that socioeconomic systems also have their tipping points, and that further research needs to be done to determine, for example, how a rapid societal transition into sustainability might be achieved (ibid., 1792).

The IPCC also examined several tipping elements, such as the overturning of the Atlantic Meridional Overturning Circulation (MOC), and the switch in the role of terrestrial soil from a carbon sink to a carbon source. Regarding the MOC, while climate models indicated a range of responses from a slight slowdown, happening currently, to a 50 percent slowdown, the MOC was very unlikely to cease flowing completely by 2100 (IPCC AR4 WGI 2007, 775). Regarding the role of soil, several studies indicated that a warmer and wetter climate could cause soil to release previously accumulated carbon, forming another positive feedback to the level of atmospheric CO_2. This switch could occur over as little as a few decades, though it is uncertain when it would begin (ibid., 777). A sudden climate shift could also cause irreversible loss of ecosystem services such as pollination, habitat provision, defense against invasive species, and increases in eutrophication (IPCC AR4 WGII 2007, 242). While it may be possible to adapt to these sudden, nonlinear shifts over the long term, the short-term impacts would be extremely disruptive (e.g., the 1997–98 El Niño caused flooding and droughts that led to thousands of deaths and billions of dollars in damages around the Indian and Pacific Oceans; Stern 2007, 97). Faced with life-threatening and home-destroying events, migration may be a logical choice. In this case, collective security can be achieved by working with other nations to mitigate the problems of climate-driven migration, since no nation can solve this problem of international migration on its own.

Disease and Public Health

There is no doubt that we have the capacity to find ways to avoid many of the worst health effects of climate change, and indeed, given the universality and potential magnitude of such effects, we have an ethical imperative to do so.

—Interagency Working Group on Climate Change and Health

Finally, when we discuss the effects that a changed climate will have on security, we must address disease and public health. Infectious disease is the third of the four horsemen of the end-times, and is responsible for approximately 25 percent of all human deaths (Cecchine and Moore 2006, 5). Humans and diseases have existed in a kind of equilibrium; disease kills a certain number of humans, and leaves the survivors immune. These survivors then reproduce, making the population as a whole more resistant, until a new disease appears. Humans have recently gained the upper hand in this balance, as the 20th century has seen a significant drop in mortality rates from infectious diseases largely due to better medical care. However, in the last couple of decades, the rate of drop is declining due in part to the spread of HIV/AIDS and the resurgence of antibiotic-resistant bacteria, indicating that the disease side of the equilibrium may be poised for a comeback. Humans have made great strides in identifying and treating infectious diseases, and we may have gotten complacent in our relationship with disease.

The links between climate change and infectious disease are clear, but the relationship between disease and international security is less so. War moves a lot of people around, and in doing so, exposes them to disease. Not every disease will have a significant security impact, and not every disease will thrive under every condition in a globally warmed world. For example, an area that experiences more precipitation may see more instances of malaria, but fewer instances of dust-borne diseases such as Lassa fever. It is important for security planners to understand the vector ecology of naturally occurring diseases, because it could be critical to differentiating whether a disease is from a newly emerging pathogen that may be spreading into an area where it has not been seen before, or has been intentionally introduced.

Climatic Aspects of Disease

A significant number of studies link climate change to increased morbidity and mortality from infectious diseases (see for example Chaves et al. 2010; Stenseth et al. 2006; Ebi et al. 2006; McMichael et al., eds 2006; Epstein 2002; NRC 2001; Kovats et al. 2001; Epstein et al. 1998). This can occur for various reasons. Increases in ambient air temperature and changes in precipitation can affect the range or behavior of the pathogen itself, the vector, or the host. More specifically, climate change can expand the geographic range of a disease by allowing vectors to thrive in areas where they previously could not due to temperature or moisture constraints. Warmer temperatures can extend the season for transmission of the disease. Changing temperatures and precipitation can increase the growth and reproduction rate of the vector or its biting behavior. Warmer temperatures are likely to change the behavior of humans in a manner that subsequently increases their exposure, such as spending more time outdoors. Finally, loss of habitat for vectors and hosts means that humans are more likely to come into contact with diseases, especially in Africa and Asia (Jones et al. 2008).

Infectious disease will spread in different places and at different rates. The areas hardest hit by the climate change–induced spread of disease are likely to be in the developing world, precisely the areas with the least adaptive capacity. Changing disease vectors are likely to increase exposure in areas that are already marginally endemic for a disease. This means the local population generally will not have built up immunity. In addition, public health services in many parts of the developing world are poor or nonexistent. The World Health Organization estimated in 2000 that 150,000 deaths per year were attributable to climate change, including deaths from diarrheal diseases, malaria, and malnutrition. This estimate is expected to double to 300,000 per year by 2030 under a 1°C warming (WHO 2005, in Stern 2006).

Diseases Affected by Changed Vectors

Climate-induced changes in vector ecology are poised to become a significant indicator of disease. A **vector** is the mechanism by which an infectious disease is transmitted from one host to the next. Common vectors include fleas, ticks, mosquitoes, and rats, but humans themselves can be vectors for human-to-human transmitted diseases like smallpox. Important properties in the transmission of vector-borne diseases include the survival and reproduction rate of the vector; the time of year and level of vector activity, specifically the biting rate; and the rate of development and reproduction of the pathogen within the vector.

Ecosystem characteristics affected by climate change such as temperature, precipitation, and atmospheric humidity have a direct bearing on the range of most vectors, particularly in areas that are on the margin of infectious zones. A climate change–induced increase in temperature or precipitation could allow vectors to thrive in previously inhospitable areas (Watson & McMichael 2001). For example, northeastern Italy saw an outbreak of the tropical disease chikungunya in July and August of 2007. The mosquito-borne viral disease was brought over from Southeast Asia and flourished in North African tiger mosquitoes (*A. albopictus*), whose range expanded into Italy due to warming temperatures (Rezza et al. 2007). In addition to chikungunya, tiger mosquitoes also carry the virus that causes dengue and dengue hemorrhagic fever.

Increasing ambient air temperatures will increase the range of diseases like leishmaniasis, plague, or hantavirus that are vectored by insects, rodents, or anything else that thrives in warm environments. Changes in precipitation will increase, or in some cases decrease, the range of diseases that are vectored by water or water-borne insects,[1] like cholera or malaria. Mosquito ranges are increased by both temperature and precipitation, since warmer temperatures allow them to overwinter in areas where they would otherwise die out, and increased precipitation results in more standing water for breeding. Mosquitoes carry dengue, yellow fever, various forms of encephalitis, and most commonly malaria. The map below shows the endemic areas for malaria extending out of the tropical zones and into the temperate zone.

Incremental changes in temperature and precipitation can have a greater effect on overall mortality by altering the baseline epidemiology of the country than extreme events could have in causing localized spikes in mortality rates (McMichael 2003, 11). This means that diseases like malaria can gain a foothold in areas where they were not able to before, and the populations of

---

[1] The Pacific Institute has classified water-related diseases in four ways: (1) waterborne diseases, caused by ingestion of contaminated water; includes cholera, typhoid, dysentery, and diarrhea; (2) water-washed diseases, caused by skin or eye contact with contaminated water; includes scabies and flea- and tick-borne diseases; (3) waterbased diseases, caused by intermediate organisms found in contaminated water; includes schistosomiasis and other helminthes; and (4) water-related diseases, caused by vectors that breed in water; includes dengue, malaria, and yellow fever (Gleick 2002, 2). Of these four categories, climate change will have the greatest effect on the fourth.

Figure 4.6 Changes in Malaria Distribution in a Globally Warmed World, 2050

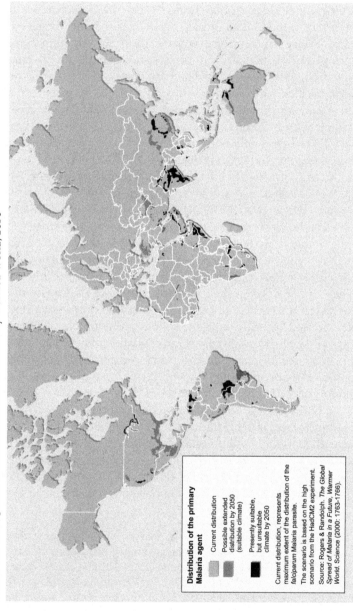

Distribution of the primary Malaria agent

- Current distribution
- Possible extended distribution by 2050 (suitable climate)
- Presently suitable, but unsuitable climate by 2050

Current distribution, represents maximum extent of the distribution of the *falciparum* Malaria parasite.

The scenario is based on the high scenario from the HadCM2 experiment.

Source: Rogers & Randolph. *The Global Spread of Malaria in a Future, Warmer World.* Science (2000: 1763-1766).

(Data from Rogers & Randolph. The Global Spread of Malaria in a Future, Warmer World. Science [2000:1763-1766]. Graphic by Hugo Ahlenius, UNEP/GRID-Arendal. Available at http://www.grida.no/graphicslib/detail/climate-change-and-malaria-scenario-for-2050_bffe. Used by permission.)

nonendemic areas can then become vulnerable. Trends of spreading disease due to climate change–altered vectors are compounded by nonclimate factors such as inadequate medical care, poor nutrition, inadequate sanitation, and bad water quality (NIC 2000, 2).

Diseases in the Wake of Extreme Events

Increasing frequency, duration, or intensity of extreme events can also extend vector ranges, though usually only temporarily. Violent storms and flood water surges can overwhelm sewers and wastewater treatment infrastructure, contaminating drinking water. High winds can damage health care infrastructure such as hospitals, clinics, or even roads for evacuation. The pitiable condition of New Orleans after Hurricane Katrina is illustrative. Due to the contaminated flood waters, breeding grounds for mosquitoes carrying malaria and West Nile virus expanded hugely. That dengue fever, cholera, and typhoid were not widely seen was only due to prehurricane, developed health care that had almost eradicated these diseases from the American population. Developing nations are often not so lucky. Bangladesh was struck by Cyclone Sidr in 2007, and suffered increases in malaria, dengue fever, and Japanese encephalitis, all of which were compounded by poor access to health services and overcrowding in medical centers (WHO 2007a).

Epidemiologists have often studied disease outbreaks during El Niño events, figuring that the El Niño–Southern Oscillation (ENSO) could act as a sort of environmental proxy for a changed climate (WHO 2000). El Niño years are marked by significant changes in precipitation, both droughts and storms, and recognized spatial variations: drier conditions in the Pacific, wetter conditions in the Atlantic. While ENSO events may become more frequent in a globally warmed world (Timmerman et al. 1999), they are not a perfect proxy for conditions under a changed climate. After an ENSO event, the climate system generally returns to equilibrium, whereas a changed climate is an incremental and permanent process. However, altered levels of disease during and after ENSO events can give epidemiologists an idea of what is likely to happen if climate should change in a similar way. For example, malaria has been shown to increase markedly during ENSO events (Hales et al. 2000), and an outbreak of hantavirus in southwestern United States followed the El Niño of 1997–1998 (CDC 2004). Hantavirus is vectored by rodents, which thrive in deserts and other dry areas and whose food supply is fed by occasional rains.

Security Aspects of Disease

The relationship between infectious disease and security is complex and multifaceted. Disease kills far more people than war. Disease affects the economic foundation of a nation, and by extension its national social order and functioning. If left unchecked, disease can undermine public confidence in a government's legitimacy, and catalyze regional instability (Brower & Chalk 2003, 7–10). Modern combat concerns offer new possibilities for the spread of infectious diseases: urban warfare, protracted low-intensity conflict, and the rapid movement of soldiers and/or civilian support personnel into conflict or disaster areas. Climate change could exacerbate any or all of these conditions.

There are two primary ways in which infectious disease will affect international security directly. First, disease can affect military readiness by reducing the health of troops, or by circumscribing the areas into which they can be deployed. Second, the spread of infectious disease can open up new areas of instability by causing the degradation of societies through the attrition of key sections of the population. The effects of infectious disease on conflict and national security are significant and robust through time, and though armed forces today have better medical protection than their counterparts in the past, disease, abetted by a changed climate, will continue to have a significant impact on global security.

Reduction of Military Capabilities and Readiness

Infectious disease, both chronic and acute, can reduce the capability and readiness of military forces. Soldiers are human, and as affected as civilians by climate change–related shifts in vector ecology and human behavior.

Disease has always served as an auxiliary force in war. Historian Elizabeth Fenn, in *Pox Americana*, describes the effects of smallpox on the conduct of the American Revolution. Smallpox affected the recruitment effort for the Continental Army, as potential enlistees feared either contracting it while serving, or dying during the lengthy and painful process of inoculation (Fenn 2001, 86–88). However, the British Army was largely immune to smallpox due to previous exposure, which gave them a significant tactical advantage in battle. Washington's decision to inoculate his troops in February 1777 (though secretly, so as not to tip his hand to the British) equaled out the comparative advantage the British troops had, leaving battle strength equal.

During World War I, the Spanish Flu (H1N1) killed an estimated 40 million people worldwide. Originally an avian virus, experts disagree about when and where it first appeared. Despite being called the "Spanish Flu of 1918," it neither originated in Spain, nor in 1918. Oxford (2001) puts its origin in France two years earlier, while Thompson et al. (2005) put its origin in the United States. It spread from military camp to military camp, both within the United States and overseas. Wartime conditions of partial starvation, stress and overcrowding, and a landscape contaminated with respiratory irritants like chlorine and phosgene allowed the disease to thrive among the troops. After the war, returning soldiers carried it home to their families and communities (Oxford et al. 2002, 113). By the time all three waves of infection had subsided, upwards of 40 million people had died.

Even today, soldiers are vulnerable, as they are not only exposed to new diseases when they are deployed, but they can also spread a disease that they themselves are carrying into areas where it is not normally found. The most recent case is the introduction of cholera into Haiti. Cholera had not been found in Haiti or anywhere in the Caribbean since the mid-19th century, but a sudden outbreak along the Artibonite River in 2010 killed more than 5,500 people and sickened more than 363,000 others (AP 2011). When epidemiologists identified the strain of *V. cholerae* as South Asian in origin, the infection was traced to a recently arrived contingent of UN peacekeepers from Nepal, who had come from Kathmandu shortly after an outbreak of cholera was reported there (Piarroux et al. 2011). Health authorities concluded that they had brought the disease with them, and inadvertently released it into the river.

It is not just soldiers who are affected by disease, but potential soldiers as well. Nations that have high rates of endemic disease, or that face increased endemicity due to climate change, can see this trend reflected in their pool of young people eligible for military recruitment (NIC 2008). Though the transmission of HIV/AIDS is not related to climate change, it can serve as a significant indicator of how infectious disease can erode military capability and readiness. For example, China, India, and the United States all test potential recruits for HIV; those who are positive are not allowed to serve. This is not to say that high rates of HIV or any infectious disease automatically lead to military unfitness. Strategies and policies pursued by military and civilian authorities—such as prerecruitment screening and medical education—can mitigate the spread of disease among soldiers and the civilians with whom they come into contact. However, high rates of infectious disease generally do not enhance military readiness or national security in any way, and in fact have the significant possibility of degrading readiness (NIC 2000).

Degradation of Government Capabilities and Social Institutions

The more widespread and long-lasting effect of infectious disease on security is that it can wreak havoc on the economic and political development of a society, rendering it unstable. Because greater levels of infectious disease correlate negatively over time with indicators of economic health, disease acts "as sand in the economic engine of a nation" (Price-Smith 2002, 80). Diseases vary in their mortality rates, but the loss of a significant number of working-age adults results in a slowdown in economic growth. The WHO reports that malaria, responsible for 2.5 million deaths per year, "has slowed economic growth in African countries possibly by up to 1.3 percent per year" over the past 35 years, leaving Africa with an overall malaria-related GDP deficit of 32 percent (WHO 2002, 16). Also, recurring bouts of disease-related illness result in lost productive hours, reducing adult work time and family income. This can cripple services in critical national sectors such as education, health care, and defense. Finally, the loss of institutional knowledge due to absent workers will reduce the productivity of almost every industry over time. Indeed, there appears to be a reciprocal relationship between the increasing prevalence of infectious disease and compromised state capacity (Price-Smith 2002, 67).

Recurrence of disease eats up already-limited public health budgets, and as states are forced to combat diseases whose exposure or virulence is exacerbated by climate change, this too can be a reciprocal relationship. The weakening of a functioning public health sector can facilitate the spread of infectious diseases, which will then further erode the government's capability to maintain public health. For example, the spread of drug-resistant tuberculosis in Russia is a direct function of a post–Soviet era drop-off in public health capacity, and a loss of critical antibiotics in outlying areas (Goozner 2008; see also Nikolayevskiy et al. 2006). While the transmission of tuberculosis is not facilitated by a climate change–influenced vector, it serves as an example of the positive feedback loop between state capacity and disease prevention. By way of contrast, the government of South Korea invested its limited public health budget in basic disease prevention, family planning, maternal and child care, and mandatory national health insurance, and it has paid off in increased life expectancy, greater economic growth, and state stability (Kim et al. 2001). If the hypothesis of a reciprocal relationship between declining public health and weakening state capacity and insecurity is true, then the very states that will be affected by resource-based conflicts and food insecurity will be made still more unstable by the loss of public health care.

Disease can stratify the social order within a country. Poorer households bear a greater economic burden from infectious disease than richer households do, and this division can reinforce social and class divisions (Price-Smith 2002, 87, 124–125), especially if there is a stigma attached to the disease. If the disease is left unchecked or escapes government control, it can undermine public confidence in the state's ability to provide for its own citizens, and hence its legitimacy. People look to their government for help in the face of a crisis (e.g., Japan and the Fukushima Daiichi disaster), and if it cannot meet basic needs such as food and water, shelter, and medical care, the people of the nation are going to ask why not. In more extreme cases, disease can embarrass governments. The case of the 2002–2003 SARS outbreak is instructive because even though the Chinese government originally kept quiet about the disease, infected individuals traveled from China to Hong Kong, Vietnam, Singapore, Canada, Ireland, and the United States. This resulted in the World Health Organization issuing a global health warning, advising people not to travel to China and other affected countries. SARS is only transmitted through close contact, which limited the outbreak to 8,000 cases and 750 deaths (a nearly 10% mortality rate), but if it had become airborne, many thousands of people could have died. Eventually the Chinese government was forced to acknowledge the disease and subsequently assisted in medical intelligence gathering and disease surveillance.

Future Issues

Of all the areas that we have discussed with regard to national security and its environmental drivers, the implications of disease are the least well known. Various scholars and government agencies have postulated that infectious disease could be a "conflict starter" (CSIS 2000), but as of this writing we have yet to see a global pandemic. It is possible that humans have seen such amazing lifespan extensions over the course of the 20th century because they have made relatively easy but significant improvements in sanitation, health care, nutrition, and clean water. If public health systems continue to improve in the 21st century to the same degree that they did in the 20th century, any increase in malaria endemicity due to climate change, for example, will be more than compensated for (Gething et al. 2010). The remaining question, however, is whether we have picked the low-hanging fruit with regard to investment in public health infrastructure. This may mean any subsequent improvements will be less easy, and future gains will be smaller and made at higher cost. If so, then the spectacular public health gains of the 20th century are unlikely to be repeated.

Perhaps we humans have gotten so good at fighting disease that we have become overconfident in our ability to prevail over nature; but we should not fall into this trap. As is said in many other contexts, "the more you succeed, the more you fail." Inoculation has protected us against many types of infectious diseases, though none have been as completely wiped off the map as smallpox, and some geographers now posit that human populations may be ripe for another virgin-soil pandemic. A **virgin-soil pandemic** occurs when a disease is introduced into an area that has had no previous exposure, and hence the population has no prior immunity. The disease then takes a high toll on an immunologically defenseless population, as smallpox, measles, and malaria did to the Native Americans after the European colonists arrived. The more the diseases we identify and prevent, the more we reduce the herd immunity of the population and make another outbreak, especially of a previously unseen pathogen, more likely.

However, this does not argue against the continuation of public health and disease surveillance, since a prevention-based approach to global health is likely to provide more wealth, development, and security than a response-based approach. The best way then, to protect against new diseases without re-exposing ourselves to old ones, is to understand to the best of our ability the climate change—global public health—international security nexus. Consequently, military personnel contribute to national security not only by protecting their nations from traditional armed threats, but also from public health threats. Military troops have an important role to play in surveilling disease by serving as ground scouts for medical researchers. This is an example of collective security at its clearest. No single nation can protect itself fully

Table 4.1. Examples of Possible Impacts of Climate Change due to Changes in Extreme Weather and Climate Events, Based on Projections to the Mid- to Late-21st Century

Phenomenon[a] and direction of trend	Likelihood of future trends based on projections for 21st century using SRES scenarios	Examples of major projected impacts by sector			
		Agriculture, forestry and ecosystems [4.4, 5.4]	Water resources [3.4]	Human health [8.2, 8.4]	Industry, settlement, and society [7.4]
Over most land areas, warmer and fewer cold days and nights, warmer and more frequent hot days and nights	Virtually certain[b]	Increased yields in colder environments; decreased yields in warmer environments; increased insect outbreaks	Effects on water resources relying on snow melt; effects on some water supplies	Reduced human mortality from decreased cold exposure	Reduced energy demand for heating; increased demand for cooling; declining air quality in cities; reduced disruption to transport due to snow, ice; effects on winter tourism
Warm spells/heat waves. Frequency increases over most land areas	Very likely	Reduced yields in warmer regions due to heat stress; increased danger of wildfire	Increased water demand; water quality problems, e.g., algal blooms	Increased risk of heat-related mortality, especially for the elderly, chronically sick, very young, and socially-isolated	Reduction in quality of life for people in warm areas without appropriate housing; impacts on the elderly, very young, and poor
Heavy precipitation events. Frequency increases over most areas	Very likely	Damage to crops; soil erosion, inability to cultivate land due to waterlogging of soils	Adverse effects on quality of surface and groundwater; contamination of water supply; water scarcity may be relieved	Increased risk of deaths, injuries and infectious, respiratory and skin diseases	Disruption of settlements, commerce, transport, and societies due to flooding; pressures on urban and rural infrastructures; loss of property

Table 4.1. (*Continued*)

Phenomenon[a] and direction of trend	Likelihood of future trends based on projections for 21st century using SRES scenarios	Examples of major projected impacts by sector			
		Agriculture, forestry and ecosystems [4.4, 5.4]	Water resources [3.4]	Human health [8.2, 8.4]	Industry, settlement, and society [7.4]
Area affected by drought increases	Likely	Land degradation; lower yields/crop damage and failure; increased livestock deaths; increased risk of wildfire	More widespread water stress	Increased risk of food and water shortage; increased risk of malnutrition; increased risk of water- and food-borne diseases	Water shortages for settlements, industry and societies; reduced hydropower generation potential; potential for population migration
Intense tropical cyclone activity increases	Likely	Damage to crops; windthrow (uprooting) of trees; damage to coral reefs	Power outages causing disruption of public water supply	Increased risk of deaths, injuries, water- and food-borne diseases; post-traumatic stress disorders	Disruption by flood and high winds; withdrawal of risk coverage in vulnerable areas by private insurers, potential for population migrations, loss of property
Increased incidence of extreme high sea level (excludes tsunamis)[c]	Likely[d]	Salinization of irrigation water, estuaries, and freshwater systems	Decreased freshwater availability due to saltwater intrusion	Increased risk of deaths and injuries by drowning in floods; migration-related health effects	Costs of coastal protection versus costs of land-use relocation; potential for movement of populations and infrastructure; also see tropical cyclones above

a. See Working Group I Fourth Assessment Table 9.7 for further details regarding definitions.

b. Warning of the most extreme days and nights each year.

c. Extreme high sea level depends on average sea level and on regional weather systems. It is defined as the highest 1% of hourly values of observed sea level at a station for given reference period.

d. In all scenarios, the projected global average sea level at 2100 is higher than in the reference period (Working Group I Fourth Assessment 10.6). The effect of changes in regional weather systems on sea level extremes has not been assessed.

(*Source:* IPCC AR4 WGII 2007, Table SPM.1)

from incursions by disease unless it seals its borders entirely, an impossible task in today's globalized world. This means that, in order to stay ahead of emerging disease threats, both developed and developing nations must cooperate (see Kickbusch et al. 2007 for a larger discussion of medical diplomacy). Developed nations may have better technological capabilities for medical analysis, but developing nations have on-the-ground surveillance capabilities in disease-prevalent areas, and they provide data to medical laboratories around the world (Chretien et al. 2007; see also Feldbaum 2009; see Cecchine & Moore 2006 for an extensive list of international disease surveillance initiatives). Continuing surveillance can provide critical early warning of a disease outbreak such as H5N1 avian flu before it becomes a global pandemic.

References

"A Cooperative Strategy for 21st Century Seapower." 2007. U.S. Navy, U.S. Marine Corps, U.S. Coast Guard, October 2007.

Abell, Nazaré Albuquerque. 1996. "The Impact of International Migration on Security and Stability." *Canadian Foreign Policy*. Vol. 4, No. 1, pp. 83–109.

ACIA. 2004. *Impacts of a Warming Arctic: Arctic Climate Impact Assessment*. New York: Cambridge University Press.

allAfrica.com. 2011. "Mozambique: No Programme for Mitigating Saline Intrusion." allAfrica Global Media, March 21, 2011. http://allafrica.com/stories/201103220919.html

Associated Press. 2011. "CDC Journal Study 'Strongly Suggests' UN Peacekeepers from Nepal Imported Cholera to Haiti." *Washington Post*, June 30, 2011.

Bates, Diane C. 2002. "Environmental Refugees? Classifying Human Migrations Caused by Environmental Change." *Population and Environment*. Vol. 23, No. 5, May 2002, pp. 465–477.

Berkman, Paul Arthur, and Oran R. Young. 2009. "Governance and Environmental Change in the Arctic." *Science*. Vol. 324, April 17, 2009, pp. 339–340.

Bi-National Planning Group. 2006. "Final Report on Canada and the United States (CANUS) Enhanced Military Cooperation." Peterson AFB, CO: Bi-National Planning Group.

Bjarnason, Björn. Minister of Justice, Republic of Iceland. 2007. "Climate Change and Iceland's Role in North Atlantic Security." Lecture at the Kennedy School of Government, Harvard University, November 26, 2007.

Brower, Jennifer, and Peter Chalk. 2003. *The Global Threat of New and Reemerging Infectious Diseases*. Santa Monica, CA: RAND, 146 pp.

Bryan, Joan H., Desmond H. Foley, and Robert W. Sutherst. 1996. "Malaria Transmission and Climate Change in Australia." *Medical Journal of Australia*. Vol. 164, No. 6, pp. 345–347.

CBC. 2007. "Imperial, ExxonMobil to Explore Beaufort Sea for Oil, Gas." *CBC News*. July 19, 2007.

CBC. 2010. "Let Cyclone Aid in 'Without Hindrance': UN Chief to Burma Leaders." Canadian Broadcasting Company, May 9, 2008. http://www.cbc.ca/news/world/story/2008/05/09/burma-aid.html

CDC, Center for Disease Control. 2004. "El Niño Special Report." National Center for Infectious Disease, Special Pathogen Branch. http://www.cdc.gov/ncidod/diseases/hanta/hps/noframes/elnino.htm.

CDC. 2005. "Current SARS Situation." http://www.cdc.gov/ncidod/sars/situation.htm.

CDC. 2010. "Frequently Asked Questions about the Haiti Cholera Outbreak." http://www.cdc.gov/haiticholera/cholera_qa.htm.

Cecchine, Gary, and Melinda Moore. 2006. *Infectious Disease and National Security: Strategic Information Needs.* Prepared for the Office of the Secretary of Defense. Santa Monica, CA: RAND, 105 pp.

Channel4News. 2010. "Pakistan Floods: Taliban Suspend Attacks." August 2, 2010, http://www.channel4.com/news/articles/science_technology/pakistani+taliban+suspend+attacks+in+floodhit+areas/3732277.html

Chaves, Luis Fernando, and Constantianus J. M. Koenraadt. 2010. "Climate Change and Highland Malaria: Fresh Air for a Hot Debate" *The Quarterly Review of Biology.* Vol. 85, No. 1, March 2010, pp. 27–55.

Choucri, Nazli. 2002. "Migration and Security: Some Key Linkages." *Journal of International Affairs.* Vol. 56, No. 1, Fall 2002, pp. 97–122.

Chretien, Jean-Paul, David L. Blazes, Rodney L. Coldren, Michael D. Lewis, Jariyanart Gaywee, Khunakorn Kana, Narongrid Sirisopana, Victor Vallejos, Carmen C. Mundaca, Silvia Montano, Gregory J. Martin, and Joel C. Gaydos. 2007. "The Importance of Militaries from Developing Countries in Global Infectious Diseases Surveillance." *Bulletin of the World Health Organization.* Vol. 85, No. 3, March 2007, pp. 174–180.

(Christian Science Monitor) Pflanz, Mike. 2011. "East Africa's Famine, by the Numbers." *Christian Science Monitor,* July 22, 2011. http://www.csmonitor.com/World/Africa/2011/0722/East-Africa-s-famine-by-the-numbers

Ebi, Kristie L., David M. Mills, Joel B. Smith, and Anne Grambsch. 2006. "Climate Change and Human Health Impacts in the United States: An Update on the Results of the U.S. National Assessment." *Environmental Health Perspectives.* Vol. 114, No. 9, September 2006, pp. 1318–1324.

Ellis, Ben. Managing Director, Institute of the North. 2007. "Arctic Marine Shipping Assessment Update." Sustainable Development Working Group, Arctic Council. October 31, 2007.

Enserink, Martin. 2011. "Cholera Linked to U.N. Forces, But Questions Remain." *Science.* Vol. 322, May 13, 2011, pp. 776–777.

Epstein, Paul R. 2002. "Climate Change and Infectious Disease: Stormy Weather Ahead?" *Epidemiology.* Vol. 13, No. 4, July 2002, pp. 373–375.

Epstein, Paul R., Henry F. Diaz, Scott Elias, Georg Grabherr, Nicholas E. Graham, Willem J. M. Martens, Ellen Moseley-Thompson, and Joel Susskind. 1998. "Biological and Physical Signs of Climate Change: Focus on Mosquito-Borne

Diseases." *Bulletin of the American Meteorological Society.* Vol. 79, No. 3, March 1998, pp. 409–417.

Fenn, Elizabeth A. 2001. *Pox Americana: The Great Smallpox Epidemic of 1775–82.* New York: Hill and Wang, 370 pp.

Gething, Peter W., David L. Smith, Anand P. Patil, Andrew J. Tatem, Robert W. Snow, and Simon I. Hay. 2010. "Climate Change and the Global Malaria Recession." *Nature.* Vol. 465, May 20, 2010, pp. 342–345.

Gleick, Peter H. 2002. *Dirty Water: Estimated Deaths from Water-Related Diseases 2000–2020.* Pacific Institute Research Report. Oakland, CA: Pacific Institute.

Goffman, Ethan. 2006. "Environmental Refugees: How Many, How Bad?" CSA Discovery Guides. June 2006, 15 pp.

Goozner, Merrill. 2008. "Prisons in Post-Soviet Russia Incubate a Plague." *Scientific American.* August 25, 2008. http://www.scientificamerican.com/article.cfm?id=prison-plague-post-soviet-russia

Hales, Simon, Sari Kovats, and Alistair Woodward. 2000. "What El Niño Can Tell Us about Human Health and Global Climate Change." *Global Change and Human Health.* Vol. 1, No. 1, July 2000, pp. 70–71.

Homer-Dixon, Thomas, and Valerie Percival. 1996. *Environmental Scarcity and Violent Conflict: Briefing Book.* Washington: American Association for the Advancement of Science.

Howard, Roger. 2009. *The Arctic Gold Rush: The New Race for Tomorrow's Natural Resources.* New York: Continuum, 259 pp.

ICRC. 2011. "Pakistan: One Year after Catastrophic Floods, Thousands Still Affected." International Committee of the Red Cross, July 26, 2011. http://www.icrc.org/eng/resources/documents/news-release/2011/pakistan-news-2011–07–26.htm

Jacobsen, Karen. 2002. "Can Refugees Benefit the State? Refugee Resources and African Statebuilding." *Journal of Modern African Studies.* Vol. 40, No. 4, December 2002, pp. 577–596.

Jones, Bryony. 2011. "What Has Caused the East Africa Crisis?" CNN. July 22, 2011. http://www.cnn.com/2011/WORLD/africa/07/20/somalia.famine.explainer/index.html

Jones, Kate E., Nikkita G. Patel, Marc A. Levy, Adam Storeygard, Deborah Balk, John H. Gittleman, and Peter Daszak. 2008. "Global Trends in Emerging Infectious Diseases." *Nature.* Vol. 451, No. 7181, February 21, 2008, pp. 990–994.

Kerr, Richard A. 2007. "Is Battered Arctic Sea Ice Down for the Count?" *Science.* Vol. 318, October 5, 2007, pp. 33–34.

Kickbusch, Ilona, Thomas E. Novotny, Nico Drager, Gaudenz Silberschmidt, and Santiago Alcazar. 2007. "Global Health Diplomacy: Training across Disciplines." *Bulletin of the World Health Organization.* Vol. 85, No. 12, December 2007, pp. 971–973.

Kim, H. J., Y. S. Ahn, and S. G. Lee. 2001. "Health Development Experience in North and South Korea." *Asia Pacific Journal of Public Health.* Vol. 13, Suppl. S5, pp. 1–7.

Kovats, R.S., D.H. Campbell-Lendrum, A.J. McMichael, A. Woodward, and J. St. H. Cox. 2001. "Early Effects of Climate Change: Do They Include Changes in Vector-Borne Disease?" *Philosophical Transactions: Biological Sciences*. Vol. 356, No. 1411, July 29, 2001, pp. 1057–1068;

Kwok, Ronald, and D.A. Rothrock. 2009. "Decline in Arctic Sea Ice Thickness from Submarine and ICESat Records: 1958–2008." *Geophysical Research Letters*. Vol. 36, L15501, doi:10.1029/2009GL039035.

Kwok, Ronald, and Norbert Untersteiner. 2011. "The Thinning of Arctic Sea Ice." *Physics Today*. Vol. 64, No. 4, April 2011, pp. 36–41.

Lacey, Mark. 2007. "UN Troops Fight Haitian Gangs One Street at a Time." *New York Times*. February 10, 2007.

Lenton, Timothy M., Hermann Held, Elmar Kriegler, Jim W. Hall, Wolfgang Lucht, Stefan Rahmstorf, and Hans Joachim Schnellnhuber. 2008. "Tipping Elements in the Earth's Climate System." *Proceedings of the National Academy of Sciences*. Vol. 105, No. 6, February 12, 2008, pp. 1786–1793.

Lindsay, R.W., J. Zhang, A. Schweiger, M. Steele, and H. Stern. 2009. "Arctic Sea Ice Retreat in 2007 Follows Thinning Trend." *Journal of Climate*. Vol. 22, No. 1, January 2009, pp. 165–176.

Lipp, Erin K., Anwar Huq, and Rita R. Colwell. 2002. "Effects of Global Climate on Infectious Disease: The Cholera Model." *Clinical Microbiology Reviews*. Vol. 15, No. 4, October 2002, pp. 757–770.

Loescher, Gil. 1992. "Refugee Movements and International Security." Adelphi Papers No. 26, Summer 1992.

Markus, Thorsten, Julienne C. Stroeve, and Jeffrey Miller. 2009. "Recent Changes in Arctic Sea Ice Melt Onset, Freezeup, and Melt Season Length." *Journal of Geophysical Research*. Vol. 114, C12024, doi:10.1029/2009JC005436.

Martin, Adrian. 2005. "Environmental Conflict between Refugee and Host Communities." *Journal of Peace Research*. Vol. 42, No. 3, May 2005, pp. 329–346.

McMichael, A.J., D.H. Campbell-Lendrum, C.F. Corvalan, K.L. Ebi, A.K. Githenko, J.D. Scheraga, and A. Woodward, eds. 2003. *Climate Change and Human Health: Risks and Responses*. Geneva: World Health Organization.

Melloul, A., and M. Collin. 2006. "Hydrogeological Changes in Coastal Aquifers due to Sea Level Rise." *Ocean & Coastal Management*. Vol. 49, Nos. 5–6, pp. 281–297.

Moreaux, M. and A. Reynaud. 2001. "Optimal Management of a Coastal Aquifer under Saline Intrusion." First International Conference on Saltwater Intrusion and Coastal Aquifers—Monitoring, Modeling, and Management. Essaouira, Morocco, April 23–25, 2001. www.olemiss.edu/sciencenet/saltnet/swica1/moreaux-reynaud-exabs.pdf

National Intelligence Council. 2000. *The Global Infectious Disease Threat and Its Implications for the United States*. NIE99–17D, January 2000, 60 pp.

National Intelligence Council. 2008. *Strategic Implications of Global Health*. ICA 2008–10D, December 2008, 54 pp.

National Research Council. 2001. *Under the Weather: Climate, Ecosystems, and Infectious Disease*. Washington: National Academy Press.

National Research Council. 2007. *Polar Icebreakers in a Changing World: An Assessment of U.S. Needs*. Washington: National Academies Press, 122 pp.

National Research Council. 2010. *Advancing the Science of Climate Change*. Washington: National Academies Press, 503 pp.

Nicholls, R. J., S. Hanson, C. Herweijer, N. Patmore, S. Hallegatte, J. Corfee-Morlot, J. Château, and R. Muir-Wood. 2008. *Ranking Port Cities with High Exposure and Vulnerability to Climate Extremes*. Exposure Estimates. Environment Working Papers No. 1. Paris: OECD.

Nikolayevskiy, Vladyslav, Krishna Gopaul, Yanina Balabanova, Timothy Brown, Ivan Fedorin, and Francis Drobniewski. 2006. "Differentiating of Tuberculosis Strains in a Population with Mainly Beijing-family Strains." *Emerging Infectious Diseases*. Vol. 12, No. 9, September 2006, pp. 1406–1413.

Norwegian Refugee Council. 2008. *Future Floods of Refugees: A Comment on Climate Change, Conflict, and Forced Migration*. Oslo: Norwegian Refugee Council, 42 pp.

Overpeck, Jonathan T., and Jeremy L. Weiss. 2009. "Projections of Future Sea Level Becoming More Dire." *Proceedings of the National Academy of Sciences*. Vol. 106, No. 51, December 22, 2009, pp. 21461–21462.

Oxford, J. S., A. Sefton, R. Jackson, W. Innes, R. S. Daniels, and N.P.A.S. Johnson. 2002. "World War I May Have Allowed the Emergence of 'Spanish' Influenza." *The Lancet: Infectious Diseases*. Vol. 2, February 2002, p. 113.

Perovich, Donald, and Jacqueline A. Richter-Menge. 2009. "Loss of Sea Ice in the Arctic." *Annual Review of Marine Science*. Vol. 1, pp. 417–441.

Piarroux, Renaud, Robert Barrais, Benoît Faucher, Rachel Haus, Martine Piarroux, Jean Gaudart, Roc Magloire, and Didier Raoult. 2011. "Understanding the Cholera Epidemic, Haiti." *Emerging Infectious Diseases*. Vol. 17, No. 7, July 2011, pp. 1161–1167.

PortNews. 2007. "Russia's First Arctic Shuttle Tanker Named 'Vasily Dinkov'." PortNews Information Agency, December 20, 2007.

Posen, Barry R. 2004. "Military Responses to Refugee Disasters." In *The Use of Force: Military Power and International Politics, 6th edition*. Robert J. Art and Kenneth N. Waltz, eds. Lanham, MD: Rowman & Littlefield Publishers.

Price-Smith, Andrew T. 2002. *The Health of Nations: Infectious Disease, Environmental Change, and Their Effects on National Security and Development*. Cambridge, MA: MIT Press.

(Reuters) Majumdar, Bappa. 2007. "Border Fence Draws Barbs from Indian Farmers." Reuters. April 30, 2007. As found at http://www.reuters.com/article/latest Crisis/idUSDEL206634.

Reuveny, Rafael. 2008. "Ecomigration and Violent Conflict: Case studies and Public Policy Implications." *Human Ecology*. Vol. 36, No. 1, February 2008, pp. 1–13.

Rezza, G., L. Nicoletti, R. Angelini, R. Romi, A. Finarelli, M. Panning, P. Cordioli, C. Fortuna, S. Boros, F. Magurano. 2007. "Infection with Chikungunya Virus in Italy: An Outbreak in a Temperate Region." *The Lancet.* Vol. 370, No. 9602, December 1, 2007, pp. 1840–1846.

Robins, Nick, and Charlie Pye-Smith. 1997. "The Ecology of Violence." *New Scientist.* No. 2072, March 8, 1997.

Sachs, Jeffrey D. 2007. "Climate Change Refugees." *Scientific American.* Vol. 296, No. 6, June 2007.

Simms, Andrew. 2005. *Africa—Up in Smoke?* The Second Report from the Working Group on Climate Change and Development. London: New Economics Foundation.

Slack, Alyson. 2003. "Separatism in Mindanao, Philippines." ICE Case Study No. 118, May 2003. http://www1.american.edu/TED/ice/mindanao.htm

Steele, Michael, Wendy Ermold, and Jinlun Zhang. 2008. "Arctic Ocean Surface Warming Trends over the Past 100 Years." *Geophysical Research Letters.* Vol. 35, L02614, doi:10.1029/2007GL031651.

Stenseth, Nils Chr. et al. 2006. "Plague Dynamics are Driven by Climate Variation." *Proceedings of the National Academy of Sciences.* Vol. 103, No. 35, August 29, 2006, pp. 13110–13115.

Stern, Nicholas. 2007. *The Economics of Climate Change: The Stern Review.* New York: Cambridge University Press.

Stroeve, J., M. Serreze, S. Drobot, S. Gearheard, M. Holland, J. Maslanik, W. Meier, and T. Scambos. 2008. "Arctic Sea Ice Extent Plummets in 2007." *EOS, Transactions American Geophysical Union.* Vol. 89, No. 2, January 8, 2008, pp. 13–20.

Timmerman, A., J. Oberhuber, A. Bacher, M. Esch, M. Latif, and E. Roeckner. 1999. "Increased El Niño Frequency in a Climate Model Forced by Future Greenhouse Warming." *Nature.* Vol. 389, No. 6729, April 22, 1999, pp. 694–696.

United States Arctic Research Commission (USARC). 2002. "The Arctic Ocean and Climate Change: A Scenario for the U.S. Navy." Special Publication No. 02–1, Arlington, VA.

Vermeer, Martin, and Stefan Rahmstorf. 2009. "Global Sea Level Linked to Global Temperature." *Proceedings of the National Academy of Sciences.* Vol. 106, No. 51, December 22, 2009, pp. 21527–21532.

Wang, Muyin, and James E. Overland. 2009. "A Sea Ice Free Summer Arctic within 30 years?" *Geophysical Research Letters.* Vol. 36, L07502, doi: 10.1029/2009GL037820.

Watson, Robert T., and Anthony J. McMichael. 2001. "Global Climate Change—The Latest Assessment: Does Global Warming Warrant a Health Warning?" *Global Change & Human Health.* Vol. 3, No. 1, pp. 64–75.

WHO, World Health Organization. 2000. "El Niño and its Health Impact." Fact Sheet No. 192, revised March 2000.

WHO. 2002. *Scaling up the Response to Infectious Diseases: A Way out of Poverty.* Report on Infectious Diseases, 2002. Geneva: WHO.

WHO. 2007a. *Communicable Disease Risk Assessment and Interventions. Cyclone Sidr Disaster: Bangladesh.* Geneva: WHO, November 2007.

CHAPTER 5

Collateral Damage

Defense and the environment is not an either/or proposition. To choose be-
tween them is impossible in this real world of serious defense threats and
genuine environmental concerns.
    —U.S. Secretary of Defense Dick Cheney, 1990

Introduction

Natural resources and the ambient environment are not only causes of conflict and insecurity; they can bear the brunt of that same insecurity. Collateral environmental damage occurs when the natural environment is damaged
during the conduct of war or in preparation for war. This damage is usually
unanticipated and unintentional, but it can range from negligible to catastrophic in scale.

The most fundamental element that makes a state sovereign in the modern
era is the inviolability of its borders. Since territorial integrity is the primary
definition of a sovereign state, the most primary duty of a state in defending its
national security is to develop the ability to counter any threat, and most nations will prioritize defense operations well above environmental protection.
Rarely will a state put environmental protection above military protection
(e.g., Costa Rica is an exception since it relies heavily on ecotourism for
national revenue but has no standing military forces). Consequently, when
these two values clash, most often a decision over resource allocation, environmental or human health, or funding will be resolved in favor of military
security. Put another way, war trumps ecology.

The natural environment has always suffered during war, but two factors
now make environmental damage from armed conflict a particular concern.

First, advancements in the lethality of military technology, particularly the increasing destructiveness of modern weaponry, can make armed conflict more environmentally devastating than ever before. Low-tech weapons such as knives, bows and arrows, and muskets have limited environmental impact. High-tech and more indiscriminate weapons such as mustard gas and other chemical agents, napalm, defoliants, and biological weapons have a much larger environmental footprint, and as such, their use has been internationally prohibited. As the largest and most indiscriminate weapon, the use of a nuclear bomb could have a global ecological impact.

Second, in the wake of unprecedented environmental degradation from peacetime activities such as economic development, the public has become increasingly aware of environmental issues and will probably find extreme environmental damage during war unacceptable, even if collaterally incurred. As global populations grow, the existing resource base becomes that much more critical to provide peacetime civilian resources, and the outcry over its damage would probably be greater.

Any discussion of collateral damage to the environment during conflict raises particular ethical questions for all nations, including those involved in the conflict and those that remain bystanders. How should the environment be treated in wartime? Is the benefit of the military objective gained worth the cost of the ecological damage done while gaining it? And should we protect the environment for our sake or for its own sake?

Negative Ecological Effects of War and Conflict

War and other military activities can have devastating effects on the natural environment, damaging land and soil, waterways, flora and fauna, and human health. Collateral damage from war compromises land integrity by eroding and compacting soil, destroying agricultural productivity, contributing to loss of forest productivity through weapons damage, and presenting a continuing danger to civilians from landmines and unexploded ordnance. Water resources are also degraded as a result of warfare, as they can be contaminated both at the surface and underground. Wildlife suffers directly through destruction of habitat, and society suffers indirectly through negative public health impacts, exposure to pollution, and loss of critical infrastructure like electricity and running water. Gary Machlis and Thor Hanson have coined the term **warfare ecology** to refer to the environmental impacts of preparation for war, war itself, and postwar activities. The concept of warfare ecology is designed "to advance ecological science; inform policy; and reduce, mitigate, or prevent the environmental consequences of warfare" (Machlis & Hanson 2008, 730).

Ecosystem services such as arable land and fresh water are needed for reconstruction of the economy and survival of the civilian population. Degradation of these services due to conflict can provide another layer of instability in war-ravaged areas, and military doctrines that call for peace ops and stability as key missions could mean that armed forces will take on an environmental protection role. Depending on the type of weapons used, recovery from a conflict could take years or decades, or the ecosystem may never recover. Different regional ecosystems are more or less robust, and each has its specific ecological weakness. The weapons used in a particular area may cause little damage in that area, but the same weapons may be more destructive when used in another area. Ecological damage from warfare can be difficult to assess properly, since the full effect of the damage may not be apparent for many years. Even when full damage can be known, it is very often impossible to know whose weapons have caused it.

In addition, "scorched earth" policies, or the intentional destruction of environmental resources during conflict, have been commonplace since the beginning of warfare. The greater the environmental destruction, the smaller the chance that the defeated population would be able to challenge the victors. In some cases, defeated territories have been destroyed completely and rendered unfit for future habitation, as the ancient Romans did to the city of Carthage. In other cases, the environmental damage has been less obvious. The 20th century contains some familiar examples of environmental destruction during war, also known as "ecocide," or the killing of the earth.

Examples of Environmental Collateral Damage

Agent Orange in Vietnam

One of the most significant examples of environmental destruction during war is the United States' use of defoliants and herbicides during the Vietnam War. From 1962 until 1971, the U.S. Air Force sprayed approximately 18 million gallons of Agent Orange and other dioxin-contaminated herbicides on the jungles of Vietnam during Operation Ranch Hand. Some two million hectares were sprayed at least once, and approximately half a million hectares were sprayed more than once (Westing 1971).

Operation Ranch Hand was designed to deprive the North Vietnamese of tree and jungle cover, and to deplete the agricultural base of their territory. These defoliants were successful in denuding the trees, but this massive defoliation caused erosion, flooding, and other ecological damage across the country. Agent Orange contained 2,4,5-T, a known teratogenic compound which was banned from use within the United States in 1970 (Stellman et al. 2003, 681). It also contained dioxin, long been known to be poisonous. Soil and sediment analysis from recent scientific studies across Vietnam have found that there are still easily detectable levels of herbicide residue, more than 30 years after the war's end. Some hugely contaminated hot spots contain dioxin and furan levels up to 20 times higher than the probable effect level in sediment, and up to 46 times higher in soil (Mai et al. 2007). In addition to long-lasting negative ecological effects, Agent Orange and the other herbicides used have been suspected of contributing to cancer and other health problems that veterans began experiencing after the war.

Oil Fires in Operation Desert Storm

Probably the most well-known and egregious example of environmental damage in modern armed conflict occurred during the 1991 Gulf War. As coalition air strikes began, Saddam Hussein's army set fire to more than 650 Kuwaiti oil wells, which burned for 10 months and consumed approximately 1.25 million tons of oil. Whether he did this to smog the skies and confuse air strikes or to deprive the Kuwaiti government of the oil and its attendant revenue is unclear. However, the environmental effect was significant: these fires released 100,000 tons of soot and 800,000 tons of CO_2 into the lower atmosphere (Horgan 1991, as found in Seacor 1994, 492) and the smoke plumes from these fires could be seen from space. More long-lasting environmental damage was caused by the released oil that was not combusted.

Figure 5.1 Aerial View of Kuwaiti Oil Fires

(National Science Foundation)

A considerable portion seeped into the ground and pooled in lakes, contaminating some 40 million tons of soil (Omar et al. 2000, 320).

In addition to setting the wells on fire, the Iraqi army caused further environmental damage as it retreated. The army damaged storage tanks and oil tankers, and opened oil taps at Mina Al Ahmadi and other coastal loading stations, discharging 2–4 million barrels (some estimates go as high as 10 million barrels; Adbulraheem 2000, 341) of crude oil into the Persian Gulf. This caused an oil slick covering 400 kilometers of coastline (Majeed 2004). Between the oil fires and the Gulf spill, Saddam Hussein may have been guilty of trying to commit **ecocide**, or killing of the earth, thereby rendering the territory in question *uninhabitable* as a political tactic, in effect saying to the Kuwaitis and the rest of the world that if he couldn't have Kuwait and its resources, no one could. In 1996, a United Nations special compensation fund awarded Kuwait $41.8 billion as war reparations for the environmental destruction caused by Saddam Hussein's invasion. To date, Iraq has paid approximately $15 billion.

Depleted Uranium Weapons

Depleted uranium (DU) has been used to make heavy, armor-piercing shells for use in war. Depleted uranium is the material left over when the fissile isotope U^{235} is removed from natural uranium for fission purposes. The resulting material is radioactive and heavier than lead, making it ideal for construction of tank-piercing shells. When fired, DU rounds not only break through armor plating, but also burn hot enough to produce uranium oxide vapor (Busby & Morgan 2005, 2). From a military standpoint, any weapon designed to halt an armored advance is very desirable and useful. Consequently, they have been used in Operation Desert Storm in 1991, in Bosnia and Kosovo in the late 1990s, and again in Iraq in 2003. It is unknown if U.S. and NATO forces used DU weapons in Libya in 2011.

The primary concerns surrounding depleted uranium are human health–related due to its longevity in the environment. However, there has been very little scientific work done on the long-term ecological effects of DU weapons. They vaporize on impact, emitting alpha particles and leaving behind radioactive residue; if undetonated, they can contaminate groundwater. The U.K. Royal Society's assessment of DU weapons indicated that the environmental contamination is limited to the immediate area of use, and other than monitoring groundwater supplies, the general population should face little risk (Royal Society 2002). Chris Busby and Saoirse Morgan point out, however, that if uranium aerosols disperse from the battlefield where they are used into an area with noncombatants, the use of DU weapons could then become a matter for international legal concern, since their effects cannot be limited to combatants only.

Ecological Effects of Nuclear War

Perhaps the most catastrophic of conflicts would be a nuclear war. In addition to the horrifying death toll and rampant physical destruction it would bring about, the explosion of nuclear weapons would have massive global ecological effects. Although the likelihood of a nuclear war between the United States and Russia has decreased significantly since the dissolution of the Soviet Union, seven other nations around the world currently have nuclear weapons, and more nations may be developing them. Even a relatively limited, regional nuclear exchange could produce enough soot and smoke to cripple global agriculture and lead to massive starvation.

In 2008, atmospheric scientists Owen Toon, Alan Robock, and Richard Turco constructed a climate model to estimate what the ecological effects would be from a regional nuclear war involving 100 15-kiloton weapons detonated between India and Pakistan. Independent of the estimated 20 million dead, they posited that approximately 5 teragrams (Tg, or 5 million metric tons) of soot and smoke from burning cities would enter the immediate atmosphere. Within five days, the smoke would cover most of South Asia, the Middle East, and eastern Africa. Within nine days, it would extend around the globe, and within approximately one and a half months, it would have blocked more than 10 percent of incoming sunlight everywhere on earth.

Similar to emissions from volcanic eruptions, this soot and smoke would increase the albedo (reflectivity) of the atmosphere, so that less incoming sunlight would reach the earth's surface. The 1815 eruption of Mount Tambora in Indonesia reduced global average temperature by 0.5°C, and the 1991 eruption of Mount Pinatubo in the Philippines did the same by 0.4°C. In the hypothetical case, 5 Tg of soot and smoke could depress global average temperatures by 1.25°C, larger than anything felt in the last 1,000 years. Soot and smoke also affect the destruction of stratospheric ozone levels (McCormick et al. 1995).

Previous studies of **nuclear winter** in the 1980s concluded that the cooling effects of the fallout from a nuclear war would be felt for only a few years. Now, due to the availability of better models developed in part for climate change analysis, recent studies show the cooling effect persisting for approximately a decade. Such cooling would depress global agricultural production by reducing the amount of sunlight available to plants for photosynthesis, by reducing temperatures and shortening growing seasons, and by altering precipitation patterns. However, the researchers insistently point out that there have been no studies done on which areas would be affected and by how much. Given that global food prices are already increasing (discussed in Chapter 3), a global supply-induced crop shortage from production failures due to soot and smoke could bring the international agricultural trade to a halt. Thus, a regional nuclear war would have environmental effects on people unrelated to the conflict, in countries on the other side of the world.

Preparation for War

Collateral damage to the environment occurs not only during war, but also during training for war. Building and testing of weapons systems, military personnel training and preparation, and routine peacetime military activities can all have huge impacts on the environment. These impacts usually occur on a local scale, but are often long-lasting and can be irreversible. Several well-known examples illustrate this type of collateral damage.

Weapons Testing and Manufacturing

The production and testing of nuclear weapons, the bedrock of international security theory during the Cold War, left an enormous environmental footprint. From 1946 to 1958, the U.S. Navy tested nuclear weapons of various sizes and configurations in the Pacific island chain of the Marshall Islands. Bikini Atoll was the site of the largest test, named Castle Bravo, in 1954. Due to larger-than-expected fallout and a major wind shift, the two inhabited atolls of Rongerik and Rongelap were exposed to radioactivity, as was a Japanese fishing vessel in the area, the Daigu Fukuryu Maru. In addition to poisoning the Marshallese islanders and Japanese crew with fallout, coral reefs in the area were damaged and persistent radioactive nuclides were found in the waters surrounding the atoll for several miles. Since these tests, the U.S. government has paid out more than $774 million to the governments of Japan and the Marshall Islands as compensation for the damages (Brookings 1998).

Before nuclear weapons can be tested, they must be created. The U.S. Department of Energy nuclear weapons development site at Hanford, WA, has long been a matter of concern to environmentalists and local residents (Gerber 1992; see also Dycus 1996). The site was established in 1943 as part of the Manhattan Project to fabricate plutonium for American atomic bombs. According to the Washington State Department of Health, releases of radioactive isotopes such as Iodine-131, Strontium-90, and Plutonium-238 have contaminated the Columbia River, as well as the air, soil, and groundwater surrounding the nearby towns of Hanford, Richland, and White Bluffs. The U.S. Environmental Protection Agency listed Hanford as a Superfund site in 1989, but plans for its cleanup have been postponed repeatedly for technological and budgetary reasons. Now, the DOE is proposing to build a unique radioactive waste treatment plant which will convert the 53 million gallons of highly toxic waste at the site into glass logs, a process called vitrification, for long-term storage at an estimated cost of $74 billion (*The Economist* 2011).

Similar contamination problems have been reported at Rocky Flats, CO, Oak Ridge, TN, and other sites involved in the U.S. nuclear weapons production chain.

Just as the United States is not the only country with nuclear weapons, it is also not the only country to suffer from nuclear contamination as a result of building and testing them. In 1954, the Soviet government established a nuclear test site on Novaya Zemlya, an island chain in the Barents Sea, and detonated weapons above ground, underground, and under water, including a 58 megaton airburst, the largest nuclear weapon ever exploded. Fallout rained down as far as Norway, 900 kilometers away. While all nuclear countries have conducted nuclear tests, the Soviet Union alone conducted 132 tests at Novaya Zemlya between 1955 and 1990 (McVicker 1998), and 456 tests at the Semipalatinsk site in Kazakhstan between 1946 and 1991 (Kassenova 2009; see also Sidel 2000). During the Cold War, information regarding nuclear tests and weapons manufacturing and deployment capabilities was generally classified and not released to the public. Even after the end of the Cold War, nuclear information is considered sensitive (see the case of Alexander Nikitin, the former Soviet nuclear inspector profiled in Part II of this volume, who was charged with treason for cooperating with a Norwegian environmental group).

Live-Fire Training and Surveillance

Weapons do not have to be used in war to cause environmental damage. The island of Vieques, off the coast of Puerto Rico, was used as a live-fire training range by the U.S. Navy for more than 60 years. Local residents claimed that the island became contaminated with lead and other heavy metals, chemical explosives, and unexploded ordnance, and protested the Navy's presence there. In May 2001, the Vice Chief of Naval Operations ADM William Fallon cited the Endangered Species Act and the Migratory Bird Treaty Act as two of the most difficult obstacles to training, and petitioned the House Committee on Government Reform to keep Vieques open. However, by May 2003, the Navy agreed to cease its use of Vieques and withdraw from the territory. The Navy has since set aside $200 million for environmental cleanup, which began in 2005; as of 2008, nearly 15,000 live munitions have been removed from approximately 775 acres of land, and in 2010, a luxury W Hotel opened up on the island, indicating the local government's desire to boost tourism.

With Vieques no longer in use, the Navy maintains a live-fire range on Farallon de Medinilla, an uninhabited island in the Northern Marianas. Defense advocates say that the military needs Farallon de Medinilla, since it is the only range that provides sufficient room for thorough training for forward-deployed forces, without which military readiness will suffer. Environmental groups, however, sought a court injunction to prevent the Navy from using the island, arguing that it is a major nesting ground for several endangered species of birds on the Pacific Flyway. In 2002, a district court for the District of Columbia argued that the Navy's activities on Farallon de Medinilla were in violation of the Migratory Bird Treaty of 1918.

Other peacetime military operations also have environmental ramifications. For example, the U.S. Navy's low- and mid-frequency active sonar is an important part of American sea-based defense, intended to detect enemy submarines. However, the high-intensity sonar has been linked to mass strandings of whales and other cetaceans in oceanic waters. Cetaceans such as dolphins, porpoises, and whales use underwater sound waves for navigation and communication, and they have been known to beach themselves after exposure to sonar. A recent study by marine scientists at the Woods Hole Oceanographic Institute revealed that the feeding, mating, and migratory behavior of whales can be disrupted at 140 decibels (Tyack et al. 2011), well below the output of many modern sonar arrays designed to detect near-silent diesel-electric submarines.

In 2008, the U.S. Supreme Court overturned a lower California court decision requiring the Navy to desist from using mid-frequency active sonar. The Court ruled that submarine training was more important than protecting cetaceans, and that the Court would defer to the Navy's judgment as to when and how best to conduct its sonar training, though the Navy is required to allocate at least $14.75 million through FY 2011 for marine mammal protection.

Military-Controlled Areas as Habitat

Not all military activities and facilities are harmful to the natural environment. Human development is constantly encroaching on wildlife habitat, and large undisturbed tracts of land such as military bases can serve as a refuge for species of all kinds. Marine Corps Base Camp Pendleton, just north of San Diego, CA, is home to the training ground of the First Marine Division. Due to the high value of land in southern California, the approximately 125,000 acres on the base is home to a number of indigenous and endangered species that have been crowded out of other land. The U.S. Marine Corps has an Integrated Natural Resource Management Plan in place to manage and conserve this wildlife while still maintaining military training.

In an unusually positive example of war's effect on the environment, an area that was formerly a war zone has now become one of the most important conservation sites in the world. The 1953 Armistice that brought the war between the Republic of Korea (South Korea) and the Democratic People's

Figure 5.2 Korean Demilitarized Zone

(Department of Defense)

Republic of Korea (North Korea) to a halt preserved a demilitarized zone, or DMZ, four kilometers wide between the two countries as a sort of no-man's-land. As a result of the area being completely uninhabited for almost 60 years, its 390 square miles have become a home for more than 1,000 species, several of which are not found anywhere else in the world. The South Korean government is now making plans to turn the DMZ and the adjacent low population area into a formal wildlife refuge, but this will not happen easily. A formal agreement will have to be reached with the unpredictable North Korean regime and more than 1 million land mines will need to be cleared before the area can be opened up for tourists.

Legal Status of the Environment during War

The conduct of war and conflict is generally governed by "rules of war" treaties such as the 1907 Hague Convention and the four 1949 Geneva Conventions, as well as arms control agreements and treaties that limit certain types of weapons (e.g., 1993 Chemical Weapons Convention) or prohibit their use in certain places (e.g., 1959 Antarctic Treaty). Limitations on the entry into war and the course of its conduct derive from what is known as Just War Theory, which governs the types of conduct that are acceptable from belligerents in a war. Restrictions that are not specifically laid out in a treaty or a convention are said to be contained in customary international law, wherein a nation will abide by guidelines out of a sense of legal obligation.

The terms and provisions contained in these treaties encompass two basic philosophical and legal principles. The principle of **proportionality** indicates that the means of war must be appropriate to the ends. Put another way, combatants can use only the minimum amount of force that is needed to attain the objective. Disproportionate use of force can include indiscriminate weapons such as landmines. What constitutes proportionality in war is decided with regard to both customary international law and current military doctrine. The principle of **discrimination** means that all targets, whether human (military personnel) or structural (bridges or airfields), must have military or strategic value. Combatants cannot target civilians, and reprisals against civilian resources are prohibited. This is a relative principle rather than an absolute principle; in other words, it is acceptable to maximize protection for noncombatants and minimize collateral damage if in pursuit of a legitimate military target.

There are conventions and protocols that protect specific groups or classes of people from indiscriminate harm during war, such as noncombatants, women and children, soldiers who are wounded or who have surrendered, and medical and religious personnel. However, there is no specific obligation to protect the natural environment during a conflict. Rather, protection of the environment falls under the realm of customary international law (ICRC 2005, 191). Principle VI of the Nuremburg Code includes in its definition of war crimes "violations of the laws or customs of war which include, but are not limited to . . . devastation not justified by military necessity."

There are several sources of customary international law that address the protection of resources during war (see the boxed text), but only two international treaties specifically address the wartime legal status of the environment.

Environmental Modification Convention

The 1977 Convention on the Prohibition of Military or Any Other Hostile Use of Environmental Modification Techniques (ENMOD) entered into force in 1980. The need for an environmental modification treaty was prompted by the use of defoliants and weather modification techniques such as rain cloud seeding during the Vietnam War. While these tactics may have conferred short-term military advantage to the side deploying them, they often resulted in persistent damage to the local environment.

ENMOD prohibits "military or any other hostile use of environmental modification techniques having widespread, long-lasting [lasting a number of months], or severe effects as the means of destruction, damage, or injury to any other State Party." ENMOD goes on to define "environmental modification techniques" as "any technique for changing—through the deliberate manipulation of natural processes—the dynamics, composition, or structure of the Earth, including its biota, lithosphere, hydrosphere and atmosphere, or of outer space."

While on its face ENMOD seems to be a comprehensive prohibition against collateral environmental damage, it has some significant loopholes. First, it only applies to the use of the environment as a weapon, that is, natural forces such as storms or drought directed against the enemy. It does not address the environmental damage arising from the use of conventional weapons. Second, its provisions are only applicable between signatories; a nation can use these techniques against a nonsignatory or against its own people. Finally, it only prohibits hostile use of these techniques. Presumably, nonhostile environmental modification is permitted, and this question has been raised in conjunction with new inquiries into the development and deployment of geo-engineering technologies.

The full text of the Environmental Modification Convention appears in Part Three of this volume, Key Documents. The United States has ratified this convention, though some critics have argued that the terms of the ENMOD do not go far enough to prevent environmental damage related to war (see Goldblat 1975).

Protocol I to the Geneva Convention

The 1977 Protocol Additional to the Geneva Conventions of 12 August 1949, and Relating to the Protection of Victims of International Armed Conflicts also addresses the protection of the environment during war, and employs language that is similar to ENMOD. Protocol I, Article 54 addresses the protection of objects specific to the survival of the civilian population. Starvation of civilians is prohibited, as is attacking or destroying food stocks, agricultural areas, and drinking water supplies. This article recognizes, under just war theory, that the civilians are nonbelligerents in the conflict and as such, the food and water necessary for their survival are deserving of the same protections afforded to their own persons.

Article 55 likewise prohibits "methods or means of warfare which are intended or may be expected to cause widespread, long-term, and severe damage to the natural environment." Protocol I uses the same terms as ENMOD, but in this case, a long-term time frame means decades, not merely one season. In addition, attacks against the environment for reprisal purposes, such as the previously discussed oil fires after the 1991 Gulf War, are explicitly prohibited.

The key concept behind both ENMOD and Protocol I is that of proportionality. As previously mentioned, this means that the damage to the environment from a weapons attack must not outweigh the military benefit gained by the attack. While current U.S. military doctrine and rules of engagement call for explicit compliance with the laws of war, it is difficult for the military to develop operational guidelines that balance military necessity with environmental protection, though these guidelines are reviewed periodically. Consequently, the determination of proportionality is extremely subjective, and at the time of the attack, relies on the judgment of the military commander in the field. Violations of these laws can be considered war crimes. As per the Nuremberg trials, not even military necessity is sufficient reason for ignoring the laws of war, not even the loss of the battle or the war itself. However, international laws of proportionality, environmental or otherwise, are still not always followed due to poor planning, bad intelligence, equipment failure, or outright neglect. The full text of Protocol I appears in Part Three. The United States has not ratified this Protocol.

Other International Agreements

Various other international treaties and agreements contain provisions that protect particular places on earth (or off earth) from warfare and conflict. The Antarctic Treaty of 1959 prohibits weapons deployment, nuclear explosions, or radioactive waste storage in Antarctica, which is to be used for peaceful purposes only. The 1968 Treaty of Tlatelolco prohibits nuclear weapons in all of Latin America and the Caribbean, the first treaty to protect a populated area; the 1985 Treaty of Rarotonga, the 1995 Treaty of Bangkok, the 1996 Treaty of Pelindaba, and the 2006 Treaty of Semipalatinsk prohibit nuclear weapons in Pacific Island States, Southeast Asia, Africa, and Central Asia, respectively. The 1967 Outer Space Treaty prohibits nuclear weapons, weapons testing, and military bases on the moon or any other celestial body.

Why attempt to outlaw war from some areas and not others? We might argue that the more the places on earth where war is prohibited, the better things will be, and it is true that none of the treaties mentioned above has been breached by any nation. However, we only have to look to the ultimate fate of the Covenant of the League of Nations to remember that most nations prize war as a method of defense, either of their borders, or their allies, or their national honor; they also prize war as a method of acquisition of land and resources. Consequently, international law is unlikely to prove to be a permanent safeguard against war's general destructiveness.

Is there something unique about the natural environment—among all the spoils of war—that should render it off limits for destruction? In 1997, a team of environmental economists led by Dr. Robert Costanza of the University of Maryland attempted to estimate the financial worth of the entire world's ecosystem services. Ecosystem services are those functions that a healthy environment provides: climate regulation, fresh water supply, nutrient cycling, pollination, food production, genetic biodiversity, recreation, and many others. Costanza and his team estimated that the natural world provided human societies all over the globe with an average of $33 trillion worth of services for free; many of these services are such that humans cannot reproduce them for themselves at any price. When we consider how critical most of these services are to human survival, their damage or decline is a threat not only to one army or even to one nation, but to the ability of the earth to support human life.

"Fifth Geneva Convention"

Legal scholars have disagreed on whether existing protections for the environment under international law and customary international law are sufficient during conflict, or whether a new and comprehensive "Convention on the Protection of the Environment in Time of Armed Conflict" is necessary to protect the environment during wartime, completely and without loopholes (Plant 1991, 184; note that this is only a proposed title, and there is no such convention currently in existence). There are both advantages and disadvantages to this.

Depending on its terms, a new convention could make it an explicit war crime to target the environment during conflict, or even to undertake a military action that might adversely impact the environment. Some argue that existing laws are not enough to protect the environment during war because operational logic on the battlefield always elevates military necessity over environmental protection and the judgment of the battle commander over legal constraints. The International Union for the Conservation of Nature has proposed a Draft Convention on the Prohibition of Hostile Military Activities in Protected Areas, but as of this date, it has not been officially adopted by any nation or government (Shambaugh et al. 2001, 19).

However, a new convention would be burdensome and contentious to negotiate among nations that have different environmental and security priorities. It might also be practically unenforceable, since an international court would give the "military necessity" argument high regard when deciding if a particular military action violated convention. Article 8(2)(b)(iv) of the charter of the International Criminal Court (the Rome Statute) does use the same language as Protocol I in defining war crimes related to the environment—"widespread, long-term, and severe damage to the natural environment"—so collateral environmental damage can already be classified as a war crime if severe enough. While no permanent agreement has yet been reached on how environmental damage during conflict might be prevented or mitigated, it is useful to know that awareness of the environmental effects of war has made its way into operational thinking, from military rules of engagement to UN treaties.

Future Issues

As weapons become more powerful, and as environmental damage that occurs during peacetime becomes more widespread, some questions will certainly arise about collateral damage to the environment during war.

First, is it appropriate to put collateral environmental damage on the list of war reparations? We may never be able to approximate war's true ecological cost due to the near-total lack of long-term environmental monitoring of warfare sites. Furthermore, determining "how much" the environment was damaged during war is problematic. Environmental economists know the myriad problems inherent in environmental valuation during peacetime—chief among them, the difficulty of measuring the nonmonetary worth of an ecosystem. Valuing economic damages to the environment as possible war reparations makes this task that much harder because how much of the damage was caused by the conflict and how much existed prior to the conflict may be unclear.

In addition, war can damage the ecosystems of entire regions, making substitutes for various ecosystem services difficult to find and creating synergistic effects between the environment, public health, and other parts of society. For example, the 1991 Kuwait oil fires resulted in air pollution, which in turn affected agriculture and public health. And while our legal system prefers to adjudicate all issues to closure as soon as possible after they occur, our current economic and scientific methods to measure damage are quite limited, and full and accurate damage estimates may take years to assess. In any case, it is very unlikely that sufficient funds would be available from a defeated nation to make postwar environmental reparations. Some scholars have proposed the creation of a stand-alone liability fund to pay for environmental damages caused by war regardless of culpability, though who would put money into such a fund prior to the outbreak of war is unclear.

Second, should wartime military activities be exempt from national or international environmental laws and statutes? The U.S. military believes they should, citing training and readiness concerns, and has already petitioned Congress to grant the services blanket exemptions from, among others, the Migratory Bird Treaty and the Marine Mammal Protection Act. On the other hand, environmental groups like the Natural Resources Defense Council and Earthjustice argue that existing laws do not impede military training, and that there are plenty of places to train and fight that are not in ecologically sensitive areas. Additional questions about environmental laws remain, such as whether peacetime environmental treaties like the UN Convention on the Law of the Sea or a belligerent nation's domestic environmental laws still apply during wartime (Plant 1991, 14; see also Dycus 1996).

Third, how should nations expect nonstate actors to behave with respect to matters of international environmental security? Traditionally, since nations are the ones that have prepared for and waged war, they have placed national security over all other national values: economic growth, human happiness, civil liberties, and ecological health. Now, in the age of nonstate warfare, groups that wage nontraditional war place their own survival or the spread of their ideologies over these same values. Current international law rests on the mutual cooperation of sovereign states; unfortunately, therein lies one of the problems with using traditional legal instruments to ensure protection of the environment during wartime. Machlis & Hanson's wartime ecology recommendations apply—as per their own admission—to traditional states with organized armed forces, and are less relevant to guerilla groups, terrorists, and rogue states (734). However, combatants of those types are exactly where the modern thrust of nontraditional war is coming from. Guerilla groups and terrorists do not have the international standing necessary to sign a treaty, nor do they have privileges in the international community to lose if they risk breaking one. Consequently, they have little to no incentive to abide by any sort of legal instrument protecting the environment during war.

Ethical Consideration toward the Environment

Given these various issues, are international legal instruments enough to protect the environment during wartime? After all, there are laws, treaties, accords, and resolutions protecting women and children, medical and diplomatic personnel, schools, hospitals, religious structures, and cultural monuments, and prohibiting acts such as torture and genocide. Yet we only have to examine current world affairs to know that monuments are destroyed by fundamentalist groups (Bamiyan, Afghanistan); women and children are raped and tortured by soldiers and sometimes peacekeepers (DRC); terrorists hide weapons in mosques and other forbidden buildings (Iraq); and medical personnel, food aid workers, and civilians are routinely fired upon (Somalia, Libya). If we cannot care for persons and things of significance to persons, how can we protect an ecosystem, whose existence is no less important than that of a hospital or church, yet seems so removed from us and our security concerns?

The idea that there are laws of war at all arises from the recognition that humans embrace some sort of ethical behavior toward each other and confer a certain level of moral worth even on their enemies. This then informs the behavior of combatants toward each other and toward noncombatant civilians. Equivalent moral worth is not conferred upon nature, however. Rather, Judeo-Christian ethics place significant emphasis on humankind's superiority over nature. This viewpoint makes abuses of the environment ethically justifiable, or at least not ethically prohibited. When our own security or that of our nation is at stake, the natural environment takes even lower precedence in our ethical calculus.

The philosophical field of environmental ethics has much to add to this debate. If humans as individuals are the referent of security and not states, then suddenly ecological health and the preservation of environmental services carry much greater weight in warfare and security decision making. Actions that can have a clear military benefit, such as bombing an oil refinery that is producing fuel for the enemy, suddenly become less of a no-brainer when the environmental damage is totted up and weighed in comparison. Ecologist Aldo Leopold articulated an environmental value known as the **land ethic**—that humankind is part of a larger ecosystem, and that "a thing is right when it tends to preserve the integrity, stability, and beauty of the biotic community. It is wrong when it tends otherwise." By this definition of right and wrong, all warfare is wrong, since there is no type of warfare that leaves the land better off after the conflict than before. Pacifists have argued this point of view for centuries, often pointing out that humans and the ecosystem suffer in tandem.

What makes an action good or bad? We think that maintaining security and/or spreading our values is good, but what if achieving this sort of security entails reaching a good end (peace) by a bad means (environmental destruction)? If we face an ethical conundrum in weighing one life against another, as in a preemptive attack that may kill a dozen fighters in an attempt to save hundreds of civilians, we can at least measure the relative worth of these two actions in the common currency of human lives. It becomes much harder to compare the worth of civilians' lives against that of a tropical forest, a desert ecosystem, or a mighty river. That humans consistently choose their own lives over nonhuman life speaks of the difficulty in embracing the land ethic when confronted with contradictory, seemingly more important values.

How could we then persuade military or combatant commanders to place the value of environmental protection and preservation above that of military necessity? On the face of it, this would seem to require a higher value for nature overall within the warring societies. Even the laws that do protect the environment do so because of its value to human society, not because of its intrinsic value. That sort of "deep ecology" philosophy, wherein the environment is valued just because it exists and not because it holds any benefit for humans, may be too large a philosophical shift for warring societies to embrace, but as the mutual interrelationship between security and environmental health becomes clearer, such a revised view of the importance of the environment may render any sort of collateral damage during war unacceptable.

Sources of International Obligations Concerning Protection of the Environment in Times of Armed Conflict

- General principles of law and customary international law
- International conventions
- Hague Convention (IV) respecting the Laws and Customs of War on Land, of 1907 (H.IV), and Regulations Respecting the Laws and Customs of War on Land (H.IV.R)
- Hague Convention (VIII) relative to the Laying of Automatic Submarine Contact Mines, of 1907 (H. VIII)
- Geneva Convention relative to the Protection of Civilian Persons in Time of War, of 1949 (G.C.IV)
- Hague Convention for the Protection of Cultural Property in the Event of Armed Conflict, of 1954 (H.CP)
- Convention on the Prohibition of Military or any Other Hostile Use of Environmental Modification Techniques, of 1976 (ENMOD)
- Protocol additional to the Geneva Conventions of 12 August 1949 and Relating to the Protection of Victims of International Armed Conflicts (Protocol I), of 1977 (G.P.I)
- Protocol additional to the Geneva Conventions of 12 August 1949 and relating to the Protection of Victims of Non-International Armed Conflicts (Protocol II), of 1977 (G.P.II)
- (United Nations) Convention on Prohibitions or Restrictions on the Use of Certain Conventional Weapons Which May be Deemed to be Excessively Injurious or to Have Indiscriminate Effects, of 1980 (CW), with:

  - Protocol on Prohibitions or Restrictions on the Use of Mines, Booby-traps and Other Devices (CW.P.II)
  - Protocol on Prohibitions or Restrictions on the Use of Incendiary Weapons (CW.P.III)

Source: Guidelines for Military Manuals and Instructions on the Protection of the Environment in Times of Armed Conflict. 30–04–1996 Article, International Review of the Red Cross, No. 311. Annex. Available at http://www.icrc.org/eng/resources/documents/misc/57jn38.htm

References

Abdulraheem, Mahmood Y. 2000. "War-related Damage to the Marine Environment in the ROPME Sea Area." Chapter 13 in *The Environmental Consequences of War: Legal, Economic, and Scientific Perspectives.* Jay Austin and Carl E. Bruch, eds. New York: Cambridge University Press, pp. 338–352.

Austin, Jay, and Carl E. Bruch. 2000. *The Environmental Consequences of War: Legal, Economic, and Scientific Perspectives.* New York: Cambridge University Press, 691 pp.

Brookings Institution. 1998. "50 Facts about U.S. Nuclear Weapons." http://www. brookings.edu/projects/archive/nucweapons/50.aspx

Busby, Chris, and Saoirse Morgan. 2005. *Did the Use of Uranium Weapons in Gulf War 2 Result in Contamination of Europe? Evidence from the Measurements of the Atomic Weapons Establishment, Aldermaston, Berkshire, UK.* Occasional Paper 2006/1, January 2005. Aberystwyth: Green Audit.

Costanza, Robert, Ralph D'Arge, Rudolf de Groot, Stephen Farber, Monica Grasso, Bruce Hannon, Karin Limburg, Shahid Naeem, Robert V. O'Neill, Jose Paruelo, Robert G. Raskin, Paul Sutton, and Marjan van den Belt. 1997. "The Value of the World's Ecosystem Services and Natural Capital." *Nature.* Vol. 387, May 15, 1997, pp. 253–260.

Dycus, Stephen. 1996. *National Defense and the Environment.* Hanover, NH: University Press of New England, 286 pp.

"Environmental Ethics." 2008. *Stanford Encyclopedia of Philosophy.* June 3, 2002, revised January 3, 2008. http://plato.stanford.edu/entries/ethics-environmental/

Gerber, Michele Stenehjem. 1992. *On the Home Front: The Cold War Legacy of the Hanford Nuclear Site.* Lincoln, NE: University of Nebraska Press.

Goldblat, Jozef. 1975. "The Prohibition of Environmental Warfare." *Ambio.* Vol. 4, No. 5/6. 1975, pp. 186–190.

Henckaerts, Jean-Marie. 2005. "Customary Law." *International Review of the Red Cross.* Vol. 87, No. 857, March 2005, pp. 175–212.

Horgan, John. 1991. "Up in Flames: Kuwait's Burning Oil Wells as a Sad Test of Theories." *Scientific American.* Vol. 264, No. 5, May 1991, pp. 17–19.

Hulme, Karen. 1997. "Armed Conflict, Wanton Ecological Devastation, and Scorched Earth Policies: How the 1990–1991 Gulf Conflict Revealed the Inadequacies of the Current Laws to Ensure the Effective Protection and Preservation of the Natural Environment." *Journal of Armed Conflict Law.* Vol. 45, pp. 45–81.

Kassenova, Togzhan. 2009. "The Lasting Toll of Semipalatinsk's Nuclear Testing." *Bulletin of the Atomic Scientists.* Web edition. September 28, 2009. http://www. thebulletin.org/node/7860

Khordagui, Hosny, and Dhari Al-Amji. 1993. "Environmental Impact of the Gulf War: An Integrated Preliminary Assessment." *Environmental Management.* Vol. 17, No. 4, pp. 557–562.

"Korean Demilitarized Zone Now a Wildlife Haven." *Christian Science Monitor.* November 21, 2008, http://www.csmonitor.com/Environment/Wildlife/2008/ 1121/korean-demilitarized-zone-now-a-wildlife-haven.

Machlis, Gary E., and Thor Hanson. 2008. "Warfare Ecology." *BioScience.* Vol. 58, No. 8, September 2008, pp. 729–736.

Mai, Tuan Anh, Thanh Vu Doan, Joseph Tarradellas, Luiz Felippe de Alencastro, and Dominique Grandjean. 2007. "Dioxin Contamination in Soils of Southern Vietnam." *Chemosphere.* Vol. 67, No. 9, April 2007, pp. 1802–1807.

Majeed, Abeer. 2004. "The Impact of Militarism on the Environment: An Overview of Direct and Indirect Effects." Ottawa: Physicians for Global Survival, 45 pp.

McCormick, M. Patrick, Larry W. Thomason, and Charles R. Trepte. 1995. "Atmospheric Effects of the Mt Pinatubo Eruption." *Nature*. Vol. 373, February 2, 1995, pp. 399–404.

McVicker, Carrie. 1998. "ICE Case Studies: Novaya Zemlya." Inventory of Conflict and the Environment, American University. http://www1.american.edu/ted/ice/novalya.htm

Moseley, Alexander. 2009. "Just War Theory." *Internet Encyclopedia of Philosophy*, ISSN 2161–0002. February 10, 2009. http://www.iep.utm.edu/justwar/.

Omar, Samira A. S., Ernest Briskey, Raafat Misak, and Adel A.S.O. Asem. 2000. "The Gulf War Impact on the Terrestrial Environment of Kuwait: An Overview." Chapter 12 in Jay Austin and Carl E. Bruch. *The Environmental Consequences of War: Legal, Economic, and Scientific Perspectives*. New York: Cambridge University Press, pp. 316–337.

Parsons, Rymn James. 1998. "The Fight to Save the Planet: U.S. Armed Forces, 'Greenkeeping,' and Enforcement of the Law Pertaining to Environmental Protection During Armed Conflict." *Georgetown International Environmental Law Review*. Vol. 10, pp. 441–500.

Peterson, Scott. 2002. "A 'Silver Bullet's' Toxic Legacy." *Christian Science Monitor*. December 20, 2002, http://www.csmonitor.com/2002/1220/p01s04-wome.html.

Plant, Glen. 1992. *Environmental Protection and the Law of War*. London: Belhaven Press, 284 pp.

Robock, Alan, and Owen Brian Toon.2010. "Local Nuclear War, Global Suffering." *Scientific American*. Vol. 302, No. 1, January 2010, pp. 74–81.

Royal Society. 2002. *The Health Effects of Depleted Uranium Munitions*. Summary. Document 6/02. London: The Royal Society, 7 pp.

Schmidt, Charles W. 2004. "Battle Scars: Global Conflicts and Environmental Health." *Environmental Health Perspectives*. Vol. 112, No. 17, December 2004, pp. A994-A1005.

http://www.ncbi.nlm.nih.gov/pmc/articles/PMC1253681/

Seacor, Jesica E. 1996. "Environmental Terrorism: Lessons from the Oil Fires of Kuwait." *American University International Law Review*. Vol. 10, No. 1, pp. 481–523.

Shambaugh, James, Judy Oglethorpe, and Rebecca Ham (with contributions from Sylvia Tognetti). 2001. *The Trampled Grass: Mitigating the Impacts of Armed Conflict on the Environment*. Washington: Biodiversity Support Program, 111 pp.

Sidel, Victor W. 2000. "The Impact of Military Preparedness and Militarism on Health and the Environment." In *The Environmental Consequences of War:*

Legal, Economic, and Scientific Perspectives, Jay Austin and Carl E. Bruch, eds. New York: Cambridge University Press, pp. 426–443.

Sills, Joe, Jerome C. Glenn, Elizabeth Florescu, and Theodore J. Gordon. 2001. *Environmental Crimes in Military Actions and the International Criminal Court (ICC)—United Nations Perspectives*. Atlanta, GA Army Environmental Policy Institute, April 2001, 61 pp.

Sills, Joe B., Jerome C. Glenn, Theodore J. Gordon, and Renat Perelat. 2000. *Environmental Security: United Nations Doctrine for Managing Environmental Issues in Military Actions*. Volume 1. Atlanta, GA: Army Environmental Policy Institute, July 2000, 46 pp.

Sills, Joe B., Jerome C. Glenn, Theodore J. Gordon, and Renat Perelat. 2000. *Environmental Security: United Nations Doctrine for Managing Environmental Issues in Military Actions*. Volume 2. Selected International Treaties, Conventions and Protocols that Address Environment-Related Issues; Selected International Organizations Relevant to Environmental Security. Atlanta, GA: Army Environmental Policy Institute, July 2000, 60 pp.

Starr, Steven. 2010. "The Climatic Consequences of Nuclear War." *Bulletin of the Atomic Scientists*. March 12, 2010. http://thebulletin.org/node/8333

Stellman, Jeanne Mager, Steven D. Stellman, Richard Christian, Tracy Weber, and Carrie Tomasallo. 2003. "The Extent and Patterns of Usage of Agent Orange and Other Herbicides in Vietnam." *Nature*. Vol. 422, April 17, 2003, pp. 681–687.

(The Economist). 2011. "From Bombs to $800 Handbags." *The Economist*, March 17, 2011. http://www.economist.com/node/18396103?story_id=18396103

Toon, Owen B., Alan Robock, and Richard P. Turco. 2008. "Environmental Consequences of Nuclear War." *Physics Today*. Vol. 61, No. 12, December 2008, pp. 37–42.

Tyack, Peter L., Walter M. X. Zimmer, David Moretti, Brandon L. Southall, Diane E. Claridge, John W. Durban, Christopher W. Clark, Angela D'Amico, Nancy DiMarzio, Susan Jarvis, Elena McCarthy, Ronald Morrissey, Jessica Ward, Ian L. Boyd. 2011. "Beaked Whales Respond to Simulated and Actual Navy Sonar." *PLoS ONE*. Vol. 6, No. 3: e17009 DOI: 10.1371/journal.pone.0017009.

U.S. Navy. 2001. "Statement of Admiral William J. Fallon, Vice Chief of Naval Operations, Before the House Committee on Government Reform on Constraints on Military Training." May 9, 2001. http://www.navy.mil/navydata/testimony/readiness/fall010509.txt.

Westing, Arthur H. 1971. "Ecological Effects of Military Defoliation of the Forests of South Vietnam." *BioScience*. Vol. 21, No. 17, September 1, 1971, pp. 893–898.

CHAPTER 6

Conclusion: Ecological Thinking

Lord, take my soul, but the struggle continues.
—Ken Saro-Wiwa, environmental activist (1995)

National security, which has been the primary driver of international relations since the 1648 Treaty of Westphalia, seems further away today than ever. Global population has passed 7 billion, more sovereign nations exist than ever before, information is transmitted around the world in an instant, and people themselves can be transported anywhere on the planet in less than 24 hours. Weapons are orders of magnitude more destructive than they have ever been, and the world's sole superpower is currently engaged in two wars. Environmental resources—from the air to the land and the ocean—are in declining health, and developed nations are struggling with financial meltdown.

At the time of this writing, the end of 2011:

- The unrest roiling across much of the Arab world is still in full swing nearly a year after it began. A few of the area's autocratic rulers have stepped down in Egypt, Tunisia, and Yemen, and tenuous new governments are still forming in these nations. Others have been forcibly routed from power by their own subjects, such as Moammar Khadafi of Libya. Still others are hanging on to power through a combination of bribery and repression, such as Bashar Assad of Syria. It remains to be seen if the so-called Arab Spring results in a new, open, democratic Middle East and North Africa region, or if renewed sectarian violence will erase any peaceful gains.
- The nation of Iran is making progress, despite various technical setbacks, in its development of nuclear technology. Iran already has working uranium centrifuges at Natanz and Qom, and a nuclear power plant at Bushehr. The international

community is asking itself what Iran's intentions are, and there are only two options. First, Iran is developing nuclear weapons in violation of the Nuclear Non-Proliferation Treaty (NPT). Second, Iran is exercising its sovereign right under the terms of the NPT and developing enrichment capability to support domestic nuclear power. Electricity demand in Iran is expected to increase 7–9 percent annually, and nuclear power is a carbon-free option.

- Over 400,000 famine refugees from the drought-stricken nation of Somalia are streaming toward relief camps in neighboring Ethiopia and Kenya. Tens of thousands of Somalis have already died from the effects of the worst drought in decades. However, the Islamic militant group Al Shabaab is again targeting food aid workers in Somalia, so the paucity of food the refugees do get is likely to be restricted further, as relief agencies like the World Food Program freeze deliveries and pull workers out of the country.

- Fatih Birol, the chief economist at the International Energy Agency, recently opined that if the nations of the world do not take immediate steps to move global energy requirements away from fossil fuels and toward renewable, carbon-free energy, we are on track for a global average rise in temperature of 6.5°C by 2100. Most of the IPCC's predictions of sea level rise, ecosystem disruption, and species extinction reach dire levels at 5°C, so if Mr. Birol is correct, humanity may only have a short window of time to avert an ecological disaster the likes of which modern humans have never seen.

Expand or Die—Ecological?

Shortages of fresh water, lootable resources going to further conflict and war, oil politics at the international level, continued food insecurity, climate change, unwanted migration, a near-constant public health risk, and the collateral environmental damage incurred by the very tools that nations use to supposedly protect themselves: many countries around the world are facing multiple environmental security stressors that look to get worse in the coming decades. This sounds like a litany of doom, but it doesn't have to be.

Ecological Thinking

It is tempting to view resources, particularly food, water, and arable land, as obtainable only in a zero-sum fashion. If my nation is concerned about food security, for example, then I might attempt to obtain as much arable land as possible, since every acre of land my neighbor has is an acre that I don't have. Yet food insecurity is only partially related to how much arable land a nation has, and depends in large part upon a host of other environmental, political, and economic factors. Given that many of these security threats are transnational, how can nations work to ensure their security without falling into the zero-sum trap?

The answer may lie in **ecological thinking**, the view that every component in a complex system is connected to every other component directly or indirectly, and that these relationships are not necessarily fixed or predefined, but change over time the way different components in living systems do. This type of systems analysis is well understood in ecology, but is not usually applied to social and political systems. For example, in traditional economics, every production process relies on inputs in the form of raw materials and produces outputs in the form of waste products. "Value" can be increased only so far as new raw materials are obtained, and wealth accrued to one party is not accrued to another—a linear, zero-sum view of value. In traditional security, most nations founder upon the security dilemma, discussed in Chapter 1. The zero-sum vision of international security means that a particular nation becomes more secure as its neighbors become less secure. "Expand or die" has been the guiding principle for any nation wishing to build an empire, yet this is a linear, zero-sum view of security. Viewing national security in this way makes a nation perpetually insecure, attempting to control as many changing political, economic, and environmental conditions as possible.

However, in ecological systems, every output from one process is an input into another process, and there is no such thing as waste. Every system is connected to every other system, and unlimited expansion isn't possible. Food, water, air, physical space—something is the limiting factor to growth. If human societies changed their view of security to bring it into line with ecological thinking, the idea of continued national geographical and economic expansion would be seen for the imperial pipe dream that it is. Water security is an excellent example. There is no substitute for water, so in order to maintain a secure and stable water supply, nations must live within the physical limitations of the ecosystem that provides them with water. The national security imperative of expansion may not be an environmental option, so ecological thinking can put us in the frame of mind that we need to accept physical ecological limits on our growth. In addition, as ecosystems degrade, nations may not even have the luxury of a zero-sum calculation when it comes to natural resources! Environmentally based threats are inherently negative-sum, since everyone is worse off in the face of environmental degradation. By contrast, the positive-sum theory of collective security is taken to a new, more comprehensive level by thinking ecologically; everyone is better off by ensuring a stable ecosystem, and collective gains can be made by investing time, money, and know-how in environmental preservation. Ecological thinking can give us a new view of national security, and of international relations in general.

Complex Interdependence—The First Step in Ecological Thinking

In 1977, political scientists Robert Keohane and Joseph Nye described a theory of international relations called **complex interdependence,** designed to synthesize elements of liberal and realist thought to form a system which would more adequately reflect the way policy decisions are made at the international level. Complex interdependence is the best framework in which to consider questions of environmental security, because it is the closest theory we have to ecological thinking in international relations, though in this case, the complexity is scientific and the interdependence is (ecologically) literal.

There are three pillars of complex interdependence theory:

1. The use of multiple channels of action between societies in international relations, including interstate, transgovernmental, and transnational channels;
2. The absence of a hierarchy of issues, with changing agendas and linkages between the issues prioritized; and
3. The objective of bringing about a decline in the use of force and coercive power.

Keohane and Nye did not use the term ecological thinking, but they implicitly recognized that international environmental issues such as ocean policy or climate warming could not be dealt with adequately by purely realist or purely liberal frameworks of international relations.

Environmental security is informed by all three pillars of complex interdependence. First, multiple channels of action are necessary to address the full scope of environmental security issues such as climate change. The IPCC, national governments, informal scientific contacts, financial and business institutions such as the insurance industry, Greenpeace and other international environmental NGOs, and concerned citizens all have their own roles to play in the discussion of whether to mitigate GHG emissions and how. Second, the absence of hierarchy is common in dealing with interconnected environmental issues. For example, climate change will affect precipitation, increasing it in some areas and reducing it in others. This affects irrigation which in turn affects food security and political stability. Farmers, the national water authority, the retailers and food markets, the national government, and the public will each take priority at some point in the decision-making process. Third, force and coercive power play little or no role in issues of environmental security because the threats to security from environment-related issues are endogenous; they arise from our own peacetime behaviors. This very complexity is the reason traditional security scholars become impatient and dismissive of interdisciplinary fields such as environmental security. Yet in an increasingly globalized world, viewing security through a traditional realist lens will not aid in understanding the complex interdependence embedded in environmental security issues, nor will it provide a path to solving them.

Growing Population and Continued Consumption—Ecological?

With the global population surpassing 7 billion in October 2011, we must consider whether continued human population growth is ecological. The 2010 estimate from the UN Department of Economic and Social Affairs places the global population in 2050 at 9.3 billion, depending on health, fertility, and other factors. By 2100, this is predicted to climb to 10.1 billion. As people get wealthier, they consume more goods and resources; according to the World Bank, global GDP has increased from roughly $11 trillion in 1980 to $63 trillion as of 2010. Furthermore, neither the population nor the consumption is spread out equally. Only 1.31 billion of the global population will live in the developed world by 2050, and this figure will only increase to 1.33 billion by 2100. The rest of the population growth will occur in the developing world, where the rate of resource consumption is already increasing. Per capita energy use in the United States has roughly held steady since as far back as 1973, whereas the same figure in China has almost doubled since only 2001, and national CO_2 emissions, growing since the late 1960s, has skyrocketed since only 2002, making China with a population of 1.34 billion people the largest GHG emitter in the world.

With populations growing around the developing world, and these same countries increasing their rates of consumption and pollution, it is relevant to ask if we might reach a point of "too much" pollution. The theory of the **Environmental Kuznets Curve** hypothesizes that as nations develop, they consume resources and pollute more until they reach a developmental tipping point, after which the population is wealthy enough to prioritize environmental health over unfettered economic growth and begins to lower its pollution levels.

The wealthy developed nations are theorized to already be past this point because they generally have strong environmental protection laws, but much more populous developing nations such as China and India are still approaching it, because their pollution levels are rising in tandem with their national GDP. Economists will rightly argue that the relevance of this theory varies with the type of pollutant emitted, and that developed nations have just outsourced the pollution intrinsic to wealth production to developing nations. However, it is important to bear in mind that the growing developing nations have significantly larger populations than the developed nations did when they went through this transition. Consequently, pollution is being emitted globally in much greater amounts. This makes ecologists wonder if there is some absolute environmental limit that we could reach where human well-being and security is permanently affected, though the exact time and amount of pollution it would take to reach this threshold is unknown.

North-South Inequity—Ecological?

Two decades ago, many environmental security thinkers argued that an expanded understanding of the threats to security, especially the links between natural resources and international behavior, was required in order to maintain peaceful relations between the developed world and the developing world. Rich nations had grown rich on their environmental resources, and now that they were wealthy, their cautionary warnings to the poorer nations about global environmental destruction fell on skeptical ears.

In order to help close the growing development gap between the global North and the global South, nations folded the principle of **common but differentiated responsibilities** into several international environmental agreements, including the 1992 Rio Declaration and the 1992 UN Framework Convention on Climate Change. This principle stated that those nations that had benefitted from natural resource consumption to develop now had a historical responsibility both to mitigate past environmental damage and to help those developing nations that were still fighting poverty to do so in a way that would avoid further global environmental degradation as much as possible. Richer nations in the North would then contribute financially toward the cost of pursuing sustainable development in the South, and this transfer of resources would help to curb the environmentally destructive development practices such as large-scale logging and fishing that would be fueling much of the coming degradation. Unfortunately, while reasonable in theory, such a resource transfer from North to South is not likely to happen in the current economic and political climate.

At present, the development gap between the North and South remains very large. Population growth is much greater in the South, but development indicators in the South such as health care, infant mortality, and literacy often lag their Northern counterparts. Trade in food and agricultural products is still skewed toward the developed nations, which often subsidize the producers of cereals and other export crops. Developing nations that cannot afford to do the same face an enduring competitive disadvantage on the global food market, as their small farmers are unable to sell their grain at profitable prices.

Finally, North-South inequity lies at the heart of the global climate change impasse over who acts first and why. Developing nations like China and India argue that the principle of common but differentiated responsibilities obligates wealthy nations like the United States, which have used expansive amounts of fossil fuels to develop, to reduce their GHG emissions first. Then when the developing nations have caught up economically, as outlined by the Kuznets Curve, they will reduce their emissions. However, the United States, which appears to be an outlier among developed nations on this issue, insists that the developing nations must reduce their GHG emissions in tandem with the developed nations, and points to the fact that China's emissions are larger than its own if measured on a national basis (the United States still leads the world in per capita GHG emissions). Until this fundamental inequity is bridged, prospects for any sort of progress on a post-Kyoto international climate regime remain poor.

Is the growing inequity between the North and the South an example of ecological thinking? No, because complex ecological systems tend toward a stable state. This is not to say they do not change; they face perturbations all the time, but large-scale inequalities do not persist because the system brings itself back into equilibrium. Large-scale human inequalities such as knowledge, wealth, or energy use will engender resentment on the part of those lacking such goods, especially if they perceive that they have been purposefully or neglectfully withheld. This gives rise to grievance conflicts of the kind currently occurring in petro-states such as Nigeria. Applying ecological thinking to developmental inequity would allow for the transfer of knowledge and opportunity, and eventually funds, from the developed world to the developing world. The material and financial resources available to the citizens of the global South may never equal to those enjoyed by the global North, but increased equity means increased security.

Geo-Engineering as a Technical Fix—Ecological?

Sometimes human societies cannot come together to adequately address problems of complex ecological interdependence such as climate change. In the face of difficult policy choices such as how to reduce population levels, consumption levels, or both, politicians often resort to the idea that there must be some scientific or technological fix that obviates the need to make a difficult or unpopular decision. In such instances, the lure of technological thinking is very attractive, because the larger systemic reasons for the problem do not have to be addressed.

Geo-engineering, which is the attempt to control the earth's climate to suit human needs, is a perfect example of technological thinking. The U.S. House of Representatives Committee on Science and Technology defines it as "the deliberate large-scale modification of the earth's climate systems for the purposes of counteracting and mitigating anthropogenic climate change." There are currently two methods of attempting geo-engineering, solar radiation management (SRM) and carbon dioxide removal (CDR). CDR involves removing CO_2 directly from the earth's atmosphere and storing it in order to allow heat to pass back through the atmosphere into space. This can be as prosaic as planting trees or as complicated as chemical storage, but it generally requires a long time horizon for the effects of carbon removal on the climate to be felt. SRM, which involves blocking incoming sunlight in order to lower global temperature, is both faster and more problematic from an environmental security perspective. Various methods, such as cloud whitening and space-based reflectors, are years away from deployment, but sulfate aerosol dispersal is possible now. Aerosols increase the **albedo**, or reflectivity, of the planet's atmosphere and lower global average temperature quickly. Volcanic eruptions cause much the same effect; the 1981 eruption of Mount Pinatubo lowered global average temperature by 0.5°C for several years.

There are several ecological and political concerns surrounding SRM. First, blocking sunlight can affect **net primary productivity** (NPP), a measure of how much photochemical energy is captured from sunlight and stored by plants. Lower NPP means less energy moving up the global trophic web. Of more direct concern to humans is the loss of agricultural output, one of the direct causes of food insecurity. Second, it is unclear as to how and where these effects will be felt. Just as climate change will cause some nations to benefit and some nations to suffer, so too will geo-engineering. Whose hand will be on the global thermostat is yet to be determined. Should the ability go to whichever nation can successfully deploy the technology, or should this deployment require global permission? Third, and something to be expected under the terms of complex interdependence, is that some methods of SRM are on the order of "only" several hundred million dollars, cheap enough for a corporation or wealthy individual to accomplish. This means the ability to fundamentally alter the earth's climate now rests in the hands of not only nations, but transnational actors.

The specter of successful geo-engineering technology raises a moral hazard problem for the citizens of GHG-emitting nations. If one or more of these technologies works, it is easy to think that the problem is now fixed, so we place less emphasis on attaining a costly Kyoto-type global climate change mitigation treaty. However, this path to fixing the problem of climate change means that SRM must be continually maintained. If GHG emissions are allowed to continue to rise and then the SRM measures fail or are discontinued, the planetary temperature could spike upwards.

All this assumes that the technology for geo-engineering is deployed from a position of mutual agreement—what if there is no mutual agreement and one nation deploys the technology unilaterally? Can one nation change its neighbor's weather (and likely its own), and if so, is this an act of war? This is not just an ecological concern, but a security concern, because a global SRM scheme makes the concept of national sovereignty further obsolete on

Figure 6.1 Joel Pett comic

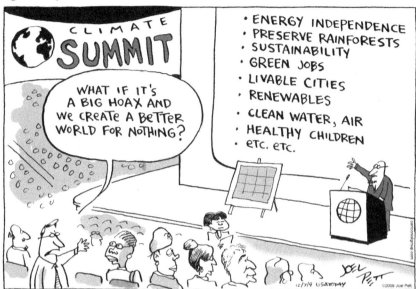

a functional level. We currently have no guidelines for how to approach the ecological, ethical, and security aspects of climate modification, but scientific research into the topic continues apace.

Is addressing the climate crisis by tinkering with the earth's atmosphere ecological thinking? In one way, yes it is. By mimicking the effects of a natural phenomenon, we are using the earth's own systems and mechanisms to achieve the desired result, that of cooling the planet's average temperature. However, in another way, attempting to geo-engineer the global climate is the most unecological option available to us. We haven't been able to live within our planetary limits, so we are using the equivalent of ecological trickery in an attempt to *change* the limits! Even now politicians are talking of geo-engineering as a possible fallback option if the global temperature begins to rise significantly and nations have not been able to agree on an international GHG mitigation regime.

Ecological Security Is Environmental Security

If our study is going to yield fruitful results in the long run, we need to be aware of all the facets of security. There are academic and policy dangers in being too pedagogical and not flexible enough in the study of environmental security. Those scholars who insist on a narrow definition of security or find nothing convincing without a statistical correlation are missing the trees for the forest. Political scientist Arnold Wolfers wrote in 1952 that "efforts for security are bound to be experienced as a burden; security after all is nothing but the absence of the evil of insecurity, a negative value so to speak." Nations that view security in this way are constantly wary of threats that may materialize and so they spend their limited time, funds, and personnel to "sweep back the ocean," counting their success in disasters avoided. I will respectfully disagree with Wolfers; ecological thinking makes national security a positive value, a direct benefit to be enjoyed by all nations.

Perhaps the fundamental difference between traditional national security and international environmental security is the difference between being secure "from" something versus being secure "in" something. Armies, weapons, and border fences can keep a nation secure "from" invading forces, refugees, smugglers, and insurgent groups. But the strongest military in the world cannot protect a nation from water and food shortages, melting ice caps and rising sea levels, floods and droughts, and infectious diseases. A nation that invests in maintaining its cropland, its water infrastructure, and its public health system is secure "in" its ability to provide for its citizens. Living within our ecological means provides environmental security to all nations, and any other security threats are manufactured by humans.

Biographies

Since environmental security is such a wide-ranging and transdisciplinary field, there are many people who have contributed to its development, both as an academic theory and as an operational concern. Consequently, I have included biographical profiles of six people and three organizations which represent the various facets of environmental security, from food to weapons to population to ecosystem integrity. There are many other worthy academic thinkers and organizations that do excellent work in the environmental security field, but they could not be included here due to space constraints.

Africom, U.S. Department of Defense Combatant Command

AFRICOM is the U.S. Africa Command, one of six regional combatant commands within the U.S. Department of Defense. AFRICOM's area of responsibility (AOR) includes the entire African continent (excepting Egypt, which remains under the AOR of CENTCOM). Officially declared on October 1, 2008, and headquartered in Stuttgart, Germany, its mission, in concert with other U.S. government agencies and international partners, is to conduct sustained security engagement through military-to-military programs, military-sponsored activities, and other military operations as directed to promote a stable and secure African environment in support of U.S. foreign policy. General Carter F. Ham is the commanding officer.

The AOR for AFRICOM was transferred from three different combatant commands: most of the African continent was transferred from the European command, Sudan and the Horn of Africa from Central Command, and Madagascar and the surrounding islands from Pacific Command. First proposed as early as 2000, a unified command for Africa seemed to be prudent given the national security interests of the United States in Africa, from oil procurement, counterterrorism, piracy, and famine relief. AFRICOM's strategic objectives are to ensure that Al Qaeda and its affiliates do not attack the United States; to maintain freedom of movement throughout Africa; to assist African states and regional organizations in developing the capability to combat transnational threats such as piracy and the illegal trafficking of weapons, people, and narcotics; to assist African states in developing the ability to respond to crises and mount effective peace operations; and to encourage African militaries to operate under civil authority, respect the rule of law, and abide by international human rights norms.

AFRICOM is unique as a combatant command that will face a multitude of environmental security issues on an operational basis, from resource-driven civil conflicts in West Africa to oil exploration in the Niger Delta to water scarcity across the Sahel. If it succeeds in its mission, environmental security could become part of the standard military AOR portfolio. Using AFRICOM as a template, ecological concerns such as protection of natural resources and deployment of green technology could be integrated into each mission profile across all the combatant commands. If it fails, environmental security as a military specialty could fail with it.

Further Information

http://wwww.africom.mil

Strategic Insights Vol. VI, No. 1, January 2007, on the strategic importance of Africa

http://www.nps.edu/Academics/centers/ccc/publications/OnlineJournal/archiveby-date.html#vol6issue1

Lester Brown, President, Earth Policy Institute

Lester R. Brown was born in 1934 in New Jersey and obtained a degree in agricultural science from Rutgers University. Having a lifelong interest in agriculture, he spent some time in India after his graduation and saw firsthand how food and population were connected.

He worked in the U.S. Department of Agriculture's Foreign Agricultural Service, the first of many government posts. In 1974, with funding from the Rockefeller Brothers Fund, Brown founded the Worldwatch Institute, a multidisciplinary think tank devoted to the analysis of global environmental issues. Brown envisioned Worldwatch as the organization to bring together many different strands of environmental knowledge and make them available to policy makers and the public. In 1986, Brown was awarded a MacArthur Fellows Grant from the MacArthur Foundation.

Some of Lester Brown's earliest connections on food, environmental health, and security focused on China. He saw China's growing population as a possible tipping point for the world food system; one or two crop failures in China and world market prices would increase to the point where poorer countries could be priced out of the global grain market. If population grew large enough, the earth would not be able to produce enough food to feed everyone, and massive famine would be the result. In May 2001, Brown founded the Earth Policy Institute, a sister think tank devoted to exploring the links between a sustainable environment and sustainable economic development.

Brown was one of the first policy analysts and writers to link environmental health, population growth, food production, and international security, as well as the critical role that large and rising developing nations like China must play in stabilizing global ecosystems. He wrote in 1977 that "the threats to security may now arise less from the relationship of nation to nation and more from the relationship of man to nature."

Books

Brown, Lester R. 1977. *Redefining National Security.* Worldwatch Paper 14, October 1977. Washington: Worldwatch Institute.

Brown, Lester R. 2001. *Eco-Economy: Building an Economy for the Earth.* New York: W.W. Norton & Co.

Brown, Lester R. 2005. *Outgrowing the Earth: The Food Security Challenge in an Age of Falling Water Tables and Rising Temperatures.* London: Earthscan.

Brown, Lester R. 2009. *Plan B 4.0: Mobilizing to Save Civilization* (substantially revised). New York: W.W. Norton & Co.

Brown, Lester R. 2011. *World on the Edge: How to Prevent Environmental and Economic Collapse.* New York: W.W. Norton & Co.

Further Information

http://www.earth-policy.org/about_epi/C32

http://www.worldwatch.org/

Environmental Change and Security Program, Woodrow Wilson International Center for Scholars

Since 1994, the Woodrow Wilson International Center for Scholars has hosted the Environmental Change and Security Program. ECSP was one of the first clearinghouses for scholarly and policy information related to environmental security. Its purpose is to explore the connections among environmental, health, and population dynamics and their links to conflict, human insecurity, and foreign policy. ECSP brings together scholars, policy makers, the media, and practitioners through events, research publications, multimedia content (audio and video) and its daily blog, *New Security Beat*. Much of the early academic and policy writing on environmental security as a topic was published in its annual report. Some of the recent topics that have been presented at ECSP include the institutional resilience to climate change in international river basins, population and health concerns in Tanzania and Kenya, the effects of a changing climate on U.S. humanitarian and disaster response, and conflict-free certification of minerals in the Democratic Republic of the Congo.

The Woodrow Wilson International Center for Scholars is a nonprofit, nonpartisan research institution, supported by public and private funds and engaged in the study of national and world affairs. ECSP currently has three primary focus areas:

1. **Integrated Development—Health, Environment, Livelihood, Population, and Security**—Global population dynamics such as urbanization, youth bulges, and migration can affect political stability and conflict dynamics. ECSP serves as a forum for presenting new research and debating practical policy options on population-health-environment connections and demographic security in developing countries.
2. **Environment, Conflict, and Security**—Natural resources are increasingly factors in conflict outcomes and the security of states. Climate change is expected to act as a threat multiplier in many security contexts. Yet environmental interdependence is proving to be a powerful incentive for cooperation and peace building. ECSP works with policy makers, practitioners, and scholars to debate new research and develop policy responses in environmental, diplomatic, development, and security realms.
3. **Water**—Changes in water availability pose fundamental challenges to the health, development, and stability of communities and states. ECSP programs and publications focus on water's potential to spur conflict and cooperation, its social and economic value, and its relationship to health and disease.

ECSP and the Woodrow Wilson Center are located in Washington, DC.

Further Information

http://www.wilsoncenter.org/program/environmental-change-and-security-program
http://www.newsecuritybeat.org/

Al Gore, Former U.S. Vice-President, Climate Change Activist

Albert A. Gore Jr. was born in Washington, D.C., in 1948. His father, Al Gore Sr., was a representative from Tennessee, and later a senator, a career path that Al Jr. would follow. He enrolled at Harvard in 1965, and in

1967, he attended a lecture on climate science by Roger Revelle, an ocean-ography professor who would spark Gore's interest in climate change and environmental issues. After graduation, he enlisted in the army and served in Vietnam for two years.

In 1976, he ran for his father's former seat in Congress and was elected representative from Tennessee. As a freshman congressman, he held some of the first congressional hearings on global warming, calling as a witness his former Harvard professor Revelle. Describing himself as a "raging moderate," he served in the House until 1984, when he was elected senator. His interest in science and the environment resulted in a number of bills supporting high technology and environmental protection, including the High Performance Computing and Communication Act of 1991 that helped fund the early development of what became the internet. In 1992, he published his first book, *Earth in the Balance*, in which he proposed a "Global Marshall Plan" under which developed nations could assist developing nations economically while still protecting the environment (some of these ideas became the forerunners of the joint implementation and clean development mechanisms in the Kyoto Protocol).

That same year, Gore was elected vice-president under Bill Clinton, and green constituents in the United States were looking forward to a new, environment-friendly administration. However, it turned out that this was not the case, as the administration faced an increasingly partisan and polarized discussion regarding environmental policy. The American negotiators pushed for many economic concessions in the Kyoto Protocol negotiations to protect the economies of developed nations, but when the Byrd-Hagel Resolution was passed in 1997 voting down any global climate agreement, further federal action on climate change was shelved for the rest of the Clinton administration.

In 2000, Gore ran against George W. Bush for the presidency. The election results were not immediately clear: Gore won the popular vote by approximately 500,000 votes, but the electoral votes, awarded on a state-by-state basis, came down to a recount in Florida. On December 12, 2000, the Supreme Court stopped the Florida recount and awarded the state's 25 electoral votes to Bush. This gave Bush 271 electoral votes to Gore's 266, handing him the presidency (270 needed to win).

After this defeat, Gore turned to other tasks, particularly those related to his environmental interests. In 2004, he launched Generation Investment Management, an investment firm for green portfolios, and continued to speak about the dangers of anthropogenic global warming. His documentary film on climate change, entitled *An Inconvenient Truth*, won the Oscar in 2007 for Best Documentary. Also in 2007, Gore shared the Nobel Prize for Peace with the Intergovernmental Panel on Climate Change "for their efforts to build up and disseminate greater knowledge about man-made climate change, and to lay the foundations for the measures that are needed to counteract such change."

Al Gore was one of the first American politicians at the national level to insist that climate change and environmental security was a salient matter for federal policy. His continued engagement with these issues has been critical in bringing environmental issues like climate change to the forefront of both the national political discussion and the popular consciousness. Some have argued that his lifelong membership in the Democratic Party has made his advocacy on this issue politically suspect, and that any recommendations he makes must be seen through a partisan lens. However, the Norwegian Nobel Institute recognized that "climate changes may also increase the danger of war and conflict, because they will place already scarce natural resources, not least drinking water, under greater pressure, and put large population groups to flight from drought, flooding, and other extreme weather conditions." Gore is cofounder and chairman of Generation Investment Management, and of CurrentTV.

Books

Gore, Al. 1992. *Earth in the Balance: Ecology and the Human Spirit.* New York: Rodale Books.

Gore, Al. 2006. *An Inconvenient Truth: The Planetary Emergency of Global Warming and What We Can Do About It.* New York: Rodale Books.

Gore, Al. 2009. *Our Choice: A Plan to Solve the Climate Crisis.* New York: Rodale Books.

Further Information

http://www.algore.com/

http://www.climatecrisis.net/

http://www.globalmarshallplan.org/index_eng.html

http://nobelprize.org/nobel_prizes/peace/laureates/2007/

Intergovernmental Panel on Climate Change

Formed in 1988 and headquartered in Geneva, the Intergovernmental Panel on Climate Change (IPCC) is the epistemic community for knowledge about the scientific basis of global warming, its impacts, and mitigation methods and opportunities. It was established by the UN Environment Program and the World Meteorological Organization to provide the world with a clear scientific view of the current state of knowledge of climate change and its potential environmental and socioeconomic impacts, and is currently chaired by Rajendra K. Pachauri.

The IPCC does not conduct its own scientific research. Rather, it is an intergovernmental body made up of thousands of physical, natural, and social scientists from 194 countries whose work relates to global environmental change in some way and whose job is to assess the scientific information relating to all aspects of climate change. It is divided into three knowledge areas: Working Group I examines the physical science basis for climate change knowledge; Working Group II studies climate change impacts on regions and societies across the globe, as well as the adaptation and vulnerability of these regions and societies to such climate change; and Working Group III assesses climate change mitigation strategies.

The IPCC is in charge of the publication of state-of-the-knowledge reports, and releases a report approximately every five years. The First Assessment Report was published in 1990 and declared that there was a 50–50 chance that human actions were contributing to global warming. The Second Assessment Report was published in 1995, the Third Assessment Report in 2001, and the Fourth Assessment Report in 2007, which had concluded that the chances of human contribution to climate change was over 90 percent. The Fifth Assessment Report, taking into account all the knowledge generated since 2007, is due sometime in 2013 or 2014. Along with former U.S. vice-president Al Gore, the IPCC was awarded the Nobel Peace Prize in 2007 "for their efforts to build up and disseminate greater knowledge about man-made climate change, and to lay the foundations for the measures that are needed to counteract such change."

In 2010, the IPCC and its chair Pachauri were criticized by some scientists for not adhering to standard peer review procedures. Some factual and numerical errors were found in the Fourth Assessment Report, and an independent review panel recommended that the IPCC overhaul its assessment process and take more care with its scientific explanations. Likewise, and as expected in an endeavor with global ramifications, the IPCC has been called both too alarmist, for making climate change sound worse than it is, and too conservative, for understating the future risks and dangers from rising temperatures.

Understanding what the IPCC does and how it does it is critical to any study of environmental security. The IPCC provides the basis for knowledge of climate change science, its impacts, and mitigation strategies vetted by the international scientific community. Without this knowledge, the links between climate change and international security will not be clear, and hence decisions about national security issues that stem from climate drivers cannot be made with trusted scientific input. All publications on the IPCC website are available to the public for free download.

Further Information

http://www.ipcc.ch

http://nobelprize.org/nobel_prizes/peace/laureates/2007/

Wangari Maathai, Kenyan Tree Planter, Founder of the Greenbelt Movement

Dr. Wangari Maathai was born in Kenya in 1940. She received a scholarship from the Joseph P. Kennedy Jr. Foundation and went to the United States for postsecondary studies, graduating with a Bachelor of Science from Mount St. Scholastica College in 1964, and a Master of Science in biological science from the University of Pittsburgh in 1966. In 1971, she graduated with a PhD in anatomy from the University of Nairobi, the first Eastern African woman to earn a doctoral level degree.

After her graduate studies, she continued her work at the University of Nairobi. Her husband's political campaign gave her the idea of linking reducing unemployment with environmental preservation, and in 1977 she founded the Greenbelt Movement, which focuses on poverty reduction and environmental conservation through tree planting. She encouraged women within Kenya to plant native trees to foster environmental protection, food security, and women's empowerment, and paid a small stipend for each tree planted.

She ran into personal and political obstacles in her career. In 1979, her husband Mwangi Mathai divorced her, saying she was "too strong minded for a woman" and that he could not control her. Much of her conservation work involved arguing for public control and preservation of public lands. This angered Daniel Arap Moi, the Kenyan president, because she protested against his plans to give away plots of public land to his political supporters, and although she was arrested and jailed several times, the movement grew.

In 1984, Dr. Maathai was awarded the Right Livelihood Award, which supports activists who support the principle of "right livelihood"; this principle says that persons should follow an honest occupation and take no more than a fair share of the earth's resources. UNEP began funding the Greenbelt Movement in 1986, and delegates from 15 countries came to Kenya to learn how to set up similar programs. In 1991, she was awarded the Goldman Prize for environmental activism at the grassroots level where positive change is created through community or citizen participation in the issues that affect them. After Arap Moi was barred from standing for president again in 2002,

Dr. Maathai ran for a seat in Kenya's parliament, and during the period 2003–2007, she held the position of assistant minister for environment and natural resources. In 2004, Dr. Maathai was awarded the Nobel Peace Prize "for her contribution to sustainable development, democracy, and peace."

Wangari Maathai and the Greenbelt Movement are important to the study of environmental security. This is because Wangari Maathai and her fellow women recognized that security in a community comes from a protected environment, a pacified people, and a democratic government, and that these things are not only not separable, but they must be achieved together. Today, the Pan-Africa Greenbelt Movement Network has programs across Africa, and has planted over 40 million trees since its founding in 1977. Dr. Maathai passed away on September 25, 2011.

Books

Maathai, Wangari. 2003 (revised 2006). *The Greenbelt Movement: Sharing the Approach and the Experience*. New York: Lantern Books.

Maathai, Wangari. 2006. *Unbowed: A Memoir*. New York: Alfred A. Knopf.

Maathai, Wangari. 2010. *Replenishing the Earth: Spiritual Values for Healing Ourselves and the World*. New York: Doubleday Image.

Maathai, Wangari. 2010. *The Challenge for Africa*. New York: Vintage/Anchor.

Further Information

http://www.greenbeltmovement.org/

http://www.rightlivelihood.org/maathai.html

http://www.goldmanprize.org/node/126

http://nobelprize.org/nobel_prizes/peace/laureates/2004/

Alexander Nikitin, Retired Soviet Naval Officer, Bellona Researcher

Alexander Nikitin is a former Soviet submarine officer and nuclear safety inspector. He served in the Soviet Navy and attained the rank of captain. He was not originally an environmentalist; indeed Soviet Russia was not known for its focus on environmental issues, preferring to put security and nuclear weapons at the pinnacle of its national interest. (The environmental NGO Greenpeace Russia has had a small presence in the USSR, but in 1990 when the MV *Greenpeace* sailed from Norway to Novaya Zemlya to protest nuclear testing there, they were turned back by the Soviet Navy.) The Russian Northern Fleet, headquartered off the Kola Peninsula, contains many nuclear vessels and decommissioned nuclear submarines whose fissile material has not been properly secured. After the demise of the Soviet Union as a political entity, the new government of Russia inherited a nuclear mess that it could not immediately afford to clean up.

After his retirement from the Soviet Navy in 1992, Captain Nikitin worked with the Norwegian environmental group Bellona Foundation to publish a report about the radioactive contamination of the Arctic environment by the heavily nuclear Russian Northern Fleet. The FSB (Russia's federal security service, successor to the KGB) attempted to confiscate the papers and computers from Bellona's Russian office and Nikitin's home, but the report was sent to Bellona electronically and published from Norway. Despite the information for the report being taken from unclassified sources, Nikitin was arrested in 1996 by the FSB and charged with treason and espionage for releasing state secrets, namely the condition of the fleet's nuclear components.

Nikitin spent 10 months in pretrial detention. Because the Russian media portrayed him as a traitor, his case did not garner much support within Russia, but the Norway home office of the Bellona Foundation released the details of Nikitin's arrest. Pressure from the Western media and NGOs such as Amnesty International grew. In 1997, he was released from custody, but the charges of treason against him were not dropped. Instead, the court sent the case back to the FSB for further investigation, and he was eventually rearrested. That same year, he was awarded the Goldman Prize for grassroots environmental work, but was not released to attend the ceremony. After 13 court hearings, Captain Nikitin was finally acquitted in 2000.

The case of Captain Nikitin is important to the study of environmental security because it puts the traditional and modern definitions of national security in direct conflict. Security during the Cold War was measured in nuclear missiles, but once the Cold War ended, the missiles served no real purpose. Rather, by contaminating the Russian Arctic, they became detrimental to the real environmental security on which Russia's future national interests depend. Nikitin's legal defense was based not only on the open source information that he used, but on the fact that Article 42 of the Russian Constitution states that environmental information may not be kept secret. Nikitin is now the director of the Bellona Foundation's St. Petersburg office and is still active in environmental security affairs in Russia.

Further Information

Nikitin, Alexander, Igor Kudrik, and Thomas Nilsen. 1996. *The Russian Northern Fleet: Sources of Radioactive Contamination.* Bellona Report Vol. 2. Available at http://www.bellona.org/reports/The_Russian_Northern_Fleet.

Handler, Joshua. 2000. "An Acquittal At Last? The Nikitin Affair." *Bulletin of the Atomic Scientists*. Vol. 56, No. 2, March/April 2000, pp. 17–19.

http://www.goldmanprize.org/node/139

http://www.bellona.org/Aboutus/Greetings_from_spb

Ken Saro-Wiwa, Nigerian Writer, Ogoni Activist

Ken Saro-Wiwa was born in 1941 in the Ogoniland region of the Niger Delta and studied English at the University of Ibadan. He was a writer of books and short stories in which he supported the autonomy of indigenous peoples such as the Ogoni from the Nigerian government. The land which the Ogoni occupy is at the mouth of the Niger River and has produced over $30 billion worth of oil for the Nigerian government and its primary partner, Shell. The area has suffered considerable environmental degradation from oil extraction, as farmland and fishing grounds have been polluted with oil.

In 1990, Saro-Wiwa helped found the Movement for the Survival of the Ogoni People (MOSOP), an umbrella group designed to represent the interests of the Ogoni people in the oil dealings between Shell and the Nigerian government. Specifically, MOSOP demanded that a fair share of the proceeds from oil extraction on their land or off their shores go to benefit the Ogoni people, and that Shell provide funds for the remediation of environmental damage to Ogoni land. Saro-Wiwa was arrested several times for his political activism, and in 1994, he was awarded the Right Livelihood Prize, for his nonviolent work in attempting to secure the environmental and economic rights of the Ogoni people.

Saro-Wiwa was arrested again by the government of Gen. Sani Abacha, the military president of Nigeria, in 1994 and held for a year. During his imprisonment, he was awarded the Goldman Prize for grassroots environmental activism in 1995. He and nine alleged co-conspirators were tried before a military tribunal on charges of conspiracy to incite murder, charges that were widely viewed as trumped-up and retaliatory for Saro-Wiwa's political activism on behalf of the Ogoni. "The Ogoni Nine," as they came to be known, were found guilty and executed on November 10, 1995, by the Nigerian military. Their deaths caused international outrage and resulted in the expulsion of Nigeria from the Commonwealth of Nations for three years.

One year later, lawsuits were filed in the United States under the 1789 Alien Tort Statute by various environmental and human rights groups against Shell and the head of its Nigeria operations for being complicit in the deaths of Saro-Wiwa and the others. After many delays and petitions from Shell, the trial was set to start in June 2009. Before it could begin, on June 8, Shell agreed to settle the suit with a $15.5 million payment to the families of the nine Ogoni leaders who were hanged. Shell admitted no liability in the deaths of Ken Saro-Wiwa or the others, or any wrongdoing in their Nigerian operations.

Ken Saro-Wiwa's trial and execution foreshadowed many of the current problems of environmental security: the economic and political instability of a petro-state such as Nigeria, the collateral environmental damage suffered due to the extraction of oil and the antigovernment insurgencies that such resentment can spawn, and the criticality of a healthy environment for the security of the state. His remains are buried in Nigeria, but a memorial to his life stands in London, where his son resides.

Books

Na'allah, Abdul-Rasheed. 1998. *Ogoni's Agonies: Ken Saro-Wiwa and the Crisis in Nigeria*. Trenton, NJ: Africa World Press.

Saro-Wiwa, Ken. 1996. *A Month and a Day: A Detention Diary*. New York: Penguin Books.

Wiwa, Ken. 2001. *In the Shadow of a Saint: A Son's Journey to Understanding his Father's Legacy*. South Royalton, VT: Steerforth Press.

Further Information

http://www.goldmanprize.org/node/160

http://www.mosop.org/

http://www.rightlivelihood.org/saro-wiwa.html

Vandana Shiva, Indian Antiglobalization Activist, Founder of Navdanya

Dr. Vandana Shiva was born in 1952 in Uttarakhand, India. She was educated as a physicist and earned her doctoral degree in physics in 1979, but became involved in issues of agriculture, soil, ecology, and environmental policy. She chronicled the endeavors of some of the women tree-huggers from the 1977 Chipko Movement in India, where village women in the Himalayas protected local trees from loggers by forming human chains around them and hugging them. (Shiva herself claims to have been involved with the movement, but it is unclear if she actually participated.) In 1982, she founded the Research Foundation for Science, Technology, and Ecology to promote local agriculture. By 1991, the resulting network of seed savers and organic farmers spread across 16 states in India had helped set up 54 community seed banks across the country. Called Navdanya ("nine seeds," symbolizing the protection of biological and cultural diversity), it continues to promote local agriculture, organic farming, and the use of native seeds.

Dr. Shiva is known for her outspoken public campaigns against industrial agriculture, biotechnology companies, and genetically modified food and seeds. Her ecological argument is that uniform production of commodity crops reduces the health and biodiversity of both the soil and the diet of the people. Socially and economically, overindustrialization of the land actually decreases food security by taking knowledge and decision-making away from local farmers and concentrating it in the hands of large multinational agricultural corporations like Monsanto. In her view, large industrial agricultural movements—such as the Green Revolution and the development of genetically modified seeds—is bad for India and for the world. She has come under some criticism for her anti-globalization views, and indeed the crop production gains made under the Green Revolution are estimated to have prevented the starvation death of millions of people. Navdanya has also campaigned against the attempts by biotechnology companies to patent genes from native seeds, plants, and animals, arguing that this local diversity is a gift from the earth and is not to be owned.

Dr. Shiva is regarded as a key eco-feminist for her linkage of agricultural health and productivity with women's empowerment and her view of the earth as female. In 1993, Dr. Shiva received the Right Livelihood Award, for "placing women and ecology at the heart of modern development discourse." She is currently engaged in a three-year project with the Royal Government of Bhutan to assist in the country's shift away from industrial agriculture and toward organic farming.

Books

Shiva, Vandana. 1989. *Staying Alive: Women, Ecology, and Development*. London: Zed Books.

Shiva, Vandana. 2000. *Stolen Harvest: The Hijacking of the Global Food Supply*. Cambridge, MA: South End Press.

Shiva, Vandana, ed. 2007. *Manifestos on the Future of Food and Seed*. Cambridge, MA: South End Press.

Shiva, Vandana. 2008. *Soil Not Oil: Environmental Justice in an Age of Climate Crisis*. Cambridge, MA: South End Press.

Further Information

http://www.vandanashiva.org/

http://www.navdanya.org/

http://www.rightlivelihood.org/v-shiva.html

Key Documents

Stockholm Declaration of the United Nations Conference on the Human Environment, 16 June 1972

The United Nations Conference on the Human Environment, having met at Stockholm from 5 to 16 June 1972, having considered the need for a common outlook and for common principles to inspire and guide the peoples of the world in the preservation and enhancement of the human environment,

Proclaims that:

1. Man is both creature and moulder of his environment, which gives him physical sustenance and affords him the opportunity for intellectual, moral, social and spiritual growth. In the long and tortuous evolution of the human race on this planet a stage has been reached when, through the rapid acceleration of science and technology, man has acquired the power to transform his environment in countless ways and on an unprecedented scale. Both aspects of man's environment, the natural and the man-made, are essential to his well-being and to the enjoyment of basic human rights the right to life itself.
2. The protection and improvement of the human environment is a major issue which affects the well-being of peoples and economic development throughout the world; it is the urgent desire of the peoples of the whole world and the duty of all Governments.
3. Man has constantly to sum up experience and go on discovering, inventing, creating and advancing. In our time, man's capability to transform his surroundings, if used wisely, can bring to all peoples the benefits of development and the opportunity to enhance the quality of life. Wrongly or heedlessly applied, the same power can do incalculable harm to human beings and the human environment. We see around us growing evidence of man-made harm in many regions of the earth: dangerous levels of pollution in water, air, earth and living beings; major and undesirable disturbances to the ecological balance of the biosphere; destruction and depletion of irreplaceable resources; and gross deficiencies, harmful to the physical,

mental and social health of man, in the man-made environment, particularly in the living and working environment.

4. In the developing countries most of the environmental problems are caused by under-development. Millions continue to live far below the minimum levels required for a decent human existence, deprived of adequate food and clothing, shelter and education, health and sanitation. Therefore, the developing countries must direct their efforts to development, bearing in mind their priorities and the need to safeguard and improve the environment. For the same purpose, the industrialized countries should make efforts to reduce the gap themselves and the developing countries. In the industrialized countries, environmental problems are generally related to industrialization and technological development.

5. The natural growth of population continuously presents problems for the preservation of the environment, and adequate policies and measures should be adopted, as appropriate, to face these problems. Of all things in the world, people are the most precious. It is the people that propel social progress, create social wealth, develop science and technology and, through their hard work, continuously transform the human environment. Along with social progress and the advance of production, science and technology, the capability of man to improve the environment increases with each passing day.

6. A point has been reached in history when we must shape our actions throughout the world with a more prudent care for their environmental consequences. Through ignorance or indifference we can do massive and irreversible harm to the earthly environment on which our life and well being depend. Conversely, through fuller knowledge and wiser action, we can achieve for ourselves and our posterity a better life in an environment more in keeping with human needs and hopes. There are broad vistas for the enhancement of environmental quality and the creation of a good life. What is needed is an enthusiastic but calm state of mind and intense but orderly work. For the purpose of attaining freedom in the world of nature, man must use knowledge to build, in collaboration with nature, a better environment. To defend and improve the human environment for present and future generations has become an imperative goal for mankind-a goal to be pursued together with, and in harmony with, the established and fundamental goals of peace and of worldwide economic and social development.

7. To achieve this environmental goal will demand the acceptance of responsibility by citizens and communities and by enterprises and institutions at every level, all sharing equitably in common efforts. Individuals in all walks of life as well as organizations in many fields, by their values and the sum of their actions, will shape the world environment of the future.

Local and national governments will bear the greatest burden for large-scale environmental policy and action within their jurisdictions. International cooperation is also needed in order to raise resources to support the developing countries in carrying out their responsibilities in this field. A growing class of environmental problems, because they are regional or global in extent or because they affect the common international realm, will require extensive cooperation among nations and action by international organizations in the common interest.

The Conference calls upon Governments and peoples to exert common efforts for the preservation and improvement of the human environment, for the benefit of all the people and for their posterity.

Principles

States the common conviction that:

Principle 1

Man has the fundamental right to freedom, equality and adequate conditions of life, in an environment of a quality that permits a life of dignity and well-being, and he bears a solemn responsibility to protect and improve the environment for present and future generations. In this respect, policies promoting or perpetuating apartheid, racial segregation, discrimination, colonial and other forms of oppression and foreign domination stand condemned and must be eliminated.

Principle 2

The natural resources of the earth, including the air, water, land, flora and fauna and especially representative samples of natural ecosystems, must be safeguarded for the benefit of present and future generations through careful planning or management, as appropriate.

Principle 3

The capacity of the earth to produce vital renewable resources must be maintained and, wherever practicable, restored or improved.

Principle 4

Man has a special responsibility to safeguard and wisely manage the heritage of wildlife and its habitat, which are now gravely imperilled by a combination of adverse factors. Nature conservation, including wildlife, must therefore receive importance in planning for economic development.

Principle 5

The non-renewable resources of the earth must be employed in such a way as to guard against the danger of their future exhaustion and to ensure that benefits from such employment are shared by all mankind.

Principle 6

The discharge of toxic substances or of other substances and the release of heat, in such quantities or concentrations as to exceed the capacity of the environment to render them harmless, must be halted in order to ensure that serious or irreversible damage is not inflicted upon ecosystems. The just struggle of the peoples of ill countries against pollution should be supported.

Principle 7

States shall take all possible steps to prevent pollution of the seas by substances that are liable to create hazards to human health, to harm living resources and marine life, to damage amenities or to interfere with other legitimate uses of the sea.

Principle 8

Economic and social development is essential for ensuring a favorable living and working environment for man and for creating conditions on earth that are necessary for the improvement of the quality of life.

Principle 9

Environmental deficiencies generated by the conditions of under-development and natural disasters pose grave problems and can best be remedied by accelerated development through the transfer of substantial quantities of financial and technological assistance as a supplement to the domestic effort of the developing countries and such timely assistance as may be required.

Principle 10

For the developing countries, stability of prices and adequate earnings for primary commodities and raw materials are essential to environmental management, since economic factors as well as ecological processes must be taken into account.

Principle 11

The environmental policies of all States should enhance and not adversely affect the present or future development potential of developing countries, nor should they hamper the attainment of better living conditions for all, and appropriate steps should be taken by States and international organizations with a view to reaching agreement on meeting the possible national and international economic consequences resulting from the application of environmental measures.

Principle 12

Resources should be made available to preserve and improve the environment, taking into account the circumstances and particular requirements of developing countries and any costs which may emanate- from their incorporating environmental safeguards into their development planning and the need for making available to them, upon their request, additional international technical and financial assistance for this purpose.

Principle 13

In order to achieve a more rational management of resources and thus to improve the environment, States should adopt an integrated and coordinated approach to their development planning so as to ensure that development is compatible with the need to protect and improve environment for the benefit of their population.

Principle 14

Rational planning constitutes an essential tool for reconciling any conflict between the needs of development and the need to protect and improve the environment.

Principle 15

Planning must be applied to human settlements and urbanization with a view to avoiding adverse effects on the environment and obtaining maximum social, economic and environmental benefits for all. In this respect projects which arc designed for colonialist and racist domination must be abandoned.

Principle 16

Demographic policies which are without prejudice to basic human rights and which are deemed appropriate by Governments concerned should be applied in those regions where the rate of population growth or excessive population concentrations are likely to have adverse effects on the environment of the human environment and impede development.

Principle 17

Appropriate national institutions must be entrusted with the task of planning, managing or controlling the 9 environmental resources of States with a view to enhancing environmental quality.

Principle 18

Science and technology, as part of their contribution to economic and social development, must be applied to the identification, avoidance and control of environmental risks and the solution of environmental problems and for the common good of mankind.

Principle 19

Education in environmental matters, for the younger generation as well as adults, giving due consideration to the underprivileged, is essential in order to broaden the basis for an enlightened opinion and responsible conduct by individuals, enterprises and communities in protecting and improving the environment in its full human dimension. It is also essential that mass media of communications avoid contributing to the deterioration of the environment, but, on the contrary, disseminates information of an educational nature on the need to project and improve the environment in order to enable mal to develop in every respect.

Principle 20

Scientific research and development in the context of environmental problems, both national and multinational, must be promoted in all countries, especially the developing countries. In this connection, the free flow of up-to-date scientific information and transfer of experience must be supported and assisted, to facilitate the solution of environmental problems; environmental technologies should be made available to developing countries on terms which would encourage their wide dissemination without constituting an economic burden on the developing countries.

Principle 21

States have, in accordance with the Charter of the United Nations and the principles of international law, the sovereign right to exploit their own resources pursuant to their own environmental policies, and the responsibility to ensure that activities within their jurisdiction or control do not cause damage to the environment of other States or of areas beyond the limits of national jurisdiction.

Principle 22

States shall cooperate to develop further the international law regarding liability and compensation for the victims of pollution and other environmental damage caused by activities within the jurisdiction or control of such States to areas beyond their jurisdiction.

Principle 23

Without prejudice to such criteria as may be agreed upon by the international community, or to standards which will have to be determined nationally, it will be essential in all cases to consider the systems of values prevailing in each country, and the extent of the applicability of standards which are valid for the most advanced countries but which may be inappropriate and of unwarranted social cost for the developing countries.

Principle 24

International matters concerning the protection and improvement of the environment should be handled in a cooperative spirit by all countries, big and small, on an equal footing.

Cooperation through multilateral or bilateral arrangements or other appropriate means is essential to effectively control, prevent, reduce and eliminate adverse environmental effects resulting from activities conducted in all spheres, in such a way that due account is taken of the sovereignty and interests of all States.

Principle 25

States shall ensure that international organizations play a coordinated, efficient and dynamic role for the protection and improvement of the environment.

Principle 26

Man and his environment must be spared the effects of nuclear weapons and all other means of mass destruction. States must strive to reach prompt agreement, in the relevant international organs, on the elimination and complete destruction of such weapons.

21st plenary meeting
16 June 1972
Chapter 11

Source: Available at http://www.unep.org/Documents.Multilingual/Default.asp?docu mentid=97&articleid=1503. Used by permission of the United Nations.

Rio Declaration on Environment and Development, 14 June 1992

The United Nations Conference on Environment and Development,

Having met at Rio de Janeiro from 3 to 14 June 1992,

Reaffirming the Declaration of the United Nations Conference on the Human Environment, adopted at Stockholm on 16 June 1972, and seeking to build upon it,

With the goal of establishing a new and equitable global partnership through the creation of new levels of cooperation among States, key sectors of societies and people,

Working towards international agreements which respect the interests of all and protect the integrity of the global environmental and developmental system,

Recognizing the integral and interdependent nature of the Earth, our home,

Proclaims that:

Principle 1

Human beings are at the centre of concerns for sustainable development. They are entitled to a healthy and productive life in harmony with nature.

Principle 2

States have, in accordance with the Charter of the United Nations and the principles of international law, the sovereign right to exploit their own resources pursuant to their own environmental and developmental policies, and the responsibility to ensure that activities within their jurisdiction or control do not cause damage to the environment of other States or of areas beyond the limits of national jurisdiction.

Principle 3

The right to development must be fulfilled so as to equitably meet developmental and environmental needs of present and future generations.

Principle 4

In order to achieve sustainable development, environmental protection shall constitute an integral part of the development process and cannot be considered in isolation from it.

Principle 5

All States and all people shall cooperate in the essential task of eradicating poverty as an indispensable requirement for sustainable development, in order to decrease the disparities in standards of living and better meet the needs of the majority of the people of the world.

Principle 6

The special situation and needs of developing countries, particularly the least developed and those most environmentally vulnerable, shall be given special priority. International actions in the field of environment and development should also address the interests and needs of all countries.

Principle 7

States shall cooperate in a spirit of global partnership to conserve, protect and restore the health and integrity of the Earth's ecosystem. In view of the different contributions to global environmental degradation, States have common but differentiated responsibilities. The developed countries acknowledge the responsibility that they bear in the international pursuit to sustainable development in view of the pressures their societies place on the global environment and of the technologies and financial resources they command.

Principle 8

To achieve sustainable development and a higher quality of life for all people, States should reduce and eliminate unsustainable patterns of production and consumption and promote appropriate demographic policies.

Principle 9

States should cooperate to strengthen endogenous capacity-building for sustainable development by improving scientific understanding through exchanges of scientific and technological knowledge, and by enhancing the development, adaptation, diffusion and transfer of technologies, including new and innovative technologies.

Principle 10

Environmental issues are best handled with participation of all concerned citizens, at the relevant level. At the national level, each individual shall have appropriate access to information concerning the environment that is held by public authorities, including information on hazardous materials and activities in their communities, and the opportunity to participate in decision-making processes. States shall facilitate and encourage public awareness and participation by making information widely available. Effective access to judicial and administrative proceedings, including redress and remedy, shall be provided.

Principle 11

States shall enact effective environmental legislation. Environmental standards, management objectives and priorities should reflect the environmental and development context to which they apply. Standards applied by some countries may be inappropriate and of unwarranted economic and social cost to other countries, in particular developing countries.

Principle 12

States should cooperate to promote a supportive and open international economic system that would lead to economic growth and sustainable development in all countries, to better address the problems of environmental degradation. Trade policy measures for environmental purposes should not constitute a means of arbitrary or unjustifiable discrimination or a disguised restriction on international trade.

Unilateral actions to deal with environmental challenges outside the jurisdiction of the importing country should be avoided. Environmental measures addressing transboundary or global environmental problems should, as far as possible, be based on an international consensus.

Principle 13

States shall develop national law regarding liability and compensation for the victims of pollution and other environmental damage. States shall also cooperate in an expeditious and more determined manner to develop further international law regarding liability and compensation for adverse effects of environmental damage caused by activities within their jurisdiction or control to areas beyond their jurisdiction.

Principle 14

States should effectively cooperate to discourage or prevent the relocation and transfer to other States of any activities and substances that cause severe environmental degradation or are found to be harmful to human health.

Principle 15

In order to protect the environment, the precautionary approach shall be widely applied by States according to their capabilities. Where there are threats of serious or irreversible damage, lack of full scientific certainty shall not be used as a reason for postponing cost-effective measures to prevent environmental degradation.

Principle 16

National authorities should endeavour to promote the internalization of environmental costs and the use of economic instruments, taking into account the approach that the polluter should, in principle, bear the cost of pollution, with due regard to the public interest and without distorting international trade and investment.

Principle 17

Environmental impact assessment, as a national instrument, shall be undertaken for proposed activities that are likely to have a significant adverse impact on the environment and are subject to a decision of a competent national authority.

Principle 18

States shall immediately notify other States of any natural disasters or other emergencies that are likely to produce sudden harmful effects on the environment of those States. Every effort shall be made by the international community to help States so afflicted.

Principle 19

States shall provide prior and timely notification and relevant information to potentially affected States on activities that may have a significant adverse transboundary environmental effect and shall consult with those States at an early stage and in good faith.

Principle 20

Women have a vital role in environmental management and development. Their full participation is therefore essential to achieve sustainable development.

Principle 21

The creativity, ideals and courage of the youth of the world should be mobilized to forge a global partnership in order to achieve sustainable development and ensure a better future for all.

Principle 22

Indigenous people and their communities and other local communities have a vital role in environmental management and development because of their knowledge and traditional practices. States should recognize and duly support their identity, culture and interests and enable their effective participation in the achievement of sustainable development.

Principle 23

The environment and natural resources of people under oppression, domination and occupation shall be protected.

Principle 24

Warfare is inherently destructive of sustainable development. States shall therefore respect international law providing protection for the environment in times of armed conflict and cooperate in its further development, as necessary.

Principle 25

Peace, development and environmental protection are interdependent and indivisible.

Principle 26

States shall resolve all their environmental disputes peacefully and by appropriate means in accordance with the Charter of the United Nations.

Principle 27

States and people shall cooperate in good faith and in a spirit of partnership in the fulfilment of the principles embodied in this Declaration and in the further development of international law in the field of sustainable development.

Source: Report of the United Nations Conference on the Human Environment, Stockholm, 5-16 June 1972 (United Nations publication, Sales No. E.73.II.A.14 and corrigendum), chap. I. Available at http://www.unep.org/Documents.Multilingual/ Default.asp?documentid=78&articleid=1163. Used by permission of the United Nations.

Convention on the Prohibition of Military or Any Other Hostile Use of Environmental Modification Techniques, 18 May 1977

The States Parties to this Convention,

Guided by the interest of consolidating peace, and wishing to contribute to the cause of halting the arms race, and of bringing about general and complete disarmament under strict and effective international control, and of saving mankind from the danger of using new means of warfare,

Determined to continue negotiations with a view to achieving effective progress towards further measures in the field of disarmament,

Recognizing that scientific and technical advances may open new possibilities with respect to modification of the environment,

Recalling the Declaration of the United Nations Conference on the Human Environment adopted at Stockholm on 16 June 1972,

Realizing that the use of environmental modification techniques for peaceful purposes could improve the interrelationship of man and nature and contribute to the preservation and improvement of the environment for the benefit of present and future generations,

Recognizing, however, that military or any other hostile use of such techniques could have effects extremely harmful to human welfare,

Desiring to prohibit effectively military or any other hostile use of environmental modification techniques in order to eliminate the dangers to mankind from such use, and affirming their willingness to work towards the achievement of this objective,

Desiring also to contribute to the strengthening of trust among nations and to the further improvement of the international situation in accordance with the purposes and principles of the Charter of the United Nations,

Have agreed as follows:

Article I

1. Each State Party to this Convention undertakes not to engage in military or any other hostile use of environmental modification techniques having widespread, long-lasting or severe effects as the means of destruction, damage or injury to any other State Party.

2. Each State Party to this Convention undertakes not to assist, encourage or induce any State, group of States or international organization to engage in activities contrary to the provisions of paragraph 1 of this article.

Article II

As used in Article I, the term "environmental modification techniques" refers to any technique for changing—through the deliberate manipulation of natural processes—the dynamics, composition or structure of the Earth, including its biota, lithosphere, hydrosphere and atmosphere, or of outer space.

Article III

1. The provisions of this Convention shall not hinder the use of environmental modification techniques for peaceful purposes and shall be without prejudice to the generally recognized principles and applicable rules of international law concerning such use.
2. The States Parties to this Convention undertake to facilitate, and have the right to participate in, the fullest possible exchange of scientific and technological information on the use of environmental modification techniques for peaceful purposes. States Parties in a position to do so shall contribute, alone or together with other States or international organizations, to international economic and scientific cooperation in the preservation, improvement, and peaceful utilization of the environment, with due consideration for the needs of the developing areas of the world.

Article IV

Each State Party to this Convention undertakes to take any measures it considers necessary in accordance with its constitutional processes to prohibit and prevent any activity in violation of the provisions of the Convention anywhere under its jurisdiction or control.

Article V

1. The States Parties to this Convention undertake to consult one another and to cooperate in solving any problems which may arise in relation to the objectives

of, or in the application of the provisions of, the Convention. Consultation and cooperation pursuant to this article may also be undertaken through appropriate international procedures within the framework of the United Nations and in accordance with its Charter. These international procedures may include the services of appropriate international organizations, as well as of a Consultative Committee of Experts as provided for in paragraph 2 of this article.

2. For the purposes set forth in paragraph 1 of this article, the Depositary shall, within one month of the receipt of a request from any State Party to this Convention, convene a Consultative Committee of Experts. Any State Party may appoint an expert to the Committee whose functions and rules of procedure are set out in the annex, which constitutes an integral part of this Convention. The Committee shall transmit to the Depositary a summary of its findings of fact, incorporating all views and information presented to the Committee during its proceedings. The Depositary shall distribute the summary to all States Parties.

3. Any State Party to this Convention which has reason to believe that any other State Party is acting in breach of obligations deriving from the provisions of the Convention may lodge a complaint with the Security Council of the United Nations. Such a complaint should include all relevant information as well as all possible evidence supporting its validity.

4. Each State Party to this Convention undertakes to cooperate in carrying out any investigation which the Security Council may initiate, in accordance with the provisions of the Charter of the United Nations, on the basis of the complaint received by the Council. The Security Council shall inform the States Parties of the results of the investigation.

5. Each State Party to this Convention undertakes to provide or support assistance, in accordance with the provisions of the Charter of the United Nations, to any State Party which so requests, if the Security Council decides that such Party has been harmed or is likely to be harmed as a result of violation of the Convention.

Article VI

1. Any State Party to this Convention may propose amendments to the Convention. The text of any proposed amendment shall be submitted to the Depositary who shall promptly circulate it to all States Parties.

2. An amendment shall enter into force for all States Parties to this Convention which have accepted it, upon the deposit with the Depositary of instruments of acceptance by a majority of States Parties. Thereafter it shall enter into force for any remaining State Party on the date of deposit of its instrument of acceptance.

Article VII

This Convention shall be of unlimited duration.

Article VIII

1. Five years after the entry into force of this Convention, a conference of the States Parties to the Convention shall be convened by the Depositary at Geneva, Switzerland. The conference shall review the operation of the Convention with a view to ensuring that its purposes and provisions are being realized, and shall in particular examine the effectiveness of the provisions of paragraph 1 of Article I in eliminating the dangers of military or any other hostile use of environmental modification techniques.
2. At intervals of not less than five years thereafter, a majority of the States Parties to the Convention may obtain, by submitting a proposal to this effect to the Depositary, the convening of a conference with the same objectives.
3. If no conference has been convened pursuant to paragraph 2 of this article within ten years following the conclusion of a previous conference, the Depositary shall solicit the views of all States Parties to the Convention, concerning the convening of such a conference. If one third or ten of the States Parties, whichever number is less, respond affirmatively, the Depositary shall take immediate steps to convene the conference.

Article IX

1. This Convention shall be open to all States for signature. Any State which does not sign the Convention before its entry into force in accordance with paragraph 3 of this article may accede to it at any time.
2. This Convention shall be subject to ratification by signatory States. Instruments of ratification or accession shall be deposited with the Secretary-General of the United Nations.
3. This Convention shall enter into force upon the deposit of instruments of ratification by twenty Governments in accordance with paragraph 2 of this article.
4. For those States whose instruments of ratification or accession are deposited after the entry into force of this Convention, it shall enter into force on the date of the deposit of their instruments of ratification or accession.
5. The Depositary shall promptly inform all signatory and acceding States of the date of each signature, the date of deposit of each instrument of ratification or accession and the date of the entry into force of this Convention and of any amendments thereto, as well as of the receipt of other notices.
6. This Convention shall be registered by the Depositary in accordance with Article 102 of the Charter of the United Nations.

Article X

This Convention, of which the English, Arabic, Chinese, French, Russian, and Spanish texts are equally authentic, shall be deposited with the Secretary-General of the United Nations, who shall send certified copies thereof to the Governments of the signatory and acceding States.IN WITNESS WHEREOF, the undersigned, being duly authorized thereto by their respective governments, have signed this Convention, opened for signature at Geneva on the eighteenth day of May, one thousand nine hundred and seventy-seven.

Annex to the Convention

Consultative Committee of Experts

1. The Consultative Committee of Experts shall undertake to make appropriate findings of fact and provide expert views relevant to any problem raised pursuant to paragraph 1 of Article V of this Convention by the State Party requesting the convening of the Committee.
2. The work of the Consultative Committee of Experts shall be organized in such a way as to permit it to perform the functions set forth in paragraph 1 of this annex. The Committee shall decide procedural questions relative to the organization of its work, where possible by consensus, but otherwise by a majority of those present and voting. There shall be no voting on matters of substance.
3. The Depositary or his representative shall serve as the Chairman of the Committee.
4. Each expert may be assisted at meetings by one or more advisers.
5. Each expert shall have the right, through the Chairman, to request from States, and from international organizations, such information and assistance as the expert considers desirable for the accomplishment of the Committees work.

Documents Pertaining to the Convention

The following understandings regarding the Convention were included in the report transmitted by the Conference of the Committee on Disarmament to the General Assembly at its thirty-first session.

Understanding Relating to Article I
It is the understanding of the Committee that, for the purposes of this Convention, the terms, "widespread", "long-lasting" and "severe" shall be interpreted as follows:

(a) "widespread": encompassing an area on the scale of several hundred square kilometres;
(b) "long-lasting": lasting for a period of months, or approximately a season;
(c) "severe": involving serious or significant disruption or harm to human life, natural and economic resources or other assets.

It is further understood that the interpretation set forth above is intended exclusively for this Convention and is not intended to prejudice the interpretation of the same or similar terms if used in connexion with any other international agreement.

Understanding Relating to Article II

It is the understanding of the Committee that the following examples are illustrative of phenomena that could be caused by the use of environmental modification techniques as defined in Article II of the Convention: earthquakes, tsunamis; an upset in the ecological balance of a region; changes in weather patterns (clouds, precipitation, cyclones of various types and tornadic storms); changes in climate patterns; changes in ocean currents; changes in the state of the ozone layer; and changes in the state of the ionosphere.

It is further understood that all the phenomena listed above, when produced by military or any other hostile use of environmental modification techniques, would result, or could reasonably be expected to result, in widespread, long-lasting or severe destruction, damage or injury. Thus, military or any other hostile use of environmental modification techniques as defined in Article II, so as to cause those phenomena as a means of destruction, damage or injury to another State Party, would be prohibited.

It is recognized, moreover, that the list of examples set out above is not exhaustive. Other phenomena which could result from the use of environmental modification techniques as defined in Article II could also be appropriately included. The absence of such phenomena from the list does not in any way imply that the undertaking contained in Article I would not be applicable to those phenomena, provided the criteria set out in that article were met.

Understanding Relating to Article III

It is the understanding of the Committee that this Convention does not deal with the question whether or not a given use of environmental modification techniques for peaceful purposes is in accordance with generally recognized principles and applicable rules of international law.

Understanding Relating to Article VIII

It is the understanding of the Committee that a proposal to amend the Convention may also be considered at any conference of Parties held pursuant to Article VIII. It is further understood that any proposed amendment that is intended for such consideration should, if possible, be submitted to the Depositary no less than 90 days before the commencement of the conference.

ENMOD has been ratified by 75 nations, excluding France. Mexico, Saudi Arabia, and South Africa.

Source: Available at http://disarmament.un.org/treatystatus.nsf/44e6eeabc9436b788 52568770078d9c0/42d4029f2edc8bfd852568770079dd99. Used by permission of the United Nations

Protocol Additional to the Geneva Conventions of 12 August 1949, and Relating to the Protection of Victims of International Armed Conflicts (Protocol I), 8 June 1977

PREAMBLE

The High Contracting Parties,

Proclaiming their earnest wish to see peace prevail among peoples,

Recalling that every State has the duty, in conformity with the Charter of the United Nations, to refrain in its international relations from the threat or use of force against the sovereignty, territorial integrity or political independence of any State, or in any other manner inconsistent with the purposes of the United Nations,

Believing it necessary nevertheless to reaffirm and develop the provisions protecting the victims of armed conflicts and to supplement measures intended to reinforce their application,

Expressing their conviction that nothing in this Protocol or in the Geneva Conventions of 12 August 1949 can be construed as legitimizing or authorizing any act of aggression or any other use of force inconsistent with the Charter of the United Nations,

Reaffirming further that the provisions of the Geneva Conventions of 12 August 1949 and of this Protocol must be fully applied in all circumstances to all persons who are protected by those instruments, without any adverse distinction based on the nature or origin of the armed conflict or on the causes espoused by or attributed to the Parties to the conflict,

Have agreed on the following:
[. . .]

Part III. Methods and Means of Warfare Combatant and Prisoners-Of-War

Section I. Methods and Means of Warfare

Art 35. Basic rules

1. In any armed conflict, the right of the Parties to the conflict to choose methods or means of warfare is not unlimited.
2. It is prohibited to employ weapons, projectiles and material and methods of warfare of a nature to cause superfluous injury or unnecessary suffering.
3. It is prohibited to employ methods or means of warfare which are intended, or may be expected, to cause widespread, long-term and severe damage to the natural environment.

[. . .]

Art 54. Protection of objects indispensable to the survival of the civilian population

1. Starvation of civilians as a method of warfare is prohibited.
2. It is prohibited to attack, destroy, remove or render useless objects indispensable to the survival of the civilian population, such as food-stuffs, agricultural areas for the production of food-stuffs, crops, livestock, drinking water installations and supplies and irrigation works, for the specific purpose of denying them for their sustenance value to the civilian population or to the adverse Party, whatever the motive, whether in order to starve out civilians, to cause them to move away, or for any other motive.
3. The prohibitions in paragraph 2 shall not apply to such of the objects covered by it as are used by an adverse Party:

   (a) as sustenance solely for the members of its armed forces; or
   (b) if not as sustenance, then in direct support of military action, provided, however, that in no event shall actions against these objects be taken which may be expected to leave the civilian population with such inadequate food or water as to cause its starvation or force its movement.

4. These objects shall not be made the object of reprisals.
5. In recognition of the vital requirements of any Party to the conflict in the defence of its national territory against invasion, derogation from the prohibitions contained in paragraph 2 may be made by a Party to the conflict within such territory under its own control where required by imperative military necessity.

Art 55. Protection of the natural environment

1. Care shall be taken in warfare to protect the natural environment against widespread, long-term and severe damage. This protection includes a prohibition of

the use of methods or means of warfare which are intended or may be expected to cause such damage to the natural environment and thereby to prejudice the health or survival of the population.

2. Attacks against the natural environment by way of reprisals are prohibited.

Art 56. Protection of works and installations containing dangerous forces

1. Works or installations containing dangerous forces, namely dams, dykes and nuclear electrical generating stations, shall not be made the object of attack, even where these objects are military objectives, if such attack may cause the release of dangerous forces and consequent severe losses among the civilian population. Other military objectives located at or in the vicinity of these works or installations shall not be made the object of attack if such attack may cause the release of dangerous forces from the works or installations and consequent severe losses among the civilian population.

2. The special protection against attack provided by paragraph 1 shall cease:

   (a) for a dam or a dyke only if it is used for other than its normal function and in regular, significant and direct support of military operations and if such attack is the only feasible way to terminate such support;

   (b) for a nuclear electrical generating station only if it provides electric power in regular, significant and direct support of military operations and if such attack is the only feasible way to terminate such support;

   (c) for other military objectives located at or in the vicinity of these works or installations only if they are used in regular, significant and direct support of military operations and if such attack is the only feasible way to terminate such support.

3. In all cases, the civilian population and individual civilians shall remain entitled to all the protection accorded them by international law, including the protection of the precautionary measures provided for in Article 57. If the protection Ceases and any of the works, installations or military objectives mentioned in paragraph 1 is attacked, all practical precautions shall be taken to avoid the release of the dangerous forces.

4. It is prohibited to make any of the works, installations or military objectives mentioned in paragraph 1 the object of reprisals.

5. The Parties to the conflict shall endeavour to avoid locating any military objectives in the vicinity of the works or installations mentioned in paragraph 1. Nevertheless, installations erected for the sole purpose of defending the protected works or installations from attack are permissible and shall not themselves be made the object of attack, provided that they are not used in hostilities except for defensive actions necessary to respond to attacks against the protected works or installations and that their armament is limited to weapons capable only of repelling hostile action against the protected works or installations.

6. The High Contracting Parties and the Parties to the conflict are urged to conclude further agreements among themselves to provide additional protection for objects containing dangerous forces.
7. In order to facilitate the identification of the objects protected by this article, the Parties to the conflict may mark them with a special sign consisting of a group of three bright orange circles placed on the same axis, as specified in Article 16 of Annex I to this Protocol [Article 17 of Amended Annex]. The absence of such marking in no way relieves any Party to the conflict of its obligations under this Article.

[. . .]

Section II. Repression of Breaches of the Conventions and of this Protocol

Article 85—Repression of breaches of this Protocol

1. The provisions of the Conventions relating to the repression of breaches and grave breaches, supplemented by this Section, shall apply to the repression of breaches and grave breaches of this Protocol.
2. Acts described as grave breaches in the Conventions are grave breaches of this Protocol if committed against persons in the power of an adverse Party protected by Articles 44, 45 and 73 of this Protocol, or against the wounded, sick and shipwrecked of the adverse Party who are protected by this Protocol, or against those medical or religious personnel, medical units or medical transports which are under the control of the adverse Party and are protected by this Protocol.
3. In addition to the grave breaches defined in Article 11, the following acts shall be regarded as grave breaches of this Protocol, when committed wilfully, in violation of the relevant provisions of this Protocol, and causing death or serious injury to body or health:

(a) making the civilian population or individual civilians the object of attack;
(b) launching an indiscriminate attack affecting the civilian population or civilian objects in the knowledge that such attack will cause excessive loss of life, injury to civilians or damage to civilian objects, as defined in Article 57, paragraph 2 (a)(iii);
(c) launching an attack against works or installations containing dangerous forces in the knowledge that such attack will cause excessive loss of life, injury to civilians or damage to civilian objects, as defined in Article 57, paragraph 2 (a)(iii);
(d) making non-defended localities and demilitarized zones the object of attack;
(e) making a person the object of attack in the knowledge that he is hors de combat;
(f) the perfidious use, in violation of Article 37, of the distinctive emblem of the red cross, red crescent or red lion and sun or of other protective signs recognized by the Conventions or this Protocol.

Protocol I has been ratified by 170 nations, excluding the United States, Iran, Israel, Pakistan, and Turkey.

Source: Protocol Additional to the Geneva Conventions of 12 August 1949, and Relating to the Protection of Victims of International Armed Conflicts (Protocol I), 8 June 1977, 1125 UNTS 3, available at: http://www.unhcr.org/refworld/docid/3ae6b36b4.html. Used by permission of the United Nations.

The Carter Doctrine, 1980

Selections from President Carter's State of the Union Address delivered before a joint session of Congress, January 23, 1980

Mr. President, Mr. Speaker, Members of the 96th Congress, fellow citizens:

This last few months has not been an easy time for any of us. As we meet tonight, it has never been more clear that the state of our Union depends on the state of the world. And tonight, as throughout our own generation, freedom and peace in the world depend on the state of our Union.

[. . .]

The region which is now threatened by Soviet troops in Afghanistan is of great strategic importance: It contains more than two-thirds of the world's exportable oil. The Soviet effort to dominate Afghanistan has brought Soviet military forces to within 300 miles of the Indian Ocean and close to the Straits of Hormuz, a waterway through which most of the world's oil must flow. The Soviet Union is now attempting to consolidate a strategic position, therefore, that poses a grave threat to the free movement of Middle East oil.

This situation demands careful thought, steady nerves, and resolute action, not only for this year but for many years to come. It demands collective efforts to meet this new threat to security in the Persian Gulf and in Southwest Asia. It demands the participation of all those who rely on oil from the Middle East and who are concerned with global peace and stability. And it demands consultation and close cooperation with countries in the area which might be threatened.

Meeting this challenge will take national will, diplomatic and political wisdom, economic sacrifice, and, of course, military capability. We must call on the best that is in us to preserve the security of this crucial region.

Let our position be absolutely clear: An attempt by any outside force to gain control of the Persian Gulf region will be regarded as an assault on the vital interests of the United States of America, and such an assault will be repelled by any means necessary, including military force.

[. . .]

The crises in Iran and Afghanistan have dramatized a very important lesson: Our excessive dependence on foreign oil is a clear and present danger to our Nation's security. The need has never been more urgent. At long last, we must have a clear, comprehensive energy policy for the United States.

Source: Carter, Jimmy. *Public Papers of the Presidents of the United States: Jimmy Carter, 1980–1981.* Book 1, pp. 194–200. Washington, D.C.: GPO, 1981.

An Abrupt Climate Change Scenario and Its Implications for United States National Security (Executive Summary), 2003

This white paper was written by Peter Schwartz and Doug Randall in 2003 for the DOD Office of Net Assessment. It is important because it was the first research paper to link climate change explicitly with U.S. national security, and was commissioned and released at a time when the prevailing U.S. Administration did not discuss climate change in public.

Executive Summary

There is substantial evidence to indicate that significant global warming will occur during the 21st century. Because changes have been gradual so far, and are projected to be similarly gradual in the future, the effects of global warming have the potential to be manageable for most nations. Recent research, however, suggests that there is a possibility that this gradual global warming could lead to a relatively abrupt slowing of the ocean's thermohaline conveyor, which could lead to harsher winter weather conditions, sharply reduced soil moisture, and more intense winds in certain regions that currently provide a significant fraction of the world's food production. With inadequate preparation, the result could be a significant drop in the human carrying capacity of the Earth's environment.

The research suggests that once temperature rises above some threshold, adverse weather conditions could develop relatively abruptly, with persistent changes in the atmospheric circulation causing drops in some regions of 5–10 degrees Fahrenheit in a single decade. Paleoclimatic evidence suggests that altered climatic patterns could last for as much as a century, as they did when the ocean conveyor collapsed 8,200 years ago, or, at the extreme, could last as long as 1,000 years as they did during the Younger Dryas, which began about 12,700 years ago.

In this report, as an alternative to the scenarios of gradual climatic warming that are so common, we outline an abrupt climate change scenario patterned after the 100-year event that occurred about 8,200 years ago. This abrupt change scenario is characterized by the following conditions:

- Annual average temperatures drop by up to 5 degrees Fahrenheit over Asia and North America and 6 degrees Fahrenheit in northern Europe
- Annual average temperatures increase by up to 4 degrees Fahrenheit in key areas throughout Australia, South America, and southern Africa.
- Drought persists for most of the decade in critical agricultural regions and in the water resource regions for major population centers in Europe and eastern North America.
- Winter storms and winds intensify, amplifying the impacts of the changes. Western Europe and the North Pacific experience enhanced winds.

The report explores how such an abrupt climate change scenario could potentially de-stabilize the geo-political environment, leading to skirmishes, battles, and even war due to resource constraints such as:

1. Food shortages due to decreases in net global agricultural production
2. Decreased availability and quality of fresh water in key regions due to shifted precipitation patters, causing more frequent floods and droughts
3. Disrupted access to energy supplies due to extensive sea ice and storminess

As global and local carrying capacities are reduced, tensions could mount around the world, leading to two fundamental strategies: defensive and offensive. Nations with the resources to do so may build virtual fortresses around their countries, preserving resources for themselves. Less fortunate nations especially those with ancient enmities with their neighbors, may initiate in struggles for access to food, clean water, or energy. Unlikely alliances could be formed as defense priorities shift and the goal is resources for survival rather than religion, ideology, or national honor.

This scenario poses new challenges for the United States, and suggests several steps to be taken:

- Improve predictive climate models to allow investigation of a wider range of scenarios and to anticipate how and where changes could occur
- Assemble comprehensive predictive models of the potential impacts of abrupt climate change to improve projections of how climate could influence food, water, and energy

- Create vulnerability metrics to anticipate which countries are most vulnerable to climate change and therefore, could contribute materially to an increasingly disorderly and potentially violent world.
- Identify no-regrets strategies such as enhancing capabilities for water management
- Rehearse adaptive responses
- Explore local implications
- Explore geo-engineering options that control the climate.

There are some indications today that global warming has reached the threshold where the thermohaline circulation could start to be significantly impacted. These indications include observations documenting that the North Atlantic is increasingly being freshened by melting glaciers, increased precipitation, and fresh water runoff making it substantially less salty over the past 40 years. This report suggests that, because of the potentially dire consequences, the risk of abrupt climate change, although uncertain and quite possibly small, should be elevated beyond a scientific debate to a U.S. national security concern.

Source: Peter Schwartz and Doug Randall, "An Abrupt Climate Change Scenario and Its Implications for United States National Security" (Executive Summary). October 2003. Washington, D.C.: The Pentagon.

Further Resources

Abbott, Chris. 2008. *An Uncertain Future: Law Enforcement, National Security, and Climate Change.* Briefing Paper, January 2008. London: Oxford Research Group.

AMTW. 2004. "Arctic Marine Transport Workshop." Results of workshop, September 28–30, 2004. Institute of the North; U.S. Arctic Research Commission; International Arctic Science Committee.

Art, Robert J. 1982. "The Role of Military Power in International Relations." *National Security Affairs.* B. T. Trout and James Harf, eds. New Brunswick, NJ: Transaction Books.

Barnett, Jon. 2003. "Security and Climate Change." *Global Environmental Change.* Vol. 13, No. 1, April 2003, pp. 7–17.

Bliss, Katherine E. 2011. "Health Diplomacy of Foreign Governments." A Report of the CSIS Global Health Policy Center. May 2011. Washington: Center for Strategic and International Studies.

Blue Planet Project. www.blueplanetproject.net

Brach, Hans Günter, Navnita Chadha Behera, Patricia Kameri-Mbote, John Grin, Ursula Oswald Spring, Béchir Chourou, Czeslaw Mesjasz, and Heinz Krummenacher, eds. 2009. *Facing Global Environmental Change: Environmental, Human, Energy, Food, Health, and Water Security Concepts.* New York: Springer.

Brown, Amber, and Marty D. Matlock. 2011. "A Review of Water Scarcity Indices and Methodologies." White Paper No. 106. The Sustainability Consortium, University of Arkansas, April 2011.

Brown, Neville. 1994. *Climate Change: A Threat to Peace.* Conflict Studies 272. London: Research Institute for the Study of Conflict and Terrorism.

Brown, Oli, and Alec Crawford. 2009. "Rising Temperatures, Rising Tensions: Climate Change and the Risk of Violent Conflict in the Middle East." Winnipeg, MB: International Institute for Sustainable Development.

Busby, Joshua W. 2007. *Climate Change and National Security: An Agenda for Action.* CSR No. 32, November 2007. New York: Council on Foreign Relations.

Buzan, Barry, Ole Waever, and Jaap de Wilde. 1998. *Security: A New Framework for Analysis.* London: Lynne Rienner.

Byerly, Carol R. 2005. *Fever of War: The Influenza Epidemic in the U.S. Army during World War I.* New York: New York University Press.

Campbell, Greg. 2002. *Blood Diamonds: Tracing the Deadly Path of the World's Most Precious Stones.* Boulder, CO: Westview Press.

Carman, Jessie. 2002. "Economic and Strategic Implications of Ice-Free Arctic Seas." In *Globalization and Maritime Power.* Sam J. Tangredi, ed. Washington: Institute for Strategic Studies, National Defense University, pp. 171–187.

Center for Disease Control. www.cdc.org

Chalecki, Elizabeth L. 2007. "He Who Would Rule: Climate Change in the Arctic and Its Implications for U.S. National Security." *Journal of Public and International Affairs.* Vol. 18, pp. 204–222.

Chalecki, Elizabeth L. 2006. "Cloudy with a Chance of War: Water Resources as a Driver of Security." *Praxis.* Vol. XXI, pp. 129–138.

Cohen, Stewart J., with Melissa W. Waddell. 2011. *Climate Change in the 21st Century.* Montreal: McGill-Queen's University Press, 379 pp.

Collier, Paul, and Anke Hoeffler. 2004. "Greed and Grievance in Civil War." *Oxford Economic Papers.* Vol. 56, No. 4, pp. 563–595.

Conca, Ken, and Geoffrey D. Dabelko, eds. 2002. *Environmental Peacemaking.* Washington: Woodrow Wilson Center Press.

Consultative Group on International Agricultural Research. www.cgiar.org

CSIS. 2000. "Contagion and Conflict: Health as a Global Security Challenge." Washington: Center for Strategic and International Studies.

Dunning, Thad. 2008. *Crude Democracy: Natural Resource Wealth and Political Regimes.* New York: Cambridge University Press.

Durant, Robert. 2002. "Whither Environmental Security in the Post-September 11th Era? Assessing the Legal, Organizational, and Policy Challenges for the National Security State." *Public Administration Review.* Vol. 62, special issue, pp. 115–123.

Energy Information Administration, U.S. Department of Energy. www.eia.doe.gov

Falkenmark, Malin. 1990. "Global Water Issues Confronting Humanity." *Journal of Peace Research.* Vol. 27, No. 2, pp. 177–190.

Fidler, David. 2004. *SARS: Governance and the Globalization of Disease.* New York: Palgrave Macmillan.

Fisher, Franklin M., and Annette Huber-Lee. 2005. *Liquid Assets: An Economic Approach for Water Management and Conflict Resolution in the Middle East and Beyond.* Washington: RFF Press.

Food & Agricultural Organization. www.fao.org

Foster, Gregory D. 2001. "Environmental Security: The Search for Strategic Legitimacy." *Armed Forces & Society.* Vol. 27, No. 3, pp. 373ff.

Foster, Gregory D. 2004. "A New Security Paradigm." *World Watch Magazine.* Vol. 18, pp. 36–46.

Garrett, Laurie. 2005. *The Coming Plague: Newly Emerging Diseases in a World Out of Balance.* New York: Penguin Books.

Gleditsch, Nils Petter, Ragnhild Nordås, and Idean Salehyan. 2007. *Climate Change and Conflict: The Migration Link.* Coping with Crisis Working Paper Series. New York: International Peace Academy.

Gleick, Peter H. 1991. "Environment and Security: The Clear Connections." *Bulletin of the Atomic Scientists.* Vol. 47, No. 3, April 1991, pp. 16–21.

Gleick, Peter H. 2008. *The World's Water 2008–2009: The Biennial Report on Freshwater Resources.* Sixth Edition. Washington: Island Press.

Global Witness. www.globalwitness.org

Gregory, P. J., J.S.I. Ingram, and M. Brklacich. 2005. "Climate Change and Food Security." *Philosophical Transactions of the Royal Society B.* Vol. 360, pp. 2139–2148.

Guterres, António. 2008. "Millions Uprooted: Saving Refugees and the Displaced." *Foreign Affairs.* Vol. 87, No. 5, September/October 2008, pp. 90–99.

Haftendorn, Helga. 1991. "The Security Puzzle: Theory-Building and Discipline in International Security." *International Studies Quarterly.* Vol. 35, No. 1, pp. 3–17.

Humphreys, Macartan, Jeffrey D. Sachs, and Joseph E. Stiglitz, eds. 2007. *Escaping the Resource Curse.* New York: Columbia University Press.

International Committee of the Red Cross. 1998. *Forum: War and Water.* Geneva, ICRC.

International Energy Agency. www.iea.org

International Food Policy Research Institute. www.ifpri.org

International Rivers Network. www.irn.org

Jacobson, Jodi L. 1988. *Environmental Refugees: A Yardstick of Habitability.* Worldwatch Paper 86. Washington: Worldwatch Institute, 46 pp.

Jervis, Robert. 1978. "Cooperation under the Security Dilemma." *World Politics.* Vol. 30, No. 2, pp. 167–214.

Kay, Sean. 2006. *Global Security in the Twenty-First Century: The Quest for Power and the Search for Peace.* Lanham, MD: Rowman & Littlefield.

Keohane, Robert O., and Joseph S. Nye, Jr. 1977. *Power and Interdependence: World Politics in Transition.* Boston: Little Brown & Co.

Kiser, Stephen D. 2000. *Water: The Hydraulic Parameter of Conflict in the Middle East and North Africa.* INSS Occasional Paper 35, Environmental Security Series. Colorado Springs, CO: USAF Academy.

Lomborg, Bjørn. 2001. *The Skeptical Environmentalist: Measuring the Real State of the World*. New York: Cambridge University Press.

Martin, P., and J. Widgren. 2002. "International Migration: Facing the Challenge." *Population Bulletin*. Vol. 57, No. 1, pp. 1–39.

Massey, Douglas, William Axinn, and Dirgha Ghimire. 2007. *Environmental Change and Out-Migration: Evidence from Nepal*. Population Studies Center Research Report 07–615. January 2007. Ann Arbor, MI: University of Michigan.

Matthew, Richard A. 2002. "In Defense of Environment and Security Research." *Environmental Change and Security Project Report*. Issue No. 8, Summer 2002, pp. 109–124.

McDonald, Bryan. 2010. "Global Health and Human Security." In *Global Environmental Change and Human Security*. Richard A. Matthew, Jon Barnett, Bryan McDonald, and Karen L. O'Brien, eds. Cambridge, MA: MIT Press, pp. 53–76.

McNeill, William H. 1977. *Plagues and Peoples*. New York: Anchor.

Morrissette, Jason J., and Douglas A. Borer. 2004. "Where Oil and Water Do Mix: Environmental Scarcity and Future Conflict in the Middle East and North Africa." *Parameters*. Winter 2004–2005, pp. 86–101.

Mouawad, Jad. 2007. "A Quest for Energy in the Globe's Remote Places." *New York Times*. October 9, 2007.

Nichiporuk, Brian. 2000. *The Security Dynamics of Demographic Factors*. Santa Monica, CA: RAND.

Ohlsson, Leif. 1999. *Environment Scarcity and Conflict: A Study of Malthusian Concerns*. Göteborg, Sweden: Department of Peace and Development Research, Göteborg University.

Parenti, Christian. 2011. *Tropic of Chaos: Climate Change and the New Geography of Violence*. New York: Nation Books.

Parry, Martin, Cynthia Rosenzweig, and Matthew Livermore. 2005. "Climate Change, Global Food Supply, and Risk of Hunger." *Philosophical Transactions of the Royal Society B*. Vol. 360, pp. 2125–2138.

Patz, Jonathan A., Diarmid Campbell-Lendrum, Tracey Holloway, and Jonathan A. Foley. 2005. "Impact of Regional Climate Change on Human Health." *Nature*. Vol. 438, No. 1766, November 17, 2005, pp. 310–317.

Pirages, Dennis. 1995. "Microsecurity: Disease Organisms and Human Well-being." *The Washington Quarterly*. Vol. 18, No. 4, Autumn 1995, pp. 5–14.

Postel, Sandra L. 2005. *Liquid Assets: The Critical Need to Safeguard Freshwater Ecosystems*. Washington: Worldwatch Institute.

Potter, Evan H. 1996. "The Challenge of Responding to International Migration." *Canadian Foreign Policy*. Vol. 4, No. 1, pp. 1–22.

Pumphrey, Carolyn, ed. 2008. *Global Climate Change: National Security Implications*. Carlisle, PA: Strategic Studies Institute.

Reuveny, Rafael. 2007. "Climate Change-Induced Migration and Violent Conflict." *Political Geography*. Vol. 26, No. 6, August 2007, pp. 656–673.

Roberts, Janine. 2003. *Glitter & Greed: The Secret World of the Diamond Cartel*. New York: Disinformation Co. Ltd.

Rowlands, Ian. 1991. "The Security Challenges of Global Environmental Change." *Washington Quarterly*. Vol. 14, No. 1, pp. 99–114.

Sagala, John Kemoli. 2006. "HIV/AIDS and the Military in Sub-Saharan Africa: Impact on Military Organizational Effectiveness." *Africa Today*. Vol. 53, No. 1, Fall 2006, pp. 53–77.

Smallman-Raynor, M. and A. D. Cliff. 2004. *War Epidemics: An Historical Geography of Infectious Diseases in Military Conflict and Civil Strife, 1850–2000*. New York: Oxford University Press.

Smith, Paul J. 2007. "Climate Change, Mass Migration, and the Military Response." *Orbis*. Vol. 51, No. 4, Fall 2007, pp. 617–633.

The Kimberley Process. www.kimberleyprocess.com

Tickner, J. Ann. 1992. *Gender in International Relations: Feminist Perspectives on Achieving Global Security*. New York: Columbia University Press.

UN Environmental Programme. www.unep.org

UNEP. 2002. *Atlas of International Freshwater Agreements*. Nairobi: United Nations Environment Programme. 184 pp.

Usery, E. Lynn. 2007. "Modeling Sea Level Rise Effects on Population Using Global Elevation and Land Cover Data." U.S.G.S. presentation to the AAG, April 17–21, 2007.

Wald, Matthew L., and Andrew C. Revkin. 2007. "New Coast Guard Task in Arctic's Warming Seas." *New York Times*. October 19, 2007.

Westing, Arthur H., ed. 1986. *Global Resources and International Conflict: Environmental Factors in Strategic Policy and Action*. Stockholm: SIPRI Publications.

Westing, Arthur H. 1991. *Environmental Hazards of War: Releasing Dangerous Forces in an Industrialized World*. Oslo: PRIO.

Whiteside, Alan, Alex de Waal, and Tsadkan Gebre-Tensae. 2006. "AIDS, Security and Military in Africa: A Sober Appraisal." *African Affairs*. Vol. 105, April 2006, pp. 201–218.

WHO—Global Outbreak and Response Network http://www.who.int/csr/outbreak-network/en/

WHO—Health and Environment Linkages Initiative http://www.who.int/heli/en/

Wilson, Thomas W., Jr. 1983. "Global Climate, World Politics, and National Security." *World Climate Change: The Role of International Law and Institutions*. V. P. Nanda, ed. Boulder, CO: Westview Press, pp. 71–77.

Wolfers, Arnold. 1952. "'National Security' as Ambiguous Symbol." *Political Science Quarterly*. Vol. 67, No. 4, December 1952, pp. 481–502.

World Bank. www.worldbank.org

World Food Program. www.wfp.org

Worldwatch Institute. 2005. *State of the World 2005: Redefining Global Security.* Washington: Worldwatch Institute.

World Water Council. www.worldwatercouncil.org

Yergin, Daniel. 1991. *The Prize: The Epic Quest for Oil, Money, and Power.* New York: Simon & Schuster.

Yergin, Daniel. 2011. *The Quest: Energy, Security, and the Remaking of the Modern World.* New York: Penguin Press.

Zinsser, Hans. 1935. *Rats, Lice, and History.* New York: Little, Brown & Co.

Index

Aerosols, 148, 172

Agent Orange in Vietnam, 146–47; Operation Ranch Hand, 146; 2, 4, 5-T, a teratogenic compound, 146–47; use of defoliants and herbicides, 146

Agro-imperialism, 97–98; cash-rich nation, 98; "private good" aspects of food, 98

Albedo, 149, 172

Al Gore (Former U.S. Vice-President, Climate Change Activist), 178–80

Al Qaeda, 4, 13, 90, 176

Al-Saud monarchy, 51

Al Shabaab, 90, 166

"American atmosphere," 13

Antarctic Treaty, 1959, 153, 156

Aquaculture, 85

Arab Spring, 165

Arctic: Arctic Thaw, 108–9; (high latitude land masses, 109; mass of sea ice lost, 109; projected winter surface temperature increase, 108); Arctic Transit, 109–13; (Arctic Transit Routes, 111; Canada and Russia plans, 112–13; increase in civilian ship and container traffic, 112; less sea ice cover; loss of summer sea ice, 110; Northern Sea Route to commercial shipping,

112; permanent Arctic base by U.S. Coast Guard, 113; sonar characteristics useful for submarines, 113; sonar signature, changes in, 113); commercial ships transporting goods, 20–21; lack of legal regime, 21; legal status of, 114–16; (circumpolar nations, benefits for, 114–15; North Atlantic Ice Patrol, 116; Northwest Passage, control claimed by Canada, 115; principle of *mare liberum* (free seas), 114; Russia's claim of seabed, 115; snow and ice melt, 115–16; UNCLOS, 1982, 114–15); loss of sea ice, 20; mineral resources, 21; security impact of oil/gas exploration, 113–14; (strategic minerals, 114; threat of militancy and in-country sabotage, 114; U.S. Arctic Research Commission, 113)

Asylum and non-refoulement, legal concepts of, 124

Auxiliary force in war, disease as, 132

Biofuels, production of, 72; fossil-based fuels for transportation, 72; World Annual Production, 73

BRICS countries, 53

Brown, Lester (President, Earth Policy Institute), 176–77

About the Author

ELIZABETH L. CHALECKI is the visiting Mellon assistant professor in the Environmental Studies Program at Goucher College. Her expertise lies in the areas of international environmental politics, climate change and security, and nontraditional security threat analysis. Dr. Chalecki has published over 20 articles and book chapters on diverse topics such as climate change and Arctic security, environmental terrorism, climate change and international law, public perceptions of environmental issues, and water in outer space. She has taught at Boston College, Boston University, California State University—Hayward, and the Monterey Institute of International Studies. She has worked for the Pacific Institute for Studies in Development, Environment, and Security; Environment Canada; the U.S. Department of Commerce; and the Brookings Institution. She holds a PhD in international relations from the Fletcher School of Law and Diplomacy at Tufts University and an M.Sc. in environmental geography from the University of Toronto.